The Gulls
Are Always Laughing

A Gay Man's Journey to Healing and Spirituality

The Gulls
Are Always Laughing

A Gay Man's Journey to Healing and Spirituality

KARLYLE TOMMS

Fresh Ink Group
Guntersville

The Gulls Are Always Laughing

Fresh Ink Group
An Imprint of:
The Fresh Ink Group, LLC
1021 Blount Avenue #931
Guntersville, AL 35976
Email: info@FreshInkGroup.com
FreshInkGroup.com

Edition 1.0 2024

Cover design by Stephen Geez / FIG
Book design by Amit Dey / FIG
Associate publisher Beem Weeks / FIG

Cataloging-in-Publication Recommendations:

POE021000 POETRY / LGBTQ+
FAM001010 FAMILY & RELATIONSHIPS / Abuse / Child Abuse
FAM056000 FAMILY & RELATIONSHIPS / LGBTQ+

Library of Congress Control Number: 2024919024

ISBN-13: 978-1-964998-24-4 Softcover
ISBN-13: 978-1-964998-25-1 Hardcover
ISBN-13: 978-1-964998-26-8 Ebooks

There are two basic motivating forces: fear and love. When we are afraid, we pull back from life. When we are in love, we open to all that life has to offer with passion, excitement, and acceptance.

—JOHN LENNON

"When I was five years old, my mother always told me that **happiness was the key to life**. When I went to school, they asked me what I wanted to be when I grew up. I wrote down 'happy'. They told me I didn't understand the assignment, and I told them they didn't understand life."

—JOHN LENNON

Dedication

This book is dedicated to my grandmother. Without her, I would not be here, not in this form or manifestation of myself, and I would have been lost.

This book is also dedicated to all those who have struggled with life, with abuse, neglect, trauma, homophobia, transphobia, racism, and all the other isms or have simply gone through severely difficult adjustments. This book is especially dedicated to those who went through any of the above and never had an anchor in the storm. When a ship does not have an anchor, the storm comes and blows it against the rocks and often destroys it. When the ship has an anchor, the storm may come; it may do damage, but the anchor holds it steady. My grandmother was my first anchor. She held me steady so I could survive the storm of my childhood.

This book is also dedicated to all those who have been my anchors through the various storms of my life. Thank you for helping me find calm waters.

My prayer for those who suffer and are trying to recover from any turmoil is that you will find your anchor. No one should ever be without an anchor in the storm, and my prayer is that those who have ever needed an anchor find something in these pages that brings them comfort and inspiration. I also pray that more and more people come to understand the true meaning of love, for within it is the resolution of all that troubles us. Like all my books, this is a book about love.

Contents

Author's Note:

It is impossible to tell your story without discussing your interactions with others. The only people named in this story are deceased and then by first name only. Others are mentioned, but not by name. This telling is from my perceptions and perspective. I understand that others may interpret it differently than I have. All these experiences have led me to where I am today and to the conclusions I have drawn about life and healing from emotional trauma. As the Twelve Steps program says, *"Keep what is worth keeping and discard the rest."*

Forward by author Forrest Lang

In the deep hollows of the Ozark Mountains, life moves slowly, bound by the rhythms of nature and the weight of tradition. For a boy growing up in the shadow of those ancient hills, the loneliness of loss and the crushing weight of rejection for his very existence made the world seem cruel. Hidden beneath the dense canopy of trees and thick whispers of family history, he learned early to keep secrets—some out of survival, others out of shame. The mountains held their silence, as did the man he would grow to be, shaped by the unyielding expectations of small-town life and the quiet ache of a boy who loved differently.

This is the story of a man who walked out of those hills carrying wounds as deep as the valleys he left behind and a heart full of poetry that only now begins to speak its truth. It is a memoir of healing, of learning to live with the scars of trauma and finding a voice in the silence that once bound him. Through verse and memory, he seeks not just to recall but to reshape—reclaiming his power while offering the hard-won lessons of survival and self-love to anyone who still feels alone in the fight for freedom from the aftereffects of trauma.

Karlyle shares his wisdom with the world in these pages, the same wisdom he freely shared with me as I struggled through my own writing process. So, sit back, grab a cup of tea, and prepare to dig deep into the wisdom and beauty of the poetry of the wounded healer.

Forrest Lang is the author of *Angel Blue, a Song of Redemption*, a tattoo artist, a combat veteran, and the founder of SPARTA Peer Support, a meditation-based non-profit suicide prevention program for veterans and first responders.
angelbluebook.com

Prologue

This is poetry written from my heart, based on multiple life experiences. There are poems about people I have known, but few are specifically identified here. Nothing is intended to discredit, offend, or demean anyone, nor is there any violation of confidentiality. These poems are simply references to my feelings, memories, and experiences when they were written.

As I have written this, I maintain my awareness that many have had trauma much worse than my own and that they have overcome it on their own. It is possible to self-heal, although most of us need help; I did. I also realize that there may not necessarily be anything special about my story except that I am telling it. Every life is a novel in the making, and every life is filled with stories, some truth, some fiction, and some stories that we were led to believe were true but may not have been the truth. Some stories are never told, and those who raised us often withheld secrets. Yet, who does not long to know the stories of how they came to be? As I tell this collection of my stories, in both prose and poetry, I have tried to give some order to it, but it still bounces around a bit. The book's introduction is a brief summary of my life. Every poem will have its own introduction, and every poem is connected to the thoughts and feelings that were going on when it was written. It may also include how the poem relates to my healing and self-love journey. Some poems were written about past events and memories. Some were written specifically about what I felt during the period they were written.

Poetry is often more of a window into our soul than a photograph. Unless it is just for humor or a class assignment, a poem reflects something deep within us that we may reveal without even realizing that we are revealing it. After my friend Larry died, his mother gave me copies of his poetry. I never knew he wrote poetry because he had never shared it with me. After reading his poetry, which was very good, I was touched, and it occurred to me that the poet paints a picture of his soul with the brush strokes of words. Poetry is an art form; it can vary from formal to abstract. The poems that follow the book's introduction are snapshots of my life. In some, I openly reveal things about myself that I have discussed only with a few of my dearest friends or therapists. In some, I may reveal parts of myself that remain unknown to me.

An Introduction:
Why this book? Why this title?

Where I grew up, there were no gulls but plenty of crows and blue-jays. Many oak trees, cedars, and pines dotted the rolling hills where the Ozark mountains blended into the Mississippi delta. There were muddy ponds, and cows waded into the middle of them on hot days to feel the cool, muddy water against their bellies. If you were to go into the center of the United States, you would find the Ozarks, where a few lakes are far too small or too removed from ocean shores to have gulls, and even those lakes are miles removed from the farm that was my childhood home. There, the rolling hills have various-sized creeks that flow across the land, but few are wide enough or deep enough to be called a river. There were ponds to gather water for the cattle to drink, but even the largest ones were maybe no more than two hundred feet in diameter and rarely more than five feet deep. Still, they were stocked with fish, occasionally yielding a cat-fish or a bass for dinner. The pastures there are often filled with dry sage grass in winter, standing about two to three feet tall and flowing tan and yellow, making waves in the wind like the petted fur on the back of a ginger cat. The winters are wet and cold, and the summers scorching. As well, in those days of my childhood, winters were only warmed by one potbellied stove, and summers were only cooled by window fans.

I grew up in the 1960s on an Arkansas farm just south of the Missouri border, and my childhood was spent traveling back and forth between the two states. That farm was ten miles from the nearest city. That city, the county seat and largest town in the county, had a population of less than 2000 and was about twenty miles from Missouri's southern border. Any city larger than that was an additional twenty miles past the Missouri Border and had only about 6,000 in population at the time. The travel time was made longer by trailing dirt roads barely wide enough for two cars to pass. However, by the time we reached Missouri, there was usually pavement from there on. Any city larger than six or eight thousand was at least a two-hour drive further away, and even those were tiny compared to such places as Chicago, LA, or New York. Contrast this with the fact that my father was from and always lived in southern California, primarily Los Angeles, but my father was not part of my life when I was growing up.

I will not bore you with all the details at this point. Suffice it to say that my family must have been the original *Beverly Hillbillies* without the oil wealth or royalties from the TV show. In the early 1950s, they loaded up the truck and moved to Beverly ... well, not quite. Somebody told Grandpa that the desert air would be good for his asthma. Apparently, my family didn't consider what a culture shock might be caused by going from the backwoods of Arkansas across the country to Los Angeles. So, they weren't there long before loading the truck and coming home. However, my mother met my father in California, who was doing bit parts for Universal Studios at the time. So, swimming pools and movie stars ... not quite. She left him while pregnant with me (also a long story—suffice it to say he had PTSD) and came back to Arkansas. She died when I was five years old. Then, my grandparents raised me and did not attempt to contact my father.

At eighteen, when Grandpa could no longer forbid it, I contacted my dad through the publishing company for a book about his experiences as a World War II Japanese POW. (*Laughter in Hell* by Stephen Marek, initially published in 1954, currently available on Amazon). When I finally met my father, he did not match the negative stories that must have been told through my mother's anguish, and we developed a good relationship. I'm sure he had PTSD when my mom knew him, but in eighteen years, he had done a lot of healing. Still, I had to build my trust, and I had my own culture shock to experience, but we maintained a good relationship after that. There were some bumps in the road, but I developed and continue to maintain a deep respect for my father, who passed in 2016.

While growing up, I was bullied at school and abused at home. My alcoholic uncle and my grandfather mistreated me (another long story—more later). I grew up gay in the 1960s in an isolated and Christian fundamentalist rural area. Even though I had siblings on my father's side, I didn't know them until after I met him, and I was raised as an only child. That, combined with everything else, resulted in a very lonely childhood where I took on the shame around me as well as that which was directed toward me. I was sixteen years old when the pastor of our church said during a sermon, "*The sin of homosexuality is worse than the sin of murder.*" What do you think that did to a lonely gay teen's mind? I knew no one else like me. I saw no depictions of anyone like me in any media, and that didn't begin happening on TV until the 1980s. I heard only negative things about "*queers,*" and being called "*queer*" was a caustic and dehumanizing insult at that time. Yes, I contemplated suicide, and had it not been for my loving grandmother, the words you are reading now might never have been written.

Throughout my childhood, my grandmother told me that my mother always wanted me to go to college. So, that's what I did, and I was the only person on her side of the family, other than some distant cousins, ever to complete a degree. College saved me. First, I was inspired by my high school counselor, although he never knew it, and we never discussed it. His influence permitted me to seek help, and I realized there was something better than how I was raised and that if I was diligent, I could find a better way. Therefore, I majored in behavioral science and started therapy soon after arriving at college. There, in that tiny college in North Central

Arkansas (Lyon, which was then Arkansas College), I met loving, wise, and compassionate mentors and teachers who began the process of guiding me to self-love. Yet, that has been an ongoing struggle throughout my life. In my elder years, I still find myself trying to shake off the conditioning and indoctrination of my childhood that taught me to believe that I could be worth less than others or that my very existence as a gay man is wrong.

Because of my authoritarian Christian upbringing, I was also indoctrinated into a specific type of religious dogma, an *us versus them* mentality where only our church can be right, and everyone else is wrong. I was told that I was going to hell because I had chosen to accept a scholarship to a Presbyterian college. Yet, a Presbyterian pre-ministerial student at Lyon first challenged me to think for myself, and all he did was ask me questions. He backed me into a corner, and I realized that until then, I had swallowed what the church fed me. I was taught that our church was the only true way and that I was not to question it. Yet, questioning and studying is what led me to spirituality versus religion.

Many of those Bible verses I had grown up with began to have a different meaning when I examined them instead of merely accepting what I was told they meant. I had always been told, *"Narrow is the way, and few there be that enter therein." Matthew 7: 13-14.* That was supposed to mean that our church members would be the only ones who would get into heaven. Later, I understood that some understand genuine love and spirituality regardless of religion, but many don't. Many are unable to divorce themselves from their indoctrination and dogma enough even to get a glimmer of what true spirituality looks like. Some will get it, but many won't. I learned that a closed mind cannot be filled, and until people are willing to open their minds to a different way of seeing things, they are stuck in whatever they were taught, which could be entirely wrong. Yet, the human ego tends to defend what we believe even if it is not the truth. Still, the only absolute truth about belief is that no belief can ever be true, even a belief about truth. Therefore, all beliefs should be questioned.

So, I had a lot to unravel from my childhood. I had a very long road to come to a point of self-acceptance and self-love. At one point, I thought that anyone who came to know that I was gay would automatically hate me, and I made multiple efforts to fit myself into heterosexuality. However, a square peg does not fit in a round hole. I couldn't make myself become what I am not. As I began to have the courage to confess my feelings, I finally discovered that many people loved and accepted me as I was and had no agenda to try to make me change. Those were not gay people. They were those compassionate mentors and teachers I talked about, all of whom were straight. Eventually, I discovered my family still loved me when I thought I would be denied if they ever knew. I realize, especially with the familial beliefs of my childhood, that I am very lucky compared to many queer people growing up in authoritarian churches. Unfortunately, many are shunned by their own families, and if you think about it, LGBTQIA+ is the only minority at risk of being shunned by their own family and friends.

Coming out of the tangle of my childhood took both therapy and spiritual study. I also read self-help books, went to lectures, attended Al-Anon recovery meetings, etc. I worked very hard on myself to come to the point where I know I am worthy, whether others realize it or not. During my therapy and spiritual study, I learned multiple skills for developing and maintaining my happiness, which I continue to maintain through ongoing practice. During times of stress, I especially have to pull those tools out of my happiness toolbox and put them to work. However, I know from my own experience that healing requires wound care, and although I hope and pray that there will come a day when I have healed all those wounds, I know that complete healing may never come. In the meantime, I have learned several skills that help me to maintain my happiness. So, I continue to practice every day. Happiness is created by learning a set of happiness skills and then maintaining those skills through regular practice. One of those skills is getting our happiness blockers out of the way. Happiness blockers include things like guilt, shame, and resentment. The more we shift our thinking away from those thoughts, the closer we come to establishing and maintaining happiness.

From college, I moved to Little Rock. From Little Rock, I moved to Nashville. After everything came crashing down there, between 1995 and 1997, when Granny began to experience dementia, I moved from Nashville back to the Ozarks to that tiny town just across the Missouri line. After Granny passed, I stayed thirteen more years. Then, Missouri Winters did not cooperate well with my aging, so I sought someplace warmer.

I had an extremely difficult and stressful transition when I moved to The Coastal Bend of Texas in 2015. I took a job and moved to a city I had never visited where I knew no one. I had no family or friends there, and I was challenged to start from scratch to build new relationships and build a support network locally. I also was adjusting to a new and stressful job. In addition, about everything that could go wrong did. I rented from an online source, sight unseen, a one-bedroom rat trap, substandard apartment that cost $300.00 a month more than my mortgage on a four-bedroom house back in Missouri, and I was still paying that. I trusted an online rental management agent and rented the apartment based on the photos that were sent, which were deceptive and misleading. When I got to The Coastal Bend, I struggled financially. I battled with the landlord, who had lied to me about the apartment, and every day, I would come home from work alone to an expensive, grossly substandard home. Because I was so stressed, I pulled the tools from my happiness toolbox and began to utilize them. One of those tools was to take meditative walks, where I began receiving healing messages. One of those messages came from the Gulls. Another tool in my happiness toolbox is writing. So, I began writing poetry again when I had not written it in a few years. That is where the idea for this book came from.

The blessing I received from my trip to Texas was that I met the man who would become my husband two weeks after I moved there. At a time and an age (sixty) when I had given up on relationships and never expected to be in another, I met a gentle, compassionate, loving, and giving man who did something for me that was the most healing thing of all. He loved me. He continues to love me and leaves me no doubt that he will never stop loving me. Guess what? I love him, too.

The following is my life (until now) in poetry. Well, at least some of my life. I have brought back poems from my teen years and reworked poetry I have written through various stages of my life. Each poem and segment has an introduction explaining what was happening in my healing process at that time. Some of the poetry is free-form and more prose than poetry. Many of these poems are merely episodes of free thinking about moments I've experienced, and some are just wordplay. I hope, in these pages, you may find pieces of yourself and experience hope for your healing.

Laughter
makes the burden lighter
when times are rough,
and gives us joyful wings
to fly over our troubles.

Karlyle Tomms

The Formative Years

My grandpa, grandma, and uncle Ray, their firstborn and only boy.

Segment Introduction

This section of the book contains poetry about growing up that I wrote during my adult years. None of this was written during my teens or young adult years. The next segment will have that early poetry. About half the poems in this segment are about experiences of my childhood, and the rest are about adult experiences and observations.

Poem Introduction - ALIVE

Some argue that we are alive from the moment of our first heartbeat in the womb. Some argue otherwise. Some want to believe that the moment the sperm enters the egg, our life begins. Yet, many fertilized eggs are not viable or are later miscarried. This poem is not an argument for or against any idea but is about an awakening to something I had not realized. In time, I understood that I wasn't mentally alive until my first memory registered. We may be physically alive before our first awareness, but our first awareness, our first memory, brings the mind to life. Our first awareness awakens us from the sleep of nothingness, which precedes the awareness regardless of age. From then on, we may forget experiences, but our awareness, perhaps even when unconscious, is always there. However, there was a time when we came out of the void into an awakening to life. Previously, we experienced the void even though we had been alive by all technical evaluations for perhaps several years. Our hearts were beating; we breathed, were fed, and had our diapers changed, but we were not yet fully aware. We became aware when we understood that we were more than a body, which occurred when our minds first encountered life. Our first memory triggered awareness of life that had not previously been there. Then, we interacted with life differently. This poem is about my first memory, my first recognition of awareness. The family story is that a pet squirrel became part of the family when my uncle and grandfather found a nest of baby squirrels after cutting a tree for firewood. They brought the surviving baby squirrel home and cared for it. It, therefore, remained tame throughout its life. It stayed about the yard, and Granny would feed it cornbread.

ALIVE

Chip, chip, chip. . .
The sound echoes in my mind.
It was the first sound I ever recall hearing.
It is a portion of the first memory

Recorded in my brain.
I was maybe three years old,
Maybe two.

Chip, chip, chip. . .
My grandma was cooing,
"Come on, lil feller. Come on, now."

Chip, chip, chip. . .
She clicked two small stones together,
And called across the yard
To a sheltering oak with a trunk so large
That two men could not reach around it
To touch the fingers of the other.

Chip, chip, chip. . .
I sat on her knee as she called.

Suddenly, down the trunk of that oak tree,
A red squirrel descended,
Tail flicking in the air like a signal flag.

Chip, chip, chip. . .
"Come on, lil feller, come on."
The squirrel descended to the ground
And hopped across the grass to the sidewalk.
Then, it hopped down the walk
To the front porch steps
Where we were sitting.
It lifted on its hind legs to receive cornbread
That Granny had tucked into a dip in her apron.

I sat on her knee with her arm around me
And squealed a toddler's squeal of delight.
Then, the squirrel scampered back across the yard.

This was my first moment of knowing life,
My first awareness,
My first experience of existence.
Born two or three years earlier,
I had been fed,
Diapered, and bathed.
I had learned to walk.
I slept and giggled,
Learned the first dregs of language,
And to them, I was alive
But I was not fully alive yet.
Mental life, you see, begins with awareness
It is the first moment that we recognize our existence.
Mental life begins when we realize that
We are alive, and that life is more
Than being fed, bathed, and diapered.
Life begins with our first memory,
And for me, life began with
Chip, chip, chip. . .
And a red squirrel descending an oak tree
While I rested in the safe comfort
Of my grandmother's loving embrace.

Poem Introduction – SCREAM

This is a poem about what happened about two years after my mother died. It was at the end of my first-grade year, around the same time of year, that my mother had been killed. Living far out into the country, we were always bussed to school. A step off the school bus threw me into a panic.

SCREAM

At seven years old, the bus delivered me home,
And there were no cars in the drive.
A car or a truck had always been there.
Someone was always there,
But no one was there.
Barely seven years old and screaming,
I remember the terror still.
I walked toward the house alone,
Slowly, at first.
Then I ran, feet pounding
The dirt driveway
Until I reached the house.
Then, I ran from room to room
Calling their names,
Checking over and over.
No resident was in the house,
Except me.

There were no cars in the drive,
No one in the house,
No one in the yard,
No one could be found anywhere.
No matter how loud I screamed,
No matter where I searched.

No one was there,
And no one called back.

Almost two years before,
My mother had been killed.
Before her funeral,
My stepdad stood in the yard
Crying crocodile tears,
Faking his love for her,
Pretending he cared.
After her funeral,
He disappeared.

They sang pretty acapella songs
And covered her casket
With piles of flowers.
When it was over,
My stepdad was gone
With almost everything.
She was dead,
And he was gone.
Grandma and Grandpa
Took me in.

There was a blank spot,
A darkness
Between her funeral
And the screaming.
I briefly remember
Meeting my first-grade teacher,
And then, one day in late May,
I stepped off the bus,

Saw there were no cars in the drive,
And the screaming awakened me.
Darkness and nothing
Became terror and anguish.
I walked through the house screaming,
Thinking, *I'm all alone now.*
They left me just like Momma.
They have all gone away.
There is no one for me,
No one ... but me,
And I'm terrified!

I screamed and cried
All through the house.
Tears dropped from my face,
A hot rain falling from the thunderstorm of my sorrow.
Tears dropped onto my shirt,
Onto the floor.
They were all gone,
And there was no one left but me.

With the house confirmed empty,
I went to the porch,
Still screaming,
Calling to the woods,
Calling to the sky,
Screaming in abject desperation.

In a moment of pause
I heard her call,
"Whoop! Hey!"
I stopped screaming for a moment,
And listened.

There it was again.
"Whoop!"
Across the farm
I heard it,
"Whoop!"
It was Grandma.

I darted off the porch;
I ran across the yard,
Across the barn lot,
Across the pasture.
We called between the distance
Until I found her coming up the cow path,
Fishing pole in hand.
A cotton dress clung to her legs as she walked.
Her straw hat was tied with rag ribbons beneath her chin,
A hickory stick was cut at the fork
To hang the fish through their gills.
She had gone fishing
and heard me from the creek
On the back side of a hundred and sixty acres.

Despair flipped to anger.
I ran toward her and screamed,
"Why weren't you there!"

She ignored my anger.
"Honey, I'm sorry.
I went fishing and lost track of the time."

Desperate anger would accept no excuses.
"No!"
I screamed and pulled away.

"You left me!"
She reached into her pocket
And pulled out a carved hickory stick.
"I didn't leave you.
I was thinking about you the whole time.
Look, I made you a toy."

She showed me
A hollowed stick
With a carved plunger in one end
And a plug at the other.
When she pushed the plunger,
It caused the plug to pop out the other end
With a sound reminiscent of a finger popped
From cheek to lips.

"It's a pop gun."
She announced.
"I made you a pop gun."

I accepted the stick
A peace offering,
A consolation.
We walked back to the house together
While I played with the stick.

From that moment on,
She would always be there.
For twelve years,
Through high school graduation,
There was never a day,
Never a time

When I got off the school bus
That she was not there.
There would never be a day,
There would never be a time,
That she would ever leave me again,
Until in my forties,
I watched her die.

Poem Introduction – ANOTHER BERRY

There were retreats during my childhood where I went to be alone or entertain myself. As an only child on a farm, secluded, even from the nearest neighbor, I had to find ways to entertain myself. We had a black-and-white television but could only pick up two channels, and often, summer weather caused so much static it wasn't worth watching. I had to be creative to prevent boredom. In warmer months, picking berries and exploring the farm was one of the ways I did that. Granny enjoyed going fishing.

ANOTHER BERRY

I sat on a branch in the mulberry tree,
One of my hiding places on the farm.
I sat and watched for passers-by
On the path that ran below.
There at that tree,
The path crossed a tiny creek
With stepping stones to cross.
I sat amid the tree limbs
And dined on the musty sweetness of slender purple berries.

Except for occasional face-puckering moments
When tasting a berry that the stink bug had visited,
The berries were good.
I could hide there and watch the farm.
I could see and maybe not be seen.
I could hide there and watch
As cattle grazed the pasture
Behind our weathered barn.

I hid, often in summer,
When the berries were ripe

And the breezes were warm.
I would hide there,
Content to be alone
Where I could watch,
Like Robin Hood,
The path that ran below.

She came by,
Walking quietly up that path.
Her wide-brimmed straw hat
Shaded aging eyes from the sun.
Her short-sleeved cotton dress,
Floral and worn,
Waved about her bare legs.
A fishing tackle in one hand,
Her fishing pole in the other
Gave clues of her intention.
She often went fishing alone.

I waited until she was about to cross
And shouted,
As I had seen in old TV movies
Of medieval lore,
"Halt! Who goes there?"

Unstartled because she must have spotted me
Before I spotted her,
She tipped that straw hat,
And looked straight up at me.
"What are you doing up there?"
She smiled.

"Eating mulberries."
I grinned at her through the green canopy.

"Better watch out for stink bugs,"
She cautioned.

"Already spit out a few. What are you doing?"
As if I didn't know.

"Goin' fishin'. Wanna join me?"
She squinted to see through the leaves
While the southern light behind me
Trickled bright amid the green.

"Nah. I'll sit here and eat mulberries
And watch the road for beggars and thieves."

"Suit yourself," she said.

Then she waded, in her canvas shoes, over the rocks
In the shallow part of the creek.
Afterward,
I watched as she walked beside the tree line
Where the creek began to deepen.
She would cross the whole back pasture
Before reaching her fishing hole.

There she would sit,
Content beneath the trees.
Watching a red and white bobber
Floating on the shaded water,
She would patiently wait for a bite.

Each of us had our hiding places,
Our escape from drama and despair.
I learned it from her.
Find peace in the uproar,
A shelter in the storm.

I thought about her sitting there
On the cool creek bank
Listening to the trickling water
As she watched her fishing line.
Then, I reached for another berry.

Poem Introduction – EYES ON THE PRIZE

My grandparents would have made the ten-mile trek into town to do laundry only if Granny's old wringer washing machine was on the blink. Otherwise, she would have washed clothes at home and hung them on the line to dry. This poem is about a memory of a childhood lesson learned at the laundry mat, the only time that I remember going there as a small child. Around the time of the county fair, a plane was flying over town, advertising the fair with a banner flying behind it. The plane dropped small paper bags attached to streamers.

In the Civil Rights movement, they affirmed, *"Keep your eyes on the prize."* On that day when I was maybe eight years old, I learned what happens if you don't.

EYES ON THE PRIZE

I was the first to hear the plane
While playing in the gravel
On the shaded side of the laundromat.
I heard it come and moved
Out into the sun, eyes to the blue sky,
And squinted.

A banner trailing behind the plane said,
"County Fair," and included the date.
The plane circled as though looking for me.
Then it swooped low over the laundromat,
And dropped something;
Brown paper bags,
Each tailed by colorful streamers,
Floating down from a blue and cloudless sky.
I could see through my squint

That a bag was going to fall
On the knoll beside the laundry.

Run, I did,
As hard and fast as I could!
Run, I did,
Up that bank
Through the grass as tall as my chest!

The grocery-sized brown paper bag
Settled into the grass at the top of the knoll,
Crepe paper streamers still clinging.
It was in my sights!
Run, I did,
Pointing myself directly at it,
Sure, of my reward!

Suddenly,
A tap on my shoulder.
An older girl,
Fifteen maybe,
Had run up behind me.
"Quick! Over there!"
She shouted and pointed to the right.

No hesitation,
With an impulse decision,
I followed the point of her finger.
Over there, to the right,
A red streamer nestled
On top of the grass.

Run, I did,
As hard as fast as I could,
With my eyes on the new prize!
Run, I did,
Excited even more!
Then,
I caught up to it,
And grabbed it!
It was nothing but a long strip
Of red crepe paper.

My heart didn't even skip across
The surface of my mood.
It sank,
Ker-plunk
Into my disappointment
And splashed
Salty water back into my eyes.

I turned to watch that girl
Marching down the knoll,
Brown paper bag in hand,
With little beggars of siblings
Becoming her parade.

From the open bag,
She pulled little pieces of candy,
And small plastic toys,
Coupons from local stores
For free stuff,
And discounts.

She pulled out everything,
Except,
Something for me.

On that hot day,
I carried the red streamer
Silently down the hill,
Sat in the shade,
My back against the cool concrete block wall,
And resented my fate.

Poem Introduction – HIS HAND

Our neighbor, who was also my school bus driver, attended our church. In my recollection, he was the only man who ever touched me with loving kindness during my childhood, and that was far too infrequent. This poem is about how much that meant to me.

HIS HAND

Standing outside after services
At our little stone country church,
My twelve-year-old timidity was evident around adults.

There we stood chatting before the long walk home,
Or rather, I was listening,
To be seen, but not to be heard.

His hand slipped round my shoulder,
Unexpected, yet welcome still.
His hand slipped round my shoulder,
And gave a comforting thrill.

Seldom touched by men or touched only in anger,
I was shocked by what he did.
This family friend and neighbor
Touched me
As no man ever had.

My heart began pounding
In the center of my chest.
I felt a nervous ambivalence
Between pull away or let it rest.

His hand lingered there for way too long
And my frightened heart did slam.
Yet, I so wanted him to touch me more,
As no man ever had.

His hand slipped round my shoulder,
A drop of water to a thirsting soul.
For a moment there, it lingered
Before it was time to go.

With laughter and exclamation,
The congregation dispersed for home.
His hand slipped into oblivion
Or it might as well have been so.

I felt the tingling presence where his hand
Once had been.
I lingered in the memory and was
Grateful for what he did.

If never again it might happen,
I would remember that touch and be glad.
His hand slipped round my shoulder
And touched me as no man
Ever had.

Poem Introduction – DON'T TELL

The Stonewall riots, which started the Gay Rights movement, occurred in 1969. I was fourteen years old then. Since we had a black-and-white TV that would only pick up two channels when the weather was good, I had never heard of anything remotely like Stonewall, nor did I realize I had any right to feel the way I felt. If there had ever been any national news coverage of Stonewall, I never saw it or didn't understand it enough to pay attention.

In my teens, I felt as though I was *"an abomination"* and unworthy even of life. I did everything I could, except marry a woman (thank God) to make myself into what society and the church thought I was supposed to be. As noted in the introduction, at the age of sixteen, I sat in church listening to the sermon when the preacher said, *"The sin of homosexuality is worse than the sin of murder."* I knew that I dared never speak what was in my heart, for if, as the preacher said, I was worse than a murderer, would they put me to death if they knew? Should I go ahead and kill myself and take care of the execution for them? Knowing that my grandmother loved me and once having seen her confront the preacher saved me from killing myself. Still, I tried desperately to make myself straight before ever hearing the term *straight*. I couldn't change what I was. So, the only option I knew to keep myself safe was to keep it a secret.

I hated when someone asked me a question that indirectly or directly related to my sexual orientation, and the only way to answer that question was to avoid it or lie. When I was an adult, the question I hated was, "Are you married?" The older I got before taking pride in myself, the more that question bothered me. If I told the truth, I would face judgment, condemnation, or worse, but one lesson I learned from Granny was not to lie. I concluded that it is better to live by omission of the truth than to commit a lie. But I wasn't supposed to be in my thirties or forties and not be married with children. I was expected to be in a heterosexual marriage. There was no other way to exist; sometimes, a lie seemed lifesaving. Worse than the first question, if I said I wasn't married, the next question, when the questioner was bold enough, was, "Are you gay?" I hated that question most of all. It made me feel like the accused on the stand in a court of law, backed into a corner and having to admit the crime, not knowing what the sentence might be. However, I am open now, married to a man, and accepting of my orientation. Yet, the fear is still there, especially with the current political climate. The age-old question for myself is, "If they know, will they attack me?" I never understood why people would hate me for who I am when I am a good and caring person. All those years of shame about being gay, all those years of silence and hiding in the shadows, feeling like an abomination and unworthy haunt me still.

DON'T TELL

I dared not say
What I was feeling.
I dared not say
What I was thinking
That a woman's touch
Was welcome and comforting,
But a man's touch
Was like nectar to a bee.

I lived a lie.
I grew up pretending
That I was someone else,
But it wasn't me.
I grew up longing to be touched by,
But never daring to touch a man.
I grew up lingering
In a brief handshake.
I grew up watching
Certain boys on the bus,
Imagining myself
Doing with them
What I knew they did with girls.

Yet,
I dared not speak it,
Dared, never ask,
Dared not give
The slightest hint
That my body
Ached for that kind of touch.
To do so
Would be damnation.
I had to have self-control.

I knew when the preacher said it
That desiring a man
Must be the worst sin of all.
I knew that I was condemned
And despised
Just for being who I am.
I knew that if they knew,
They might beat me,
Or kill me.

There were no Gay Rights
In the Ozark Hills
During the sixties.
Even heterosexual sex
Was condemned
And considered dirty
If not within a marriage.
It was obvious that
Some were disgusted by it
Even within the permissions
Of marriage.
To sexually desire another male

Was the most horrible kind of dirty,
And the shame that accompanied it
Was the most horrible kind of shame.
To think that I would be better off dead
Was a very short distance from that shame.
Were it not for Granny,
Dead might be
Where I would be right now.

I did everything I could to force a change.
I dated girls,
Made out with girls
And had sex with girls … much later.
But, like trying to speak a foreign language,
It never felt as comfortable
As speaking my native tongue.

It was not until college
That I began to awaken.
It was long past college
Before I realized
That I cannot force myself,
This square peg,
Into a life
Which wasn't meant for me.

It was long past that
Before I actually accepted
This secret longing.
Even today, as I write these words,
A voice within me pleads,
Don't tell.

Poem Introduction – THE WHIPPOORWILL

Amid all the chaos of my childhood, there were peaceful moments. I don't think I realized fully until years later how much nature comforted me. It still does. So, I ensure I get some little piece of nature almost every day. I listen to the birds, look at my flowers, take a walk, listen to the rain, have lunch outside, and generally do what I call rocking in the arms of Mother Nature. This is a poem about one of my fond memories of nature in childhood.

The whippoorwills would sing during summer nights on the farm, which was one of my comforts. The whippoorwills sang me to sleep as I lay in bed with the windows open to bring in the evening breeze.

THE WHIPPOORWILL

The whippoorwill calls in the dead of night,
A mournful but peaceful sound.
Across the farm, in the dead of night,
The whippoorwill calls, "Chip butter white oak."
The melody repeats like a metronome,
Rhythmically calling, "Chip butter white oak."

The whippoorwill calls in the dead of night,
And sings the world to sleep.
"Chip, butter white oak," Granny used to say.
"Chip, butter white oak" is the sound it makes.
"Chip, butter white oak",
All night long,
All night long,
All night long.

The whippoorwill calls from out my window,
A symphony of the night,

"Chip, butter white oak"
A symphony,
Yet, out of sight.
"Chip, butter white oak"
A concert that I both hear and feel,
As sleep seduces my eyelids to conceal.
Then, my eyelids begin to dance
As my soul creeps into the night.
And dreams of a whippoorwill across the dark field.

This was a soothing solace to a lonely child.
A whippoorwill calling, distant and mild.
The memory echoes within me still,
The whippoorwill calling, "Peace, be still."
"Chip, butter white oak" is the sound it makes
Soothing the wounds of a fitful day.
"Chip, butter white oak" in the dead of night.
Softly melting my cares away.

Poem Introduction – I AM A STONE

Most of us do not realize we are much stronger than we think. Those who grow up with abuse or tragedy, if they are lucky, find ways to cope other than self-destruction, and hopefully, in time, even those who chose self-destruction will learn a better way. Yet, I would admonish anyone who has ever been through any abuse or trauma: Never do to yourself what they did to you. Never abandon yourself, no matter how you were abandoned, when, or by whom.

My grandfather was a controlling tyrant, so controlling that the first check Granny ever signed on their joint checking account was to pay for his funeral. Yet, because of her upbringing in that authoritarian church, she was committed to her marriage *"for better or for worse."* In addition, there wasn't much chance she could make it alone in those days if she left him. She wasn't allowed to drive, so she never learned how, and many of the rights that women enjoy today were not available to women then. It wasn't until 1974 that women were even allowed to open their own bank accounts. So, Granny had to find a way to deal with Grandpa. In many ways, she was as much his prisoner as I was.

There were times when I saw Granny become furiously angry with him. Yet, she would stop, leave the house, and be gone for an hour or so. When she came back, the anger was gone. She wasn't pretending not to be angry anymore. It was easy to observe that she had let it go. So, when I got upset, I would also leave the house. I would go to a boulder on the back side of the farm that sat on the hillside above the creek. There, I would sit and watch nature until I could calm down. As an adult, I mentioned to Granny that I had seen her leaving the house and coming back without anger, and she said something very insightful. She said, "Yeah, I noticed that every time I got mad, my stomach would get upset, and I knew that if I didn't let it go, I was going to make myself sick." She had listened to her body and recognized the effect of emotions on her physically. I would have to have a lot more practice before I could stop carrying anger and anxiety around with me.

I AM A STONE

A crisp chill blew across the tan Arkansas sage grass,
And waved it across the hills.
Stark winter wind played
Among the red berries and cedars
That grew along the rusty fence.
The diamond-blue sky was devoid of clouds,
And the dogs huddled near the front door for warmth.
Grey branches of oak, yet bearing
A few clinging brown leaves
Appeared to crack the crystal sky.
Winter days were seldom white in northern Arkansas,
Although there were times
When the snow drifted against the doors,
And the dogs retreated to the barn.

In summer,
The temperatures climbed well above the nineties,
And cicadas hummed an annoying chant.
On summer nights, I would often sweat more than sleep.
In the day, a walk, if only across the yard,
Could leave my legs spotted with brown yearling ticks
That left itching bumps, which I would claw until they bled.

This was the land that bore me and tore me,
The land that gave me refuge from anguish,
Yet exacted payment of sweat, endurance, and labor.
This was the land that made me who I am.

I feel like my veins still flow with muddy pond water,
That has seeped into my soul.

I can't escape it,
Though I both cherish and loathe it.
Those rocky hills became my backbone
Forged to strength through anger and abuse.
Yet, in those rocks, I also hid from danger,
Retreated from anger and listened to the creek trickle
Around the foot of the hill below.

I sat for hours atop the largest stone.
I climbed it like a monkey when I was young.
There, I watched the squirrels dance along the branches.
Atop that rock, the birds sang,
The leaves floated about on gentle breezes,
And I became calm.

But in winter, I could not go.
The chill cut my face,
And drove me back to the potbellied stove.
In winter,
I tolerated their rage, criticism, and contempt,
Yet, I could discern no reason for it.
Perhaps they excreted contempt for themselves.

In time, I fought back.
In time, I adopted
The same rage and self-loathing as my own.
In time,
Resentment hardened around my heart,
And I forgot who I was.

Yet, I was lucky.
I got away.
I found loving guides

Who saw through my stone facade
To the tender heart still beating inside.
I found those souls who refused to return anger for anger,
Who returned love for my sullenness
Until the stone around my heart
Began to crack and fall away.

Then, I learned to become a different kind of stone.
I became my own refuge.
Then, I learned that my past may have influenced me,
But it does not have to define me.
Then, I learned that I am my own freedom,
I am my own peace,
And ultimately,
No one
Can shatter
That peace
But me.

Poem Introduction – THIS BOY

Who, even in this day and age, has not heard the admonishment, "*Big boys don't cry.*" What stupidity is taught to our children when they are conditioned to ignore rather than regulate their emotions? What damage is done when anyone is taught that there is something wrong with feeling? Emotions are one of the most integral parts of being human. Unless there is something wrong with the wiring of the brain, human beings feel emotions, and gender is irrelevant in that truth. Studies have shown that until about three years old, little boys tend to be more emotionally expressive than girls, but what happens by the age of three? We have learned language. Then, generally, if a little girl is smacked on the playground, parents or others sympathize with her. However, if a little boy is smacked on the playground, he is told to buck up, "*be a man,*" and that boys don't cry. We, therefore, rob children of their natural inclination to have emotions, which is one of the most integral parts of being human. Society typically talks feelings into girls while talking boys out of theirs. So, as adults, you have women who can be mad as hell and cry, while men can feel afraid or vulnerable and get angry.

Of course, we feel. When we grieve, we need to cry. When we are sad, and sometimes, even when we are happy, we need to cry. When I was a child, I was taught, as most males are taught, that crying was a sign of weakness. Later, I realized that the mind does not stop thinking just because tears come. We do not stop deciding just because we are grieving. We may need to set some time aside to allow for it, but crying is as natural as any other bodily function. Now, if I happen to cry, so what! We need to start teaching our children that it is okay to be human, sometimes humans cry, and there need be no shame in expressing what we feel.

THIS BOY

The boys on the bus
Are cruel with
Harsh words,
Putdowns and slurs.
Too much for an only child
With no sense of self-worth.

The boys on the bus
Torment and pick,
Bully and abuse,
But this boy
WILL NOT CRY,
Will not give them the satisfaction
Of gloating victory.
This boy
Will grit his teeth,
And take it,
Hold it like a mountain lake,
Hold it in
At home,
At school,
On the bus.
Hold it
Trembling and silent,
Hold it
For as long as it takes.
This boy
WILL
NOT
CRY!

Back up behind that dam,
Grief,
A reservoir of tears,
Presses hard against the barricade.
Up behind that dam,
The waters stir
And will not
Be still.

Though cracked,
The dam holds.

At last,
This boy
Steps down from the bus.
One shoe into the gravel,
Then another,
Slow,
Methodical.
Back turned to the bus,
This boy
Does not run,
Walks slow,
Determined they will not see.

The bus pulls away.
Then ...
Only then,
Those steps pick up speed,
And run the rest of the way.

Dust pops from the soles of cheap shoes.
Those steps slam
Across the porch,
Into the house,
Through the living room,
Into the bedroom,
Up to the bed.
This boy
Falls,
Face into a pillow,
And the dam
Breaks.

Poem Introduction – I LEARNED TO FIGHT

By the time I was eighteen, I was a very sullen and angry boy, and it took a lot of therapy and mentoring to weed that out of me. Before that, I had reached a decision, after dealing with my uncle's abuse as well as bullying at school, that I wasn't going to take it anymore. I trusted no one besides my grandmother and didn't trust her with everything. After all, I never told her that I was gay, even though I knew she loved me anyway, and I knew that she knew. Any new person that I encountered was met with initial contempt. Yet, they may never have known it. In the end, it was not fighting that saved me. It was something else.

I LEARNED TO FIGHT

I learned to fight when I was young.
It was fight or be conquered,
Fight or be bullied more.
I learned to respond with quick rage.
I wasn't going to put up with it anymore.

Out on the baseball field one day,
A flick of my knee, heaving my foot to the groin
Brought an end to the threat of one
Who thought he might conquer me.
I refused to be conquered.
He lay on the ground, curled in a ball
Crying and groaning, "Sissy fighter!"
My pointed response
was more of a statement than a question,
"I won, didn't I?"
I walked away and left him lying there groaning
With his friends all standing around
Doing nothing.

I learned to fight when I was young,
Kick, claw, bite, whatever it took.
My sixth-grade book was slammed
Flat into a senior's face
When he would not stop pulling my hair.
A bloody nose was his sentence
For the crime.
When thrice, he had been warned.

He sought to tell on me,
"Did you see what that kid did to me?"
The bus driver responded,
"Seems I heard that kid say,
'You'll be sorry if you do that again.'
Are you sorry, now?"

I learned to fight when I was young.
At thirteen years old, I challenged my abuser.
His boot hurled into my ass in the kitchen one night,
Brought a volcanic rage that had been intensifying
Since I was five years old.
I tore into him with everything I had,
But I did not win
That time.

Physically, I beat him when I was eighteen.
I finally made a believer out of him,
And he dared not touch me again.
After beating his head into the door facing,
I drug him out of my room, into the kitchen
And stood over him as he lay drunk and defeated
On the kitchen floor.

I pointed my raging finger in his face,
And snarled,
"You set foot in my room one more time,
Mother fucker, and you are a dead man!"

I learned to fight when I was young.
Bullied at home and bullied at school,
It seemed to be a necessity.
I could protect my body,
Sometimes.
The physical wounds healed,
But the wounds inside would not heal.
The wounds to my heart
Went on and on.
Like a belfry ghost,
The wounds to my spirit haunted me.

What they said could not be deflected
By a kick, a punch, or a slam.
What they said made me doubt
My worth and my worthiness.
What they said crumbled the foundations
Of my spirit, and left me doubting
My reason to exist.
No fist could fight that demon.
No angry punch of rage could stop it.
As anger rose, so rose
The fear and doubt behind it.
Nothing could prove my worthiness.
No matter how hard I tried
To cover my doubt with pride,
I could not bring myself to believe
That I was worth saving.

Accomplishments were nothing.
A fight won, so what?
The bottomless pit of my heart
Could not be filled
By the applause of a nation
Or the adoration of the world.
Still, I fought to fill it,
But I could not entertain my way
Out of the pain.
I could not achieve my way out of it.
The more I dumped into my empty heart,
The greater the void became.

I learned to fight when I was young,
But a different kind of fight
Was needed for an internal foe.
So, I learned to stand up for myself
When I grew up.
I learned to challenge my inner bully
Who constantly told me that
I would never be enough.
I learned to challenge doubt,
And affirm the truth.
I learned to relinquish fear
And recognize that courage
Often means standing your ground
Without fighting.
I learned to stand up for myself
When I grew up.
I learned that another person's behavior
Is never about me.
What they think and what they do
Does not define me.

I define myself.
I learned to stand up for myself
When I grew up.
I learned that my worth
Is equal to all worth.
I learned to comfort and console myself.
I learned to appreciate myself
For who I am.
I learned that I am worth more
Than fighting for.

Poem Introduction – MORE THAN ADMITTED

My great-grandfather, my grandmother's father, was deep into his eighties when I was a teenager. He had been born in the 1880's. After my great-grandmother died, typical of men in those days, he was unable to keep a household or cook for himself. When he was becoming so feeble that he needed assistance with practically everything, his four daughters and one son decided that they would rather share him amongst themselves than send him to a nursing home, each keeping him for a month at a time. However, our home had only four rooms. A fifth had been added by converting the back porch when I was a teen. Still, there was no extra bedroom. So, I gave up my normal comforts when he stayed with us, slept on the couch, and resented it. None of Granny's siblings had kids living in their homes, so they always had an extra bed available. I thought I was the only one who was truly inconvenienced. Yet, my great-grandpa on Granny's side was congenial and kind, unlike Grandpa and my Uncle Ray. He never mistreated me or spoke an unkind word to me. Later, I found myself regretting having been resentful of him.

MORE THAN ADMITTED

The old man frustrated me.
Because his five children traded him off
A month at a time to share the burden,
He came to our house to stay for a month,
Every five months for several years before he died.

He sat the whole time in a rocking chair
By the kitchen door.
He annoyed me with stories
That he told me practically every time I passed by.

There he sat, feeble and old,
With hair of purest white.
He set his cane hooked over the arm of the chair
To keep it handy
And fondled it as he talked.

He talked, and talked, and talked,
"The first woman who ever painted her lips
Was eaten by dogs.
The Bible says so."
"I once saw a man walk five miles
Carrying his guts in his arms
Because his belly got cut open in a knife fight."
"The town where your grandma was born
Is a ghost town, now.
Nobody lives there."
On
And on
And on.

I resented giving up my bed to him,
Then, having to sleep on the couch.
I resented having to shave him,
My chore when he was there.
I resented having to walk him to the bathroom
And stand there while he peed.
I resented that he got special meals cooked,
"Doctor's orders."
In the opinion of a young teen,
I had to give up too many things.
I suppose that I was a little selfish.

When he died,
I went on about my business
As though nothing had happened
Until one day,
When my anger boiled over,
The tears came.
The grief came,
And the knowledge came
That I had loved him more
Than I had admitted.

Poem Introduction - HATRED

Like an infecting virus, hatred is an evil, parasitical seed propagating by eliciting the host to produce more hate. Those who return hate for hate help that evil multiply. It took me a while to see that when I hate, I am taking on the same mental attitude as the one I hated, the one who hated me and hurt me. When I hate, I attach myself to what I despise. Hatred repeats itself from one host to another until we recognize it for what it is and give ourselves a chance to heal. A friend of mine said her father used to tell her, "*When you forgive, you set a prisoner free, and that prisoner is you.*" The only inoculation for hate is love. Hate for hate brings only hate. Love for hate brings healing.

HATRED

I thought of killing him once when I was fourteen.
I had had way more than enough.
I was done with his torment,
Done with his violence,
Done with his drunkenness,
Done with his contempt.

I WANTED HIM GONE!

The first abuse that I recall must have been
When I was maybe three.
I played with a spinning top on the floor
And for no apparent reason,
He began thumping me in the head with his finger.
It might be a small abuse compared to some,
But it was a huge affront to a three-year-old
When innocent play became anguish.

It went on.
Sometimes, it was only psychological torture
Such as walking by the TV set and turning it off
While I was watching my favorite show.
Sometimes, it was some little torment that
He would not admit
When Granny stepped back into the room,
And asked why I was crying.

No one asked why I began to torture animals
As a very small boy.
The pecking order went from my mother's older brother
To me and then to the animals.
The torment of a child was passed down to the
The next most vulnerable.
Had there been some little brother or sister,
They might have been the first to receive
The brunt of my anger,
But I grew up alone.

Hate begets hate.
No one seemed to realize,
Or, in those days, admit
That my behavior indicated
A reaction to abuse.
I was on my own.

I concluded, as an adult,
That he must have been jealous of me.
He never married,
Never left home,
Was the only boy of five children,

And had gotten his way for his entire life …
Until I came along.

When my mother died,
They said they didn't know where my father was.
I was orphaned,
And taken into their home
Where he had always been the prince,
Always the one
Who sucked up all their attention.
Suddenly … he had to share.

When I was left alone with him,
That was the worst.
To be slapped was the least of it.
To be held down on the couch
With a pillow over my face,
And have him sit on that pillow
Bouncing his ass into my face
Wasn't the of the worst of it.
Maybe he only stopped holding the pillow on my face
When he realized that he might kill me.
It certainly felt like I was going to die.

When I was thirteen,
I had had enough.
At first, I returned violence for violence.
One night, in the kitchen,
He kicked me in the ass with pointed cowboy boots,
And that was the final straw.
I flew into him with all the rage I could muster;
All the rage that had been building since the age of five.
The next thing I knew,

He had me on the floor
with his knees on my shoulders
while he beat me in the head with his fists.
Grandma grabbed him by the collar,
Tried her best to pull him off me,
And finally succeeded,
But the damage was done.
Hatred had infected me for years,
And that night, it festered into a boil.

One day, when Grandma and Grandpa were out of the house,
I caught him passed out in a living room chair.
I carefully snuck out into the yard,
And lifted a very large rock
From the border of Granny's flower bed.
I held it carefully under one arm
And opened the screen door as quietly as I could.
Then, I slithered up behind him
With the evillest intent I have ever contemplated,
I held the rock above my head
Intending to lower it with enough force
To crush his skull.
Yet, as I held it there,
A question ran through my mind,
"What will happen if you do this?"

There were images of prison,
Images of any hope for a better life halted,
But there were also images of grief,
For as much as I hated him,
I knew others loved him,
Especially Granny.
Although I intended to hurt him,

I could not hurt her.
I slowly lowered the stone,
Carried it back to the flower beds,
And told no one how close I came
To killing him until my adult years.

Then, I patiently waited,
Tolerated him as much as possible,
But finally, at the age of eighteen,
I beat him so badly
That he dared never touch me again.
Yet, in the end, it wasn't my fist that won the war,
It was loving, detachment, and forgiveness.

In time, I pitied him.
Pitied that he had not become
The man he could have been,
Pitied the hatred he had, more toward himself
Than anyone else,
Pitied his misery, his life of constant torment
Which he created for himself,
and others.

At the age of sixty-two,
He lay dying of lung cancer,
Slowly smothering.
I couldn't help wondering
If it had been
Some karmic punishment
For trying to smother me,
But it was more likely
Due to years of smoking unfiltered cigarettes.

I drove from Nashville,
Seven hours,
To help Granny.
Grandpa had died the year before,
And she had contended with my uncle alone.
When I arrived,
He still accused me of being selfish,
A projection of what he could not admit
Within himself.

One day, near the end,
When I was sitting with him alone,
He mumbled something.
I got up from my chair,
Leaned over the bed rail
And said, "I'm sorry, I couldn't hear you."
He mumbled again.
I said, "I'm sorry, I still didn't hear you."
The look on his face was one of complete rage.
He drew in as much air as he could hold
And said very clearly, "You're a Goddammed liar!"
I softly replied,
"Ray, no amount of anger is going to improve my hearing.
I honestly did not understand you,
But I'm willing to try again if you are."
He paused a moment,
Tried to fill his lungs one more time,
And enunciated, "I want a drink of water."
I walked around the bed,
Poured a glass of water
And held him up to drink.

That was the last interaction I ever had with him.
I have no way of knowing
If maybe,
Just maybe,
In those last moments,
He might have finally realized the truth,
But I don't know.
Yet, this is something that I will always find comfort in.
My last interaction with him
Was one of kindness and forgiveness
Because I realized the truth.

Poem Introduction – THE HURT DOG BITES

In the *Tao*, they teach that every lesson we need to learn can be found in nature. Yet, we have to be open to receiving the lesson. I learned from this childhood experience but didn't realize until adulthood that anger is never the real emotion. Hurt, fear, or feelings of vulnerability always drive anger. When animals or people feel vulnerable, they lash out. It is a natural response to intense and overwhelming pain, a natural response to being terrified. It occurs with both physical and psychological pain. We get grumpy when we get the flu or when we are exhausted. We are more likely to snap at things we might otherwise overlook when overly stressed. When we have unhealed trauma, we are more likely to verbally or physically attack others. *A Course in Miracles* says that anything that is not love is a cry for help. Beneath all anger is a cry for help.

I was about eight or nine years old when I learned that the hurt dog bites.

THE HURT DOG BITES

On the shaded summer porch wedged against the house.
We hull black-eyed peas into a bowl,
And drop the hulls into a zinc bucket.

Grandma smiles but doesn't say much,
And hulls twice the peas that I do.

Inept, immature, content, knowing nothing else,
I hull peas and watch the sunlight glisten
On the drying summer lawn.

Grandpa passes with a grunt,
"Goin' into town."

"Mumm Hmmm, pick up some bread," Granny says.
She drops another handful of peas into the bowl.

A moment later, the truck starts.
Summer silence breaks with warps and yelps.
My dog drags himself from the weight
Of the truck tire that crushed his back legs.

My heart breaks.
Startled and frightened, I run across the yard.

Grandma stands screaming,
"DON'T GO NEAR THAT DOG!
DON'T GO NEAR THAT DOG!
DON'T GO NEAR THAT DOG!"

Ignoring her, I reach to comfort "poor Brownie"
Only to have canine teeth
Sink deep and hard into the soft flesh of my right arm.

Blood drips, and I scream with pain.
The dog dangles from my arm as I tug it back,
But it refuses to let go.

Both adults,
Beside me now,
Careful, attentive, and mature
Distract the dog,
But keep their distance.

The bite releases,
Yet, left in its place,
Is an inch-long gash

That remained slow to heal.
Having never been stitched,
It left a lifelong scar.

I seldom notice it now.
More often than not
It is forgotten
But the scar remains.

Yet, moments occur
When I glance at that scar
And I am reminded,

The hurt dog bites.

Poem Introduction – THE BIRD STOPPED SINGING

I was given a gun when I was in the ninth grade. Yet, I was not like other boys who could go out to hunt and kill animals for sport or food. Hunting was yet another mold that I tried to fit myself into, another thing I did because other boys and the men in my family were doing it, not because I really wanted to. In those days, the school even let out for a day when deer hunting season started because most boys would skip school to hunt anyway. After the girls protested that they should be given equal treatment, they were granted a *"shopping day"* in early December. My need to fit myself into the male expectation of having guns and hunting didn't last for long, and I still feel sadness about how it came to an end. That moment of transition when I stopped trying as much to be like other boys occurred when the bird stopped singing.

THE BIRD STOPPED SINGING

When the bird stopped singing,
It broke my heart.

Moments before, the bright red cardinal's
Mating call filled the forest with nature's melody.
Moments before, I heard the singing
And wondered where it might be coming from.
I followed my ears in the direction of the serenade
And finally spotted it.

There, on an oak limb above our muddy pond,
The bird sat joyfully warbling.
It hopped from one side to the other
Lifting its beak with a bewitching sound.
I spotted it, watched it for a moment,
And wondered.

The bullfrogs croaked around the edge of the pond.
Their song was nothing in comparison.
Their muddy heads could not equate
Nature's most colorful artistry.
The cardinal was bright red elegance
And a symphony on an oak limb.

My twenty-two-gauge rifle,
A gift on my fourteenth birthday,
Felt warm and smooth in my hand.

Bullfrogs were easily popped in the head
At the edge of the pond
And became fried frog's legs for dinner.
That was my goal,
But I watched the cardinal as it sang,
And wondered.

Finally, my decision made, I held the gun aloft
And found the bird square in my sights.
Before I could give it a second thought,
I pulled my curled finger.

The crack of my gun echoed through the trees,
And the singing stopped immediately.
The bird fell onto rocky ground, completely silent,
Completely still.

That moment shattered me.
Waves of grief ran through me, and tears came.
When the bird stopped singing,
It broke my heart,
And I never fired that gun again.

Poem Introduction – REJOICE

I am very lucky to have had the positive spiritual and loving influences I encountered throughout my life. I am so lucky to have mentors, teachers, and guides. I know that many went through even greater torment than mine and had no one as a child, encountered no one in their young adult years, and suffered ongoing internal torment for most or all their lives. Some remain so wounded by their childhood that they never dare trust and, therefore, seek the slightest reason to push someone out of their lives, even if that person sees through them and is trying to help. Far too many LGBTQIA+ youth commit suicide or attempt suicide because they don't have someone to love and support them. We all need an anchor in the storm. We all need those who know how to love genuinely and are willing to extend it. I won the love lottery. Despite what I went through as a child, I won the love lottery, and I will be eternally grateful for all the anchors I have had in my storms.

This poem is about my friend, Marcy, who mentored me in college and beyond. She was older and had returned to college after dropping out to work and help put her husband through getting his PhD in psychology. The deal was that she could return to school when he graduated and got his first job. His first job happened at our college town's community mental health center.

When I first met Marcy (college choir), I avoided her. She seemed goofy and weird to me. I made a mental note to stay away from that strange woman. Yet, she wouldn't stay away from me and repeatedly placed herself in my company. She must have seen something in me and later told me she thought I had been her child in a former life. Perhaps that's true since she became like a surrogate and loving mother to me. She very lovingly refused to let me get away with my bullshit.

REJOICE

The moon looked green
Through the tinted windows of our tour bus.
She sat between me and the window, holding my hand.
Her humor calmed my anger as I bitched about
This infraction or that.

"You're fuming again."
She grinned her gleaming grin
With dimples dipping
On either side of her face
when she smiled.

I couldn't get away with it,
Not with her.
I couldn't piss and moan,
Lament the unfairness of my life.
She met every fume with a reminder
That I need not be negative.

She had taken me under her wing, this older woman,
Not so much older, but certainly wiser.
She had mentored me,
Given me options to anger.
Most often, the option was humor.
Laugh it off and go on.
Enjoy all of life that you can
While you can
For as long as you can.
Learn to revel in the simplest beauty
Of the simplest thing
On your worst day.

Rejoice!
Be grateful.
She was an expert at it.

Having been ill from birth with a prognosis
Never to live beyond young adult years,
She had beaten the odds and returned to college
After her husband completed his PhD.
She would never let her genetic illness
Or a prognosis slow her down.
She rejoiced in life,
And learned to milk it for all it was worth.

The college choir tour was over.
We were headed home,
And I was bitching
Which was common for me.

After reminding me that I was fuming again,
She had turned her attention to the moon.
"Isn't she beautiful tonight?"

I watched the green moon
Glowing round and full
Behind the green-tinted window of our bus.
It appeared to stay still,
Hang constantly in place
While everything else moved around it.
She was like that.
She was steady like the moon.
We gazed at the moon together that night.
Then I felt her fat, warm hand
Squeeze gently on top of mine,
And I relaxed.

Poem Introduction – GET AWAY

Following are the lyrics to a song I wrote in 1981 after my cousin committed suicide. My cousin and I had been close when we were growing up, but I didn't learn that she was lesbian until after we became adults, and she showed courage that I could not yet muster. Still, there can be consequences to courage. Two years older than me, she joined the Army, and I chose to go to college. Shortly after, she came home with her female lover and could get no peace about it from her mother and father, who would not accept her for being lesbian even though she was an adult. They harassed her, tried to control her, and demanded that she could not touch her partner. So, she moved as far away as she could, to Sacramento, California. Later, I learned that she had been gang raped in the military, perhaps because she was lesbian. All of it was far too heavy for her to carry. So, she gave up, and I will forever grieve that she could not have found a better way.

GET AWAY

When you were a little girl
Learning all about the world
You were playing with the little boys
Not paper dolls or sissy things,
None of those so-called normal things.
They told you early on that you were
Different from the others in the world.

Growing up was such a bore,
And Momma's wishes were such a chore.
All the demands they forced on you
Made you forget your humanity.
You spent your life trying to flee
From monsters placed into your mind
But you could never leave those fears behind.

Did you ever really get away?

Sometimes crap ran through your head
Making you wish you were dead.
Seemed like everywhere you turned,
Another lesson for you to learn,
Crazy makers manufacturing
A vice-grip mind that made you want to scream.

Little girls don't play with boys.
Big girls ought to tease the boys.
Keep away; don't get too close.
What's the matter, girl?
Don't you like boys?
Crazy makers manufacturing
A vice-grip mind that made you want to scream.

Did you ever really get away?

The first chance that you could get,
You moved away to another state
Where you thought you could be yourself
But wherever you went, you carried the hell.

Trapped in yourself, wanting out.
One day, when you thought you'd had enough,
You took a gun and blew it all
Away,

Away,

Away.

Did you ever really get away?

Poem Introduction – NEVER EXPECT

In addition to the previous song lyrics, I wrote this poem after my cousin's suicide. I received a phone call at work shortly after graduating from graduate school in 1981. My cousin's partner informed me that my cousin had walked into their living room the night before, put a gun to her head, said, "What's the use," and pulled the trigger. Because of the way they had treated my cousin's partner, she was unwilling to contact my cousin's parents. I became the one who called my aunt to inform her that her oldest daughter had committed suicide.

I had spoken to my cousin the week before. I was living in Little Rock, where I had attended graduate school. She was unhappy with her situation in California, and I suggested she live with me for a while. She refused, saying, even though I was a four-hour drive from her mother, that if she lived even that close, her mother would be up in her business and trying to control her. That was one of those *I wish I had known* phone calls. Yet, sometimes, even when we know that someone is having thoughts about killing themselves, our best efforts cannot stop them. Ultimately, it is a choice they make. What I know is that I expressed my love for her, and I offered compassion.

NEVER EXPECT

When you answer the phone at work,
You don't expect that the person on the other end
Will be your cousin's lesbian girlfriend.

You don't expect her to tell you
That the only other person in the family
You were almost as close to as your grandma
Is dead.

You don't expect that she will tell you that
Your cousin walked into the living room the night before,

Put a pistol to her head,
And pulled the trigger.

You don't expect the shock
Of hearing those words
Will freeze you in place
With no breath,
Speechless,
Not knowing what to say,
What questions to ask,
Or what to do next.

You probably wouldn't even notice
How numb you feel
As you sit staring at a blank space on the wall,
Or that the receiver is still in your hand,
Until you almost drop it.

You never think that your cousin's lover
Will ask you to call your cousin's mom,
The one who rejected her and drove her away
For living a life of "*sin*."

You don't expect a few minutes on
That you will avoid making that call to your aunt
While you wonder if you might divert the responsibility
To someone else in the family.

When you finally,
Hesitantly,
Make that call,
You don't expect
That you will be asked to be a pallbearer at the funeral,

Or that you will say "yes,"
Knowing it will be one of the most difficult things
You will ever have to do.

You don't expect,
When you hang up that call,
And make another to your boss,
That your voice will quiver,
And your hand will tremble
When you ask for time off.

You never dream that,
In a couple of days,
You will be standing outside a funeral home
Listening to your aunt swear
That your cousin was murdered by her lesbian lover.

You don't expect that you will bite your lip,
And rock in place
As you struggle to keep your mouth shut
Knowing that your cousin moved as far away as she could
To escape your aunt's control.

You never think that you will sit through a funeral service
That will become a blank space in your mind,
A totally forgotten episode of your life
In which no memory resides.

You don't expect that the next memory you will have
Will be of pulling your cousin's casket from a hearse
At a tent-covered burial site,
Or that you will walk,
Stone-faced,

Hand on a bar,
Holding a coffin
Carrying it to a hole in the ground
Where you stand with five other men,
Some you don't even know.

You don't expect that the one thing,
The straw that will break the camel's back,
The one thing
That will make you burst into uncontrollable tears
Will be watching that silver coffin
Sinking slowly into a hole.

You don't expect
That the one person
Who will rush to comfort you and hold you
Will be the same aunt
Who drove your cousin away in the first place.

You never, ever
Expect
How much your heart will hurt
Or that you will never, ever
Forget
That one day at work
When you answered that one call,
Where you were told
That one thing
You would never,
Ever
Expect,
And never,
Ever
Wanted to know.

Poem Introduction – A POEM FOR MARCY

Marcy, the older woman I had met in college who had taken me under her wing, mentored me, loved me, and mothered me, died at the age of fifty-eight. This was twenty years past the date that her doctors had predicted her to die. Yet, it was not her lifelong auto-immune illness that finally got the best of her. It was undiagnosed diverticulitis that ruptured into her peritoneum and poisoned her from the inside. As she lay dying, she could only lie on her back with her abdomen open under a tent so her intestines could be lavaged. While I and others sat visiting her, she suddenly said, "I love my magnolia tree."

When she said that, I searched my mind. I never recalled seeing a magnolia tree at or around her house. I said, "Magnolia tree? What magnolia tree? You don't have a magnolia tree."

She said, "Yes, I do."

I asked, "Where?"

She said, "Out there," and pointed toward the window.

I got up and moved to her bedside to follow the direction of her point, and through the window of her third-floor room, in the distance between two buildings, was a magnolia tree in bloom. She had taught me mindfulness, to focus on and be grateful for any blessing to be found in the moment. She practiced that until the end, finding a magnolia tree in the distance to claim as her own and appreciate its simple beauty as she lay dying. This was the one last lesson she taught me.

I will be grateful for all my life that I met her and that she loved me.

A POEM FOR MARCY

Oh, my restless soul
Where will I come to rest?
Will I rest beneath the grass,
In deep soil and stone?
Will I rest amid the grave sites
Where others lie row upon row
bone upon bone?

Oh, my restless soul
Where will I come to rest?
Will I rest high in the rafters,
In the homes I used to know?
Will I rest in echoes through the halls
Or in still garden solitude
Among the seeds that I have sewn?

Oh, my restless soul
Where will I come to rest?
Will I rest in the sunlit sky,
In breezes through the hills?
Will I rest in bird calls from the trees
Or in nature's song of silence
as evening settles soft and still?

Oh, my restless soul
Where will I come to rest?

I will rest in memories of joy
In laughter and in tears.
I will rest in sacred love
That endures through all the years.
I will rest in lessons learned,
In comfort and in peace.
For I will rest forever and ever
In the hearts of those who loved me.

Poem Introduction – THE OBJECT

Even though my uncle often managed to ruin it by getting drunk, Christmas was one of the things I treasured about my childhood. I remember trudging through the sage grass with Granny, looking for the perfect Cedar tree to cut for Christmas. When we found it, we put it in a bucket and held it in place by putting rocks around the trunk inside the bucket. The bucket, with water poured over the rocks, would keep the tree fresh for a few days, hopefully until after Christmas. Of course, putting up the tree had to be done shortly before Christmas, for it wouldn't last too long.

Granny's Christmas tree was usually sparse, with bits of ornaments collected from here or there, often worn-out hand-me-downs from others who didn't want them. Still, the tree meant something. However, my friend Marcy and her family taught me what a treasure a simple Christmas ornament could be.

When I was in graduate school, Marcy's mother was dying of cancer at Christmas time. We visited her parent's house in the Heights area of Little Rock. They had a beautiful Victorian home with beveled glass windows on either side of the door and a large front porch. Through the front door was a very large foyer. On the back side of that was a set of stairs leading to the second floor. To the right were white double French doors with beveled glass. This led to the living room, where a fireplace was directly across from those French doors.

Inside the foyer, to the left, was what her father called "*The Sugar Plum Tree.*" (I've written about this on the blog page of my website.) He had cut the top of a bare elm tree, spray painted the branches silver, strung it with lights and angel hair, and hung various ornaments from the bare limbs. Beyond the fact that it was beautiful, what fascinated me was that every ornament on the tree had a memory and a story. They weren't just there for decoration. Marcy's aunt made ornaments from old medicine bottles from the 1940s and 50s. There was a small pagoda lantern sent to them by friends in Taiwan, but my favorite was a little red plastic Santa Claus that had likely been a candy container, which her mother found in a gutter in New York in 1934.

That tree gave me an idea. Since, on my graduate school stipend, I had little money for Christmas that year, I decided to give friends and family ornaments. I wrote about the Sugar Plum Tree and how I had been touched by the memories contained in each ornament on the tree. I then made copies of that story and bought inexpensive Christmas ornaments. That year, I gave friends and family the story of the Sugar Plum Tree and an ornament.

After that, those close to me began giving me ornaments for Christmas. When I moved to The Coastal Bend in 2015, I had around three hundred ornaments and a huge tree to put them on. However, some were more special to me than others, including ornaments that Marcy and Granny had given me.

When I moved to The Coastal Bend, I had to whittle the contents of a four-bedroom house with eleven-foot ceilings down to a one-bedroom apartment with an eight-foot ceiling. So, my eight-foot, extra-wide Christmas tree had to go. Cutting back included giving a huge number of my ornaments to charity. However, I kept the ones given to me by those closest to me. When it came to my first Christmas in South Texas, I bought a four-foot Christmas tree and began decorating it with some of the keepsake ornaments I had left. However, there was an ornament from Granny that I could not find, and I was heartbroken. Before moving, I had had three-yard sales, and several boxes had also gone from my Missouri house to charity shops. I assumed Granny's ornament must have mixed in with those, and I would never see it again.

As I cut my possessions to less than a quarter of what I previously owned, I said, "Sooner or later, it all ends up in a landfill." I had been working on detachment and letting go years before doing this. So, I gave about twelve of Granny's quilts to family members. I parted with plants I loved and had kept for 30 years (they got good homes), and I let go of ornaments that meant something to me but that I could simply no longer hang onto. In all the confusion, it was easy for things that I intended to keep to get lost. For instance, I never found my chef's knife even though I remember wrapping it and putting it in the box labeled *kitchen*. We always lose something when moving, and I thought I had lost Granny's ornament. It challenged me to practice my detachment skills. However, after writing this poem, when I moved out of that tiny apartment, I found Granny's ornament in a box I had forgotten and had stored under the bed. After grieving for its loss, I was grateful to find it again. When I thought I had lost it, I wrote this poem.

THE OBJECT

Gathering dust,
The heirloom was unaware of the emotional baggage
Cast upon it by my grieving heart.
It could not see,
Nor understand the bond that causes grief to cling
To an object that only fades with time.
Packed in a box, unpacked at Christmas,
The object that my grandma gave to me,
Felt nothing when grieving tears fell upon it
After she died.
Yet each year I brought it forth,
And considered it precious.

With my tender care, it had never fallen to break,
But was lost in my upheaval and transition,
The wrong box was carted off to charity.
It has likely ended up in a flea market somewhere.

Perhaps someone who never knew the story
May feel something—
Some unspoken loving magic that draws her to it.
Perhaps she will add it to her own Christmas bounty,

And also cherish it, year after year.
Perhaps a similar emotional spell
Will be cast over other lives.

In some unforeseen future, some fumbling hand
Will touch the object one last time before it falls
And shatters against a hard and uncaring floor.
It will be swept away with other debris,
And tossed into the trash.
If I am gone when that day comes,
There will be no one to remember
What it meant to me,
Or that it symbolized
How much my grandma comforted
And cherished me.

Poem Introduction – TOUGH

Although I didn't meet my dad until I was eighteen, he was integral to my childhood. There had always been a longing to know him. My mother was missing, and I could never get her back, but perhaps my father was someone I could find someday.

I used to gather the few things that were left of my mother's possessions after she died, sit with them and think about her. My stepfather had taken everything except what was retrieved after her funeral and a silverware set that Mom had, for some reason, left with Granny. What had been retrieved was her purse, the police report about the accident, her watch, and jewelry, including her wedding and engagement rings. A small cedar jewelry box contained her jewelry. As an adult, I kept those things wherever I moved. However, all that except her purse containing paperwork was stolen during a house break-in when I lived in Nashville. My entire life has been about learning to let go. Technically, if you think about it, letting go is the primary lesson of everyone's life.

The only thing I had of my father was one photo and a copy of the book written about him, which he had autographed for my mom. (*Laughter In Hell* by Stephen Marek – available on Amazon) I would often get it out, thumb through it, and look at the black-and-white photographs of servicemen so thin that their bones showed through their skin. However, I never read it until I was an adult. I don't know if I thought it was too complicated to read as a kid or if I was afraid of what might be revealed in those pages. Even after meeting my dad, I avoided reading it until I was in my thirties.

I longed for and hoped for my dad all during my childhood. I didn't know what I might uncover if I were to find him. My grandparents' minimal amount of information about him was not positive. My uncle apparently knew, and my father later confirmed, that my mom had gotten pregnant before they were married. This is why my uncle loved gloatingly, referring to me as "the little bastard."

When I finally found my father, however, I was not disappointed. He confirmed his bad behavior that had occurred when he knew my mother. Like many servicemen with PTSD, he drank heavily early on, among other things, but finally concluded that he didn't need to continue doing that. He had changed over the eighteen years between knowing my mother and meeting me. Unlike many who suffered trauma, he had not kept it in. He had talked about it, shared stories, and continued to live a life as a civilian without the hypervigilance and public paranoia that many who suffered trauma experienced. There have been several stories that he has shared with me about his POW experience that are not contained in his book, and he didn't seem to mind talking about it with practically anyone. I think talking about it is part of what helped him heal.

Viktor Frankl, a Jewish Psychiatrist whom the Nazis also imprisoned at Auschwitz, wrote the book *Man's Search for Meaning*. In it, he talks about observing those fellow prisoners who he thought were most likely to survive the death camps. He identified three fundamental traits of survivors. First, they did something for themselves daily, even if only to wash their face. Second, no matter how little they had, they shared at least some of it with someone else, and third, they always talked positively about the future and had plans for what they would do when they got out of the camps.

If I look at those traits as applied to my father, he had all three. I'm fairly certain he did whatever he could to care for himself. He told me about eating insects or whatever protein could be found, including any animal wandering into the yard, which was caught, skinned, and eaten raw. He also did what he could to help his fellow servicemen survive. POWs were put to work unloading trains, among other things, and used as slave labor by the Japanese. So, my dad had access to food at times. He had learned how to pick locks and began finding ways to steal food. Even then, there had to be caution about gaining weight, attracting suspicion from certain officials, and sharing food with fellow POWs. Self-discipline was lifesaving. He struck up bargains with some guards who would look the other way when he stole food because he would also share it with them.

They were happy to receive it because, even though they had more than the P.O.W.s, they and their families were also rationed. Last, he kept a journal throughout his time as a P.O.W. and hid it from the Japanese officials lest they torture him or perhaps kill him. He told me there is a copy of his journal at the National Museum of the Marine Corps, although I have never been there. He looked forward to being able to get out and tell his story. He had the traits of a survivor, as identified by Viktor Frankl. The book about him, *Laughter in Hell*, by Steven Marek, initially published in 1954, was the first book ever published about Japanese prisoners of war in WWII.

This is a poem about my dad and about a strength that I don't think I could ever even imitate.

TOUGH

Captured by the Japanese in the Guam invasion,
Post Pearl Harbor attacks,
The jungle had been a temporary refuge.
Captured, tortured, humiliated,
They were placed in front of a fake firing squad,
Intimidated down to the order of "fire!"
"Ready …
Aim …"
But "fire" never came.
There were, he said, no dry pants
In the lineup of about ten enlisted
And some had lost bowel control.
Then, they were stacked in a pile,
Locked in a closet for three days
With
No food,
No water,
Marinating in the stench of

Urination and defecation,
And gasping at the stale air
Before being shipped to Japan
In the hull of a cargo ship.
This was his introduction to
spending the duration of World War II
In Japanese P.O.W. camps.

A cockroach is a nasty thing,
Unless you're starving.
Raw rat meat is disgusting,
Unless you're starving.
Squalor and filth,
Starvation, beatings, and illness
Can be tolerated briefly,
But for four years?
He did it.

Malaria, malnutrition, and beatings
Took their toll.
Six feet tall,
He was down to seventy-eight pounds
At one point.
Yet, he was surviving,
Barely.
Others did not.
About a third did not survive.

I guess you could say
He was tough,
Tougher than I ever dreamed of being

And he never seemed to realize
How much I admired him
For that and many other things.

The prison camps never left him.
The damage seeped into his bones
And tortured him for life.
A wheelchair became his transportation,
But he was tough,
Tougher than I ever dreamed of being.

At ninety-three years old,
Still tough,
Still pushing on,
Still hanging onto life,
He was finally forced to succumb.
My dad was tough.
He was tougher than I ever dreamed of being.

Perhaps,
I should think of him
The next time
I smash my finger and cuss,
The next time, some petty frustration
Torments me
And I feel sorry for myself.

Perhaps,
I should think of him
The next time a restaurant
Delays serving my meal,
The next time I worry or regret
Or think that life hasn't treated me right.

Perhaps,
I should thank him
when I exercise my right to vote
Or protest something that I perceive to be injustice.
I should thank him for
The freedoms that he served to protect.

Perhaps,
I should think of him
A little more than I do,
And remember that no matter how difficult
My life might have been,
It was never as bad as that.
It can always be a lot worse
And gratitude for what I have
Is a far greater reward
Than regret for what I don't.

Indeed,
My father
Was tough.
Tougher
Than I ever dreamed
Of being.

Poem Introduction – INVISIBLE

Growing up gay in the hills of Arkansas in the 1960s while attending an authoritarian church was not easy. The message came to me all too clearly from society and the church that I should not be gay. It was not allowed. When the preacher of my church said, *"The sin of homosexuality is worse than the sin of murder,"* it was a shot straight to the heart of a lonely sixteen-year-old kid. The conclusion was that I either needed to kill myself or keep my mouth shut lest they kill me or torture me for simply being.

I struggled with that spiritual monster for much of my life until I found people who would love and accept me for who I was and until I found ministers of other churches who disagreed with the preacher of my childhood. For the longest time, I thought I had to swallow what the authoritarian church fed me. I never considered that there could be different interpretations of the Bible. Besides, the other authoritarian message I received was that the church's word was not to be questioned. Later, I asked myself why authoritarian churches focus so vehemently on a few passages about homosexuality that have been debunked by many theologians while ignoring so many other passages of the Bible admonishing them to love their neighbors, treat others as they would wish to be treated, not to judge, and to mind their own business.

As my spirituality developed, I wondered how Jesus's message of love got turned into condemnation and judgment. *"He that is without sin among you let him first cast a stone."* (*John* 8: 7-11) Why was I and others like me supposed to hide? Why was my "sin" (and I no longer believe it is a sin) worse than theirs? *"For all have sinned and fall short of the glory of God."* (*Romans* 3: 23-24) Besides, who I am is not a sin. In time, I understood and accepted that God loves me as I am and that I don't have to prove anything to anyone, be invisible, or live according to their prescribed rules. If they want to believe that, the rules are for them to practice, not try to force on others. *"Why do you look at the speck of sawdust in your brother's eye and pay no attention to the plank in your own eye?"* (*Matthew* 7: 3-5)

The myth perpetrated by the authoritarian church is that sexual orientation is a choice, but those who believe that never stop to ask themselves how easy it would be to try to force themselves to change their sexual orientation. They never wonder why anyone would choose to be invisible, to be despised by a huge chunk of society, and to risk violence just for being visible as who they are. Heterosexuals who believe that being gay is a choice, a sin, need to put some effort into trying to make themselves be attracted to the same sex and see how far they get. LGBTQIA+ people have been trying to force themselves out of their attractions for centuries. It has never worked. We had to put on a mask and play a role because we couldn't change who we were, and society would not accept us; we had to remain invisible.

In the era of my childhood, I had to be invisible. In the 1960s, in rural Arkansas, being raised attending an authoritarian church, I had to be invisible. Since they made it potently clear that queer people were to be despised, and as far as I knew, I was the only one anywhere around there, in my mind, I had to be invisible or risk being attacked or kill myself. Oh, but suicide is considered a sin, too. So, If I stayed alive, I might have some chance of redemption before I died, and maybe I could save myself from eternal damnation. I chose to live even though that meant living a miserable, invisible life. Finally, I allowed myself to stop being invisible and stop worrying about the approval of others.

Unfortunately, far too many queer people, especially queer youth, choose to die because there is a danger and a threat to being visible. The judgment and condemnation get to be too much for them. Maybe, unlike myself, they don't have an anchor, someone who loves them and holds them steady. They should. Since LGBTQIA+ is the only minority at risk of being rejected and shunned by their own family and friends, if more families and friends stood up and offered the love and support that queer people, especially queer youth, need and deserve, perhaps fewer would choose suicide. In fact, research shows that fewer attempt suicide when they have an anchor of love and understanding. Ultimately, society should be their anchor because they (we) deserve to be visible and deserve a place in society like everyone else.

I have never understood the hatred of queer people. We don't maraud about as gangs attacking people. Most want to be left alone and live in peace without being attacked overtly or covertly. If there were any gift we could be given, it would be the gift of being allowed to be a visible and normal part of society instead of being demonized and hated simply for being who we are or being despised for no good reason. After all, we all deserve to be visible.

INVISIBLE

It had to be hidden.
The real me unseen.
For I was forbidden
As nature created me to be.
I had to remain invisible.

I wasn't supposed to feel it.
I wasn't supposed to know it.
I wasn't supposed to be it.
I was supposed to be invisible.

I wasn't supposed to step out of bounds
Or feel what I was feeling.
I wasn't to utter a single sound
Of what I was concealing.
I was supposed to be invisible.

They taught me that I was horrible,
That I had no place in life.
They taught me that I was an abomination,
A source of conflict and strife

A plague to be abolished
If ever I were visible.

Like a witch to be burned at the stake,
Despised, tormented, and shunned
I was taught that I was a mistake
That I should be unloved
And forever remain invisible.

I dared not love myself
For that was not allowed.
I dared not be myself
Or, worst of all, be proud.
I must remain invisible.

I dared never let my feminine side be seen
For that was most despised.
I had to be what they wanted me to be
A role that they prescribed
And always remain invisible.

My terror grew as time went on
That some part of me might show
That they would conclude who I was
And my secret would be known.
What then might become of me
If ever I were visible?

It took great courage when I admitted
First to myself before anyone else
That I deserved more than permitted.
That I deserved to be myself.

I deserve to be visible.

I deserve what they take for granted
To be seen and known
Loved, welcomed, open, and candid.
I deserve to hold hands in public
With the man who is my love.
I deserve to be visible.

I deserve the same rights as them
And the same respect.
For I have learned to love myself
Regardless of what they expect.
I deserve to be visible.

I am here the same as you,
The same heart, the same blood,
The same longing, too.
I deserve to be visible.
I refuse to believe that I am worth less than you
Just because of who I am.
I refuse to believe that I deserve less than you
Because I am a man who loves a man.
I deserve the same rights,
The same privileges, too,
For no matter what you think,
I
Am not
Less
Than you.

See me as I am.

I am here.
I am visible.
See me as a human being
Not as your judgment or condemnation
For I am not here for you.
I am here to live my life for me.
I will no longer play a role for you.
I will no longer be invisible.
I will be myself whether you like it or not
For just like you,
I deserve
To be
Visible.

Poem Introduction – WHY I AM HERE

I wish that every troubled child could have an anchor in the storm, someone who would be consistent and loving with them, no matter what, someone who would cherish rather than hurt and betray them. I wish that every suffering child could have someone like my grandmother.

What we know from research is that when LGBTQIA+ youth have someone who loves and respects them and who accepts them, they are far less likely to attempt suicide. Knowing, genuinely knowing, that you are loved is one of the most life-affirming and life-saving experiences anyone can have. That doesn't mean that it is a save-all or that there aren't those who have love and respect and don't attempt or succeed with committing suicide, but love and acceptance make a huge difference, especially for youth.

My grandmother was my first anchor in the storm.

WHY I AM HERE

What was I supposed to do with my uncle's spitting rage,
His resentment that life had not become what he wanted,
His self-imposed misery
And the self-hatred that he took out on me?
What was I supposed to do with that?

I was only a little boy,
Only trying to figure things out for myself.
For the longest time,
I took his resentment and jealousy
As an indication of my worthlessness.
After all,
I was discarded.
My mother was dead.
My father was nowhere to be found,

And my uncle called me "the little bastard,"
A mistake of lust.

For the longest time,
I thought something was wrong with me.
After all,
My uncle wasn't the only one who was disappointed in me.
My Grandpa despised me, as well,
Or at least,
I thought he did.
He resented having to raise
The discarded kid,
And didn't mind letting me know
That I was his burden.

The kids at school mistreated me,
And found it easy to bully.
They picked at me and taunted me,
But worst of all,
They shunned me.
My childhood was an experience
Of tremendous loneliness.

There was torment at home,
Torment at school,
And loneliness abounding.
Grandma seemed to be the only one
Who said or did loving things.
She was my anchor,
My shelter in the storm,
Holding me steady
In my tempest-tossed childhood.

She was the one
Who held my hand
When we walked to church.
She was the one
Who saved Easter egg coloring
To decorate the icing on my birthday cake,
And she was the only one
To celebrate it with me.

She was the one
Who encouraged me,
"Your mother always wanted you to go to college."
She was the one who was there for every graduation
When Grandpa never came.

She was the one light
In my darkness,
The one hand
Reaching out to hold my own
So, I would not sink
Into the vortex
Of anguish and despair.

She is why I am here.

Learning to Live

Segment Introduction

In the Biblical book of Genesis, Adam and Eve are described before eating the forbidden fruit as innocent, unaware of their nakedness, and not knowing good or evil. Who do you know who is like that? The answer is small children. You see, symbolically, we have all been cast from Eden, which occurred at the point of our first shaming, the first time we came to know the concept of wrong. For example, if a two or three-year-old child runs through the house naked, everyone thinks it is cute. The child is not shamed for it and, for a time, remains in the mental state of Eden. However, if the child runs through the house naked at age five or six or older, the child is scolded, "Get back in there and put some clothes on! You should be ashamed of yourself!" The child is made aware of his/her/their nakedness and that it is no longer accepted. Now, it's wrong; before, it wasn't. It is at our first moment of shaming that we are all cast from Eden, and most of us spend our lives subconsciously thinking that we are outcasts, whether we are Judeo-Christian or not, whether we are aware of it or admit it or not. When a child is abused, in addition to that first shaming, they feel even more cursed and outcast. The younger the child when the abuse or trauma occurs, the more they may struggle with shame. Yet, even abused children, when younger, cling more closely to innocence. If you ask small children if they can sing, draw, or dance, almost all will say 'yes.' The older they get, the fewer the numbers who will proclaim that they can sing, draw, or dance. Very few adults retain that connection to joy and creativity. No one gets away without dealing with shaming, even if they are loved and have not been abused. Those who grow up in abusive homes are affected by it and have to deal with it more than others.

The poetry in this section was all written when I was young. Some of it was written in junior high and high school, possibly as young as twelve or thirteen, when I was still trying to cling to some innocence and joy. Some were written in college and a bit later, but none were past my mid-twenties.

The poems here were written during the years that I discovered myself, first learning about life, love, attractions, and feelings. These were the years that I first began emerging from the abuse and isolation of my childhood into the recognition that there is another way of life, another way of looking at things, and that obtaining release from limiting beliefs of the past is not only possible but attainable. When I became convinced there was a better way, I did not stop until I found it. Now, I continue to practice the skills for that better way regularly.

Some of these poems are just wordplay for fun, clinging to my innocence; some are experiments in poetry, some are observations of the time, and some are expressions of emotions I was experiencing during those periods. You will likely notice a progression from the early poetry to the poetry I wrote in my early 20s, reflecting how I was changing and what I was facing.

I wrote poetry by hand in a bound record book/journal that I bought with my saved allowance at the local five-and-dime store. I must not have been too prolific because I started it when I was thirteen or fourteen and didn't fill in the last page until after graduating college. I have also written poetry in other places, but those are lost. Moves and computer crashes without backup have destroyed those. However, I still have that record book, which is now over fifty years old. A lot of the poetry in it does not seem worthy of repeating, but I have pulled some of the ones that I like or think have merit and some that are just for fun. I have also taken the liberty of tweaking some of them slightly.

Poem Introduction – THE FLY

Okay, in junior high school, I did a little poetic experimentation. This was one of those experiments. I may have written it after watching a cat chase a fly. More than anything, it was my mind enjoying itself. I've always loved wordplay, and this is an early example of that.

THE FLY

Flip it!
Flop it!
Beat it!
Bop it!
Stomp it!
Chomp it!
Squeeze it!
Tease it!
It's going to die!
It's going to die!
Poor little fly. . .

Poem Introduction – THE TOAD

Here is another junior high school experiment. This is more wordplay experimentation.

THE TOAD

Stationed along life's weary road
It felt the warmth,
Experienced the cold.
An ugly, scaley, bug-eating toad.

Poem Introduction - HIDDEN

This is another youth experiment. Perhaps it was related to my first aware-ness of needing to be invisible. I hid many things growing up, especially as a teen.

HIDDEN

The bird may chirp,
The wolf may howl,
Our hearts may nurse
A hateful scowl,
Yet our lips smile wide
And all this we hide
At the coming of the feast.

Poem Introduction – CRADLE TO GRAVE

A lot was happening nationally when I was in high school and before. It was, after all, the 1960s. Even though I grew up in an all-white, rural area of the country, I was not shielded from television news broadcasts of the civil rights movement, race riots, and the assassination of Dr. Martin Luther King Jr. Although, I paid less attention than I now wish I had.

In the summer of 1968, after the Kansas City race riots of April 1968, which occurred after the assassination of Dr. King on April 4, I went to Liberty, Missouri (a suburb of Kansas City) to spend a couple of weeks with my aunt and uncle and cousins who lived there at the time. I was thirteen years old and had never been further than 40-50 miles from home. I had never seen a Black person in the flesh, only on television. The Ozarks region today is still 87.11% White, and the part of Arkansas where I grew up is, to this day, 97.67% White.

My aunt and uncle decided to drive the kids through the rioted area to show us what the Black people "did to their own neighborhood." I don't know about my aunt, but my uncle, by marriage, was most assuredly a racist, and this was supposed to teach us how "stupid" Black people were. I had no clue at thirteen years old, but my grandparents, even Grandpa, taught me to respect other races. As an adult, I figured out why. Granny used to talk about going to *"the bottoms"* to pick cotton for extra money when they were trying to raise kids during The Great Depression. Along the Mississippi Delta, *"the bottoms"* where a lot of cotton was grown were down around West Memphis, Arkansas, and the Black population in that area is now 50.1%. I realized that my grandparents had not been racist because they had drug cotton sacks alongside Black people and didn't consider themselves to be superior. So far as I know, no one in our family was ever a slave owner, and they had a different perspective than other whites of the time who might have been from other places. On the other hand, I recall my Uncle, who married into the family and drove us through the area of Kansas City where the riots occurred, making many bigoted statements.

When we drove into the rioted area, my aunt called over into the back seat, where I was sitting with my cousins, and told me to lock my door and roll the window up. Very few cars had air-conditioning in those days, and rolling up the window meant it would get hot. I asked, "Why?" She said, "Just do it." I complied, and shortly after, we stopped at a stop sign. I looked up to see a little Black boy, maybe seven or eight years old, leaning out of the second-story window of a brick building. I smiled and waved at him, and he stuck his tongue out at me. At the time, I was confused. I had no idea why he reacted that way. It made no difference to me what color he was. I had never encountered racism, even though that's what my uncle was trying to teach me. Later, I realized what was going on in America and wrote this poem. Today, I can say that I don't blame that little boy for sticking his tongue out at me. If I had been him and some arrogant White family came through my neighborhood gawking after such horrible events, I might have reacted with hostility, as well.

CRADLE OR GRAVE

Cartwheels, jumping ropes and hopscotch boards,
They play baseball and dragons like knights and lords.
Children play together, not noticing each other,
One black as night, the other white as a swan feather.

Smoke, bombs, fires, guns, and hate.
Death will come to those who tempt fate.
Adults will fight, murder, and kill each other.
One black as night, the other white as a swan feather.

Poem Introduction - AWAKE

I have no idea where this came from or exactly when it was written, but I found it in my poetry record book. Sometime during my high school years, I must have seen a beautiful sunrise.

AWAKE

Magenta morning creeps above the treetops,
Lingers on the hills,
Spills onto the world,
Cool and still.
Magenta morning beacons the sun in silence,
Awake, awake, awake.
Behind it, the sun ascends,
Golden, gleaming
Spreading colors across the clouds.
It glistens across the water.
Awake, awake, awake.
The day arrives with no trumpet, no fanfare.
In silence and stealth, it seeps into existence,
And then the morning birds begin their music,
A worldwide serenade.
Awake, awake, awake.
Meet the coming day.

Poem Introduction – TOO LATE

This was probably an early attempt to recognize my identity and accept the way that nature made me.

TOO LATE

I have broken my bonds
And sailed through time.
I have found myself
Within my own life.
I have looked down roads of love
And walked on roads of hate.
I have done so many things
Only to find that I was too late
To save my own identity.

Poem Introduction – OLD MAN

There were subtle signs beneath my writing, feelings I had suppressed, and thoughts I was forbidden to express. This poem tells of a high school boy who felt tired of life before he was old. It describes much of what I was feeling when I was in high school. Because of bullying, I didn't relate to or fit in with other kids. Because my grandfather was so strict, I was not allowed to attend events or engage in activities other high school kids took for granted. I was held back and limited. I did what they expected of me, and I was not bold. I didn't talk about my true feelings. I did fight with my grandfather to finally get my driver's license at seventeen. Even then, I was restrained and rarely allowed to take the car. My self-loathing was not overtly evident, and I dared not speak what was in my heart, but I quietly wrote in my poetry book.

OLD MAN

The old man would sit crippled and forlorn;
Cry for himself and his pain.
He would listen and long for the calling of death,
But it would not come.
The old man despised himself and the world,
But he could not shed a tear for his own soul.
He cried without tears and sang without songs.
He sighed the sigh of agony and lived on.

Now, do you want to know the funny ending?
The old man was not really crippled at all.
He could stand up and be bold,
But the world forbade it;
Forbade the truth be told,
And here is the secret from deep in my soul,
The old man is me, and I am sixteen years old.

Poem Introduction - TURNED

Again, there are hints of a kid who felt like he could not be himself, who felt like he had to put on a mask and pretend to be something he was not.

TURNED

Can a bluebird turn gray on a single day
When all of God's angels have turned away
And love has turned to clay?

Can a frog really turn into a prince,
Or say, "Hey! Look at me! I'm a frog!
Why can't you accept that?"

Can the wind always blow free
And never be,
When we must see our shattered dreams
All wrapped up in string
To be thrown away
When all the bluebirds turn gray
On a single day
And all of God's angels turn away,
Because love has turned to clay …
Or am I bound,
All wrapped up in string,
To be imprisoned in this binding
Forever?

Poem Introduction - IF

My first love occurred when I was in high school, but he never knew it. It was a secret love that I dared never speak and barely admitted to myself. Besides, he was an older man, heterosexual, married with a child of his own who was slightly younger than me. There was no way I could ever have anything more from him than a handshake.

IF

If, when the dark and dreary world is through,
I have never known you,
I don't know what I'll do,
For I love the love I see in you.

If, when the dark and dreary world is through,
I have never touched you,
I don't know what I'll do
For I cannot bring myself to say
The feelings I have hidden away.

If, when the dark and dreary world is through,
I have never been with you,
I don't know what I'll do
For if your love I have never tasted,
I might conclude that my life was wasted.

Poem Introduction – JUST ENOUGH TIME

This is more along the same lines of wanting what I knew I could never have.

JUST ENOUGH TIME

Is it right that life should go
And never leave a mortal soul
To think about love?
Is it right that life should go
And never leave a soul to ask
Why are we given just enough time
To burn with love,
But never enough time to forget?

Poem Introduction – THE KITTEN

There was precious little affection or demonstration of love in my family, not even from Granny. She didn't become physically affectionate with me until my college mentor, Marcy, taught me to hug and be affectionate and encouraged me to express affection to Granny. Then, when I started being affectionate, she took to it like a duck to water, and our relationship blossomed even more. We were affectionate with each other for the rest of her life. When she was spending her last days in a nursing home with her mattress on the floor due to her tendency to fall out of bed, I would go every Sunday afternoon and lay on the floor beside her mattress, holding her hand. Sometimes, we would nap, and sometimes, we would chat, but chatting was diluted by her dementia.

My grandfather and uncle, however, were not about to be affectionate with me. In fact, until I met my father at the age of eighteen, almost all the physical contact with men had been abusive. When I was eighteen, upon meeting my dad, he was the first man who ever hugged me.

When Marcy encouraged me to show affection to Grandpa, I hugged him one day and told him I loved him. He stood there like a fence post, unmoving, seemingly terrified that I had embraced him. I might have felt more return of affection from a post. He did, at least, eventually say, "I love you, too," but that was the only time he ever said it, and likely more the expected protocol response than his actual feeling.

In my childhood, there were times when it felt like no one wanted to be near me. I spent the majority of my life feeling abandoned and separate, feeling like an outcast and lonely, even in a group of people, even around family. I had a good friend briefly in the fourth grade, but his family moved away, and I never saw him again. However, the cats, especially the kittens, were affectionate with me. They loved to cuddle on my lap and purr or sit nearby. They loved to be touched and would nuzzle a cheek to me in return. The majority of the affection that I received while I was growing up was from them, and unfortunately, not from human beings.

THE KITTEN

The kitten purrs
In and out
A tiny motor
Going constantly.
If the kitten dies,
The music is gone,
And I'll have no reminders,
As life goes on,
That, at least something,
Wanted to be near me.

Poem Introduction – WINDSONG

I think I wrote this poem when I was in college, finding myself, longing and hoping for love but fearing that in my haste, I might fall in love too easily, and I did. I was still trying to at least appear straight at that time, so I'm not sure if this had any specific reference.

WINDSONG

My life is just a fairy tale
My living a dream.
My heart is just a piece of clay
Unmolded and green.
My Love is a wind song
Whistling through the trees
Searching for a place to land,
A place to be.
So, shelter me, shelter me,
Will you please?
Give me a place to land.
Keep me, oh keep me
Will you please?
Give me a place to stand.
Tether this unseasoned heart.
Tie it to a tree,
That I will not just blow away
On any alluring, frivolous breeze.

Poem Introduction – SILENT MASQUERADE

When I was in college, at eighteen, I fell in love and confessed it for the first time. I was in love with an older, straight fraternity brother, and it was at a time when I was still struggling to get anywhere near acceptance of my sexual orientation. He was a truly beautiful man but didn't realize it. He knew that he was physically attractive. He was so attractive that he got a tremendous amount of attention, and therefore, he thought that his physical appearance was the only thing that others could see. He had been affectionate and spent time with me, and I cherished our time together. I didn't know that he was just one of those straight guys who are naturally affectionate, even with other men. I had never really encountered that before college. My best friend of the last thirty years is like that, and that's one of the things I love about him, but my best friend and I understand each other, and that relationship began during my maturity. I love him, but I feel no romance toward him, and he feels safe to be affectionate with me. We respect each other's boundaries. I didn't have a good understanding of myself or others when I fell in love at the age of eighteen, but in addition to loving this upperclassman, I began to trust him.

One night, on a walk around campus in the spring rain, with our one umbrella hoisted as shelter, I mustered tremendous courage and confessed to him that I was in love with him. I lowered my mask and allowed him to know my feelings. His reaction was far kinder and gentler than it might have been from most men, especially in those days. Still, his response was conditional rejection. We would remain friends and nothing more, but he was much more to me than a friend. In retrospect, his tears told me that he did love me, but he couldn't be attracted to me or make love to me. Nonetheless, the experience broke my heart. These are the lyrics of a song I wrote when enough time had passed that I could let go.

SILENT MASQUERADE

Were you in love?
You pulled me close as we walked in the rain.
Reflections caught the evening lights,

The rhythms tapping out your name.
In my mind, we made love,
And our friendship never was the same.
I fell in love with you, lost in a silent masquerade.

All my fears, all my dreams
Went walking with you through that night.
As we walked, I told the truth.
You stopped, stared at me, and cried.
In my mind, I blamed myself
That you could never give a return.
Watching the tears you cried,
I felt the rain begin to burn.

Love was a dream, a silly game that children play.
Then, I was a child, lost in a silent masquerade.
In the night, I told it all.
I took my dream and gave it all away.
Breaking my heart must be a game that grownups play.

It took a while to let you go,
But every fire burns to an end.
Yet, if you could hear these words right now,
Would you be looking back again?
In my mind, there is a place
Where you will always be with me.
I fell in love with you
But loving meant setting you free.

Love was a dream, a silly game that children play,
And I was a child lost in a silent masquerade.
In the night, I told it all.
I took my dream and threw it all away.
Breaking my heart was a game that grownups played.

Poem Introduction – THE MIDDLE

During my years of college from 1973 to 1977, I struggled painfully between my authoritarian Christian upbringing and the fact that I was gay. After falling in love with the straight upperclassman (note the poem above) who rejected me but was still affectionate and accepting of my attraction to him, I struggled for several years to let go. I was confused about how he could be straight but still be so affectionate, especially with attitudes toward gay men at the time. I struggled through the rest of my time at college and for several years after that, knowing that, after college, I would probably never see him again, and I longed for him like heroin. This was my first true love. The feelings I had for him were powerful, and unlike falling in love with the older man in high school who never knew how I felt, there was a hint of hope that he might actually reciprocate. He was, at least, affectionate, and returned affection was, for me, like an oasis in a dry forbidding desert. Even though I controlled myself, I felt like I could never get enough, and every arm across my shoulder, every hug, or hand rubbed across my back was both torment and exhilaration.

While my relationship with him occurred, I watched as he dated girls, both of us knowing how I felt about him. He even agreed to room with me for the last semester of his senior (my sophomore) year. I don't know if that was more torture than bliss, but it was certainly both. It meant that I got to be around him a lot. It meant having conversations in the evenings before bed. It meant realizing that I would have that brief time between January and May, and then he would be gone. It meant that I would have to let go, but letting go was the last thing I wanted. I desperately wanted him. Still, those few months were precious to me, even though letting go was easier said than done. However, those months also meant getting to know his tortured side, the part that didn't trust anyone truly loved him or desired anything other than his good looks. This part never could feel like he had lived up to his father's expectations, the part that was tormented to the point of tears by every exam, lest he should fail and disappoint his dad.

I knew that I was stuck. I knew that I could not feel for a girl the way I felt for him, and I knew that I could never really have him. As I was struggling to let go, I wrote this poem. In reviewing this now, fifty years later, I admit that I was also angry that I couldn't have him and that he could never reciprocate my attraction. I was angry for being gay, that I couldn't be like other guys. For them, it seemed so easy. Not only were they comfortable with their attraction to girls, but the world didn't despise them for it. I was angry that the rest of the world seemed to hate me simply for having same-sex attraction, angry that the world couldn't seem to realize that attractions are not just about sex and that in authentic relationships, the heart is involved more than the genitals. I was angry that I couldn't be one of those pretty girls for him, angry that I would never be able to feel his kiss or feel him make love to me. I was angry that I couldn't have a life with him, be married to him, or have a home with him, and I was angry that I couldn't let go and accept the reality of the situation. In addition to being angry, I was terrified that by loving him, I had committed the most grievous sin.

The summer after he left, I fought bitterly between my feelings and the indoctrination of the church. It started the week before my last sophomore semester ended. I had gone to see *The Exorcist* with a friend. I ridiculed the movie and thought that I had not taken it seriously, but that night, I had my first dream about being possessed by demons, and that continued all summer. I realize now that I either was psychotic or was becoming psychotic because I could not make peace between my feelings and my anti-gay authoritarian indoctrination. Before the summer was over, I would stay up as long as I could and try not to fall asleep because I knew that I would have a nightmare about being possessed by demons. I didn't like walking by windows at night and felt constantly on edge. Also, that summer, it seemed like vermin kept getting into my room: spiders, wasps, worms, etc. One night, I was sitting up reading, trying to stay awake, when I heard a splat on my pillow. I turned to see a six-inch-long millipede crawling around my pillow. I leaped out of bed and freaked out. I managed to kill it, rather decimate it, but I couldn't lay in that bed again or sleep that night. Having fallen in love with a man meant that I was going to hell, and in my mind, it had already started. Everything that was happening convinced me that, by loving a man, I had sold my soul to the devil.

About two weeks before I was to return to school for my junior year, I had a terrible nightmare. In the dream, a storm came out of the south containing demons. The window of my room blew out, shards of glass and ripped curtains flew across the room, and demons were flying over my bed, screeching. I fell out of bed and began climbing the walls made of hardwood planks. As I climbed, I split the wood with my fingers and screamed, "God, please help me!" Suddenly, everything went silent and dark. I was sitting nude on a ledge with my knees pulled up to my chest. Below, I could see two men dressed in white lab coats under a spotlight, and they were talking about what a shame it was that I had to be committed to a mental institution. When I woke up, I told myself that if I didn't get a grip, a mental institution was where I was going to end up.

Two weeks later, I met Marcy, and among other things, she began teaching me skills for lucid dreaming. After some practice, I had one last demon dream. I was walking through an ancient Egyptian crypt, and a mural was painted on the wall of a goddess walking a black leopard on a leash. When I passed, the leopard came to life, stepped out of the mural, and began stalking me. I realized that the leopard was a demon. Rather than being terrified as I had been in other dreams, I turned to the leopard and said, "You have no power over me." Then I strangled it. This was one of my first steps toward loving and accepting myself and breaking away from the shame of my childhood indoctrination. To this day, I keep a black leopard figurine in my home to remind me that fear has no power over me.

After I had had enough time and healing, I wrote this poem about the power of that first love and how confusing it was. It almost overwhelmed me, and it almost took me under. Yet, I firmly believe that my cry for God to help me was why Marcy was sent.

THE MIDDLE

In winding up my plastic toy
I find a thought of the greatest joy
To sit you down and sing
A blue—blue song or two for you.

You freak me out when I'm insane
Then, pick me up and toss me in the drain.
You make me feel for you.

You give me swans that lay golden eggs,
Pretty hens with ugly legs
And I want to smile for you.

You dig me up when I'm dead and gone.
When I'm off track, you put me back on,
And I appreciate you.

Smack dab in the middle.
I'm smack dab in the middle.
I'm in the middle—the middle.

She said, "Love me."
And you said, "Sure, dear."
But you didn't—and yet—you did.
I'm in the middle—the middle.

You said, "Befriend me."
But I wanted to love you,
So, I didn't,
But I did.
I'm in the middle— the middle.

You eat popcorn
And smear butter across your lips,
So nice—I glance twice.
Yes—I desire you.

When I am crying,
You won't stop denying
That I have nothing to cry about.
Yet—you cry, too.
I have compassion for you.

I love you when I should love another,
Just do what I'm supposed to do.
I love you while you desire another.
Still, I love you,
And I love you.
I'm in the middle—the middle.

When you smile, I smile.
When you frown, so do I,
But I'm in the middle of a vast pond,
Floating in circles,
Waiting for you to walk by.
Then—you do,
And I smile,
But so what?
I'm in the middle,
The middle,
The middle.

With my nose in a book—I think of you!
With my feet in a brook—I think of you!
Everywhere I look—I think of you!

I think of you!
I think of you!
I think of you!
Just all the damn time,
I think of you,
And think of you,
And think of you!

I'm in the middle—the middle.

When the white bird meets the fairy queen
And snow is black as night,
I eat up all my salad greens
And wish that you were by my side.
I long for you.
I want you,
But I'm in the middle—the middle.

The guillotine beheaded
Many a handsome Frenchmen,
But none as beautiful as you.
You have the features of Jesus,
Hair of a raven—black as night,
Eyes of a dove—blue on white
Does the Bible say that?
The Bible says a lot.
The Bible says—I shouldn't love you,
But I do,
I do.
I'm in the middle—the middle.

Yet, you are not Jesus,
And I am no disciple.

You are not pure, and neither am I
You're just a man,
Just like me.
You're nothing special,
Just like me,
No miracle worker
or God-like quality.
Then why—do I
Worship you
So
Damn
Much?

I'm in the middle—the middle.
Eternally stuck—in the middle.

Poem Introduction – BOTH SIDES

A couple of years after having been in love with the upperclassman described in the previous two poems, I began to question if I had fallen in love with him or had fallen in love with the illusion of what I had hoped he would be. He was a wonderful, beautiful man who treated me with kindness, respect, and affection even after knowing that I was in love with him, but he was also a very troubled man. I heard rumors, a couple of years after graduating college, that he had become psychotic and thought that people could hear his thoughts through walls. He didn't keep up with me or respond to letters. So, all I got was gossip from other former classmates.

The truth is that there had been very little I had known about him. The psychosis, I was told, came after multiple times of being turned down for medical school and being unable to fulfill his father's demands on him to become a doctor. I know that, in the last semester of his senior year, when he let me room with him, he would take a test, come back to the dorm room, throw himself into bed crying, lamenting that he had flunked the test when he set the curve on most of the tests he took. Something was going on between him and his father, some anguish that caused him to think that he could never be good enough for his father. In the meantime, I was in love with him, which was no good for either of us. It was additional pressure on him and a torment for me as I fought myself over my feelings.

I had only one brief visit with him several years after college, and in time, I realized that I had never really known him. My brief experience had been merely the tip of an iceberg, and everything else had been hidden beneath the surface, his and mine. One day, I looked up at the clouds while remembering him and thought of the song *Both Sides Now* by Joni Mitchell. Then, I wrote this poem.

BOTH SIDES

I saw the clouds and remembered a song,
Only the words are different now.

I've looked at you from both sides now,
From win and lose, inside and out.
I've looked at you from all sides now,
Your smiles, your love, your life, your frowns,
And still, somehow,
It's your illusion that I recall.
I never really knew you at all.

Poem Introduction – NOTHING

This poem was written about the same relationship as those written above. It intensely impacted me, and I wrote about it a lot. These words symbolically attempt to express what I was going through then. At this point in life, I have a different understanding of love, and I no longer see it as a sacrifice, but this is about what I felt then.

NOTHING

On the threshold of my life, I sit,
And dream away the hours,
And never give myself a chance
To reach the Ivory Towers.

Here I am, world,
You son-of-a-bitch!
You chew me up and spit me out,
Toss me in a ditch.
Come on, world!
Come on, God!
Just one chance,
That's all I need.
Give me life,
and give me love,
Just one chance,
Lord, please.

When I was three,
I planted a tree
And watched it climb toward the sun.
Then came a man with a gleaming ax
And, alas, my tree was gone.

When I was four,
I looked at hate
And got all wrapped up in despair.
Then, I threw it out and went about
Finding something that I knew should be there.

When I was five,
I learned to drive
An Oldsmobile Delta 88.
Then the tire went flat with some damn nail
And that kindly sealed my fate.

Now, I'm dead, though I try to live.
I beg the world for love.
I never had anything, no way, no how.
I lost everything I ever loved.

When I was six, I took a drink
Of fine, enchanted wine.
Then, I felt myself float from heaven,
Down among the swine.

When I was seven, I loved a man.
His name was Jim or something like that.
For a little while, he accepted me,
And that, my friends, was that.

When I was eight, that same friend
Who I loved more than anything at all,
Denied me over and over
And so, I died of a love that's lost.

Oh, give me three pennies, three pennies, three pennies.
Oh, give me three pennies and destroy my soul.
For a crumb from your table, I'd die, I'd die.
Oh, give me three pennies.
You killed me ...
right?

Oh, why am I longing?
Oh, why?
Oh, why?
You're nothing but human.
Oh, why?
Oh, why?
Love is my only reason,
But I get no decision.
Oh, why?
Oh, why?
Oh, why?

I want to sit close to the fire, Mommy,
I want to sit close to the fire.
Don't care if I get burned or die, Mommy,
I want to sit close to the fire.
I don't care if he hurts me or kills me.
I don't care if he steps on my soul.
I don't care about nobody or nothing,
I want my love to be close.

Poem Introduction – APRONED COACHMAN

Throughout my life, I have loved wordplay. Currently, the social media term seems to be *"word porn."* I love letting words flow to see where they go. I wrote this poem while working as a grocery carry-out boy between my Junior and Senior years of college. In those days, they hired kids, almost always boys, to take the groceries to the customer's car and load them. Little old ladies would give us tips, but often no more than a dime. Grocery "carry-out boys," in those days, wore aprons similar to a butcher's apron, and the aprons had the store logo embroidered onto them. Writing this poem was more for fun than anything else, but it was also about my observations while working in that store.

APRONED COACHMAN

Shinning tile floors, glass doors, chores
For the aproned ones.
Son of a bitch!
Listen to me, and I'll let you see what really stands
Amid the aisles and the cans.

Glittering sunlight beats down outside.
Rolling carriages, I take yours for a ride.
In the cold room, air-conditioned suite, I walk the beat.
They "oooh" and "ah" over the produce, "so nice."
Look twice.
They're gone.

Women are walking, talking, in choking summer air.
Their modern vehicles await them there
While nosey children with glassy eyes
Only sit and scrutinize.

Here, old grey women stand,
Tired and old,
Tired and cold,
Legs collapsing on the floor, barely holding them up.
Porcelain, fake, milky-white teeth grin at me and …
Odors of the world come assaulting me.

Men, clothes caked with concrete, street worker-wise,
Who might beat their wives,
Buy meat, I surmise
For canine satisfaction.

Out there,
Steaming, wet, hot, creamy, summer air I feel.
Cracking sidewalks over turn the wheels.
"Feels hot today."
"Might rain, you say?"
Over and over, conversation is spoken this way.
Nothing else to say.

Middle-class mothers peck at checkout machines.
Across the counter, their peers buy beans
To feed their teens who drive the streets,
And waste their lives on ketchup highs.

Then here am I,
Too unsure to move,
Too broke to groove,
Too tired to be smooth,
Crying without a tear.
I ask myself, "What am I doing here?"
It doesn't come out,

A silent shout within my mind.
I look at people who stare back at me,
And wonder what they're thinking.
A thousand faces, always separate,
Unique.
I see every face, every physique.

Rolling carriages all day long,
The aproned coachman
Steps into the sun.

Poem Introduction – LIFE CYCLE

In addition to a brief stint as a carry-out boy, I worked as a nurse's aide through college. Most of the time, I worked in nursing homes over the summer to make enough money to pay residual tuition when I returned to classes in the fall. While there, I learned about an entirely different side of humanity that most of us never see. Our elderly are, too often, placed in facilities where many families seldom visit and where they are cared for by strangers. Working there also attuned me to the finality and fragility of life.

LIFE CYCLE

He was a baby once,
As Shakespeare said,
"Mewling and puking in the nurse's arms."
Then, he was a child,
Then, an adult. . .
Then, an old man,
Now, a baby, again
In a room with gadgets and tubes
Mewling and puking in the nurse's arms.

Poem Introduction – FUMBLE HANDS

As I said in the introduction of the previous poem, working in nursing homes gave me a perspective that I had not previously considered. Even though I was raised by my grandparents and spent most of my young life around people their age, they were still too young for a nursing home. I was still very young when I was working there, under the age of twenty. I realized that anyone who lives long enough without dying of an accident or some tragedy will eventually reach the point when the body no longer functions as it once did or the way that the possessor of that body wants it to. This poem was written after I had watched an old man try with angst and determination to button his shirt. He didn't want me to do it for him, but when he was finally unable to button the shirt himself, he gave up and allowed me to help him.

FUMBLE HANDS

Fumble hands
Press the button,
Twist the button,
Push the cloth.

Fumble hands
Are old and shaking,
Shaking,
Trembling,
Button and cloth.

Fumble hands
Are old and feeble,
Once strong
And smooth,
Strong no more.

Fumble hands
Like wrinkled spiders
Miss the buttonhole,
Push the cloth.

Knotted hands,
Old and aging,
Are strong, no more,
Smooth, no more.

Fumble hands
At last, give up.
The button wins.
Time wins.

Once proud,
Now weary,
The old man sighs.

Poem Introduction – THE TRAILER PARK

I almost lost my scholarship in my first semester of college. I had to maintain a 2.0 GPA to keep the scholarship, and I managed that by the very skin of my teeth. The algebra and trigonometry teacher had been about to fail me. If I failed any class, I lost my scholarship. If I lost my scholarship, I was out with insufficient funds to pay for college. I went to her and begged for something I could do to keep from failing her class. She gave me thirty-two pages of extra credit work to complete the night before grades were turned in. I stayed up all night, completed the assignment, and delivered it to her when her office door opened the next morning. Then, she gave me a pity 'D,' the lowest possible 'D' percentage she could give me without failing me. I don't think she even looked at the work. The fact that I had done it was enough for her to take pity. To this day, I have never used any algebra or trigonometry (that I know of), and I still managed to get a master's degree. In my opinion, algebra, trigonometry, and calculus should all be considered profanity. Yet, in the very next semester, I got a 98% out of 100% semester grade for statistics and a 'B' in chemistry. Perhaps the near 'F' in the algebra and trig class was not entirely my fault. I had a very hard time staying awake in that class, but the chemistry and statistics teachers were entertaining.

One of the reasons that I did poorly on my grades during that first semester was that I thought I was stupid. I thought I was an ignorant hick from the sticks and that I could not compete with people who came to *Arkansas College* (now *Lyon College*) from all over the country and all over the world. I assumed that they had all been educated at sophisticated, big city schools and that my pre-college education in a backwoods, little town was nothing in comparison. When I discussed this with the campus counselor, he gave me the *Wexler Intelligence Scale* and then informed me that I had an above-average IQ and there was no reason that I could not make good grades like anyone else.

In the second semester of my freshman year, I joined a fraternity with upper-class fraternity brothers, who showed me how to study for college classes and helped me with my studies. The fraternity prided itself on being intellectual and having high average grades for the chapter. I brought my grade up to a 3.25 the next semester, but for all the remaining semesters of college, I could not seem to get much above that. I was determined to get a 4.0 GPA for at least one semester before graduating, but I assumed it would be much more difficult to achieve if I lived on campus with so many distractions. So, I rented a trailer, the cheapest place I could find, and moved into a trailer park for the last semester of my senior year. That way, I could live alone, not have the temptations of campus life, and I could devote myself to my studies.

I had never lived in a trailer park before, even though I had grown up with less accommodating living arrangements. I had grown up where I thought I was poor, but the trailer park was a different kind of poor. Other than dorm life, I had never lived in a place that was so crowded with neighbors, and the dorm seemed, in many ways, more private than the trailer park. Where I grew up, it would have taken at least a few minutes to drive to the nearest neighbor's house and at least ten or fifteen minutes to walk there. However, in the trailer park, there was only enough room between the trailers to park a car.

My trailer was on the back side of the park where the train tracks passed, just on the other side of the space where I parked my car. When the train came through at night, I could feel the train's rumbling shaking my bed. I opened my windows in the spring weather to get a breeze into the trailer. Then, I could hear dogs barking, TVs blaring, and neighbors fighting or having sex. The neighbor and his wife in the trailer beside me could bounce the bed for an hour. I found myself, under my breath, begging him to climax so he would stop distracting me from my studies. When he did, I'm sure no one in the trailer park missed the crescendo of his grand finale. I know I didn't. There was little privacy for them or me, but I was not engaging in those activities at that stage.

One evening, I wrote this poem. Even though I experienced a different kind of distraction from dorm life, it was not a tempting distraction that might have caused me to sit around and chat with friends instead of working on my studies. So, I did pull a 4.0 GPA for my last semester of college.

THE TRAILER PARK.

There is dank, dark, dusty air,
Still as a whisper,
Heavy,
Lying there,
Unfortunately, not
undisturbed.

"Quiet in the park!
Quiet in the park!"
I heard her shout.
Scream all you want.
It does no good.
It has no clout.

There are noises
Everywhere.
Squeaky bed springs,
Car doors slammed,
TV's blaring ... distant ...
But always heard,
And now and then,
A bird.

The smell is heavy and warm
Like a greased and sweaty
Sunburned back,
Sweet, suffocating,
Oily, garage floor steam
Melting my nostrils. . .
I can't breathe!

In the distance, a dog
Barks in a fervent uproar,
And a train comes
To shake the bed
And wake me in the night
As it jiggles my head.

The sounds of mankind
Rule the air,
Voices,
Motors,
Radio blare.
This isn't nature!
It's a sickening joke
Someone, please help me,
I'm about to choke!

Poem Introduction – DON'T TOUCH

Who, having been hurt, rejected, betrayed, and denied the return of love, has not tried to protect their heart by swearing that they would never love again? It never worked for me. The longing for intimacy, connection, and relationship always burned stronger than any desire to protect my heart by refusing to love again. The illusion is that we can love only once or only one person, but that is not true. Once we have truly loved, we can never unlove, despite all our efforts, rejection or betrayal, and future experiences of love. Even when they are gone, and we acknowledge that we could never have had a life with them, we still love them. If we ever truly loved anyone, we still do.

When we are rejected young, we think, "That's it! That was too much. I never want to go through that pain again!" Yet, if we give ourselves half a chance, we do love again and again unless we are among the incredibly lucky few who manage to hit Love's home run the first time up to bat. I can assure you that those people, gay or straight, are rare. When we get older, we think, "That's it! I've had my last chance at love, and no one would want me now." Yet, if we give them half a chance to love us, they do.

At the time that I wrote this poem, I was obviously afraid of loving again, obviously afraid of letting anyone get close, and obviously afraid of intimacy, but time taught me lessons. I learned that no matter how shattered I was over losing a relationship, I could give myself another chance. I learned how to have relationships, and eventually, I lucked out and met a wonderful, giving, and loving man who loves me and is committed to me. Though doubts still besiege my mind occasionally, they become less intense and less frequent. I have been abandoned far too often not to doubt, but he repeatedly proves himself to me. If I had not gotten over my fear of intimacy long before we met, I might never have given him a chance.

This is a poem about fearing love.

DON'T TOUCH

Don't touch me!
Don't hold me!
Don't love me!
My shell is too thin.
One touch would crush it,
It would open my heart,
Open my soul,
And scatter me,
Unprotected,
Onto the emotional minefield of intimacy.

Poem Introduction – PITY

You might never have known how lonely I felt when I was young. You might not have seen it in my eyes that I felt as though I didn't fit into the world or belong to anything or anyone. I was even popular in college, but it didn't matter what group I was around or where I was; I felt like an outcast. I greatly enjoyed college, and it was about the best four years of my life, but I still felt disconnected even though I met some of my best and most endur-ing friends at that time. From family and friends to church and later around gay culture, I felt like I didn't fit in. I felt like a stranger no matter where I was or who I was around. I could be standing in a room full of loving, compassionate people who liked me, maybe even loved me, and I still felt alone, not because I was alone, but because I felt as though I was a member of no one's club like there was nowhere that I belonged. One of the things that can happen to people who are abused is that they feel separate from everything and everyone, lonely in any situation and with anyone, discon-nected from life. Feelings of worthlessness and self-loathing deny that the acceptance of others can be trusted, that it means anything, or is even real.

There were people I felt safe with and people who I knew would love me no matter what. Marcy and Granny were the primary ones. Even then, I would never be completely, openly myself around Granny or anyone except Marcy. I still felt like a square peg in a room with only round holes everywhere else.

In my late twenties, because I had been backed into a corner about it, I confessed to two of my aunts that I was gay. I never wanted to tell anyone, and I retained my shame about it until I was middle-aged. My indoctrination into authoritarian Christianity haunted me about the *"sin of homosexuality,"* and sometimes still does. I don't know if I will ever fully get over a twinge of shame about being the way that nature created me, but I'm more open about it and free with it now than I have ever been. After I had confessed to my aunts, who were not supposed to tell anyone, Granny said to me one day, as I sat at her kitchen table while she was fixing dinner, "You know Madge (my most untrustworthy and troublesome aunt) says that you are a homosexual."

I neither confirmed nor denied the statement. I said absolutely nothing. Then, after a moment of silence, she said, "I don't know if you are or you aren't, but I want you to know that I love you, anyway." Still, I never confessed to Granny that I was gay. Yet, she knew. Her acceptance came from the woman who attended the same church where the minister proclaimed me among the worst of sinners. She was a true Christian. She was capable of loving beyond Biblical admonitions and filtered interpretations based more on the human ego than spiritual truth. She knew that her religion was for her to follow, not something she was to push on anyone else, and her religion was about love.

After telling me that she loved me anyway, I remained silent. I neither confessed nor denied. *"Don't ask, don't tell,"* right? We left it at that. Years later, without a word spoken about it, she accepted my first long-term partner into her home and was as kind to him as she ever would have been to anyone. One of the primary fears that gay people have is that LGBTQIA+ is the only minority at risk of being shunned by their own family and friends. That was never going to happen with my grandma. It was knowing that she loved me that got me through.

I think many people, like myself, who grew up with bullying and abuse, whether they are gay or not, feel like they don't fit in and like they don't matter. I get it, and I know its source. When we are treated like we don't matter, we begin to think we don't matter, and then we begin to feel like we don't belong in the world itself. Those who most feel like they don't matter often begin to act like they don't matter. Yet, we all matter, and we all have worth. If we are here, it is because we are meant to be here.

It took me a very long time to recognize that my worth is equal to everyone, no matter what they may think, whether they praise me or judge me. It took me a very long time to realize that I belong in the world and have as much right to be here as anyone else. It took me a very long time to realize that another person's behavior or opinion is never about me, even if it is directed at me and blamed on me. Their behavior is always about what is going on inside of them at the time it occurs. Their judgment does not define me. I define myself, and no matter where I am or who I am around, I am now well aware that *"Those who matter don't mind and those who mind don't matter."* (Dr. Suess quote) For every person who does not love and accept me as I am, many will. Others are welcome to move on if they don't love and accept me. It's the ones who love me who matter, and I now know that I absolutely belong with them and I deserve my place on this planet as much as anyone.

This poem is about how I felt for almost half of my life before I began learning to love myself the way Granny and Marcy loved me.

PITY

Pity to be lonely,
To love and never say it,
Never show it,
Never try.
Pity to be lonely,
To be nothing in a crowd,
To be only a wish for love,
Be silent and alone.
Pity to be lonely
And cry inside
A million tears
And never take
That one fleeting chance
To STOP!
And cry out loud.

Poem Introduction – HALF A MAN

In my efforts to fit myself (this square peg) into society's round hole, I am grateful that I never married. I am grateful that gay marriage is now legal and that I married the man who matches me instead of marrying someone I didn't really want just because that is what society (the church) wanted me to do. However, back in the day, there were multiple gay men and women as well as transgender men and women who married into unfitting situations in their quest to fit with what the church and society expected of them instead of being true to themselves. Some pulled it off, some remained married, probably loved their wives or husbands, had children, and maintained a lifestyle where they never really fit. I don't know if those gay or transgender men and women lived a lie or admitted who they were within their relationships. Maybe they wanted a traditional family more than they wanted to live as themselves. However, there were more who could not maintain a demanded lie and could not ignore the nagging at their soul that they were not being true to themselves.

Many heterosexual men and women went through feelings of betrayal (understandably so) when they found out that the person they had been married to, sometimes for many years, and had children with had been living a lie. Sometimes, this came when a gay person was caught with a lover. Sometimes, it occurred when the gay or transgender person finally got so tired of pretending that they confessed and asked for a divorce. Many don't realize that acting is a much more difficult job than it seems. If you have to act every moment of every day and never step off that stage and rest, it becomes very taxing, especially on one's emotions. There is a constant fear of being found out, shunned and rejected, booed off the stage, so to speak. Nonetheless, no one knows what kind of effort it takes or what kind of strain it creates to constantly pretend, except for gay people who have tried it. The whole idea of Gay Pride and *"coming out"* is to counter this institutionalized and internalized bigotry, self-hatred, and pretense based on what society and some religions demand. Gay people deserve to be proud of who they are, *"born this way,"* rather than being pressured to fit some obscure mold that others prescribe for them. If you are straight, imagine having to spend your life playing a role that doesn't fit with who you are instead of being allowed to be yourself, living up to authoritarian demands rather than being free to live as your authentic self. If you are heterosexual, imagine yourself trying to fit yourself into a homosexual relationship and maintain that for life. Put the shoe on the other foot and see how that feels.

I dated a man, for a short while in the early 1980s, who had been married, divorced, and had a child with a woman who vacillated between bulimia and anorexia. Not only was she not feeding herself and was dangerously thin, but she was not feeding their two-year-old son, who was losing weight. Despite testimony from the child's pediatrician that the baby should be in the custody of his father, the Arkansas courts refused to grant custody to someone who was gay, even though he was the biological father, and there was clear evidence that his child was being neglected by his mother. My friend had not divorced his ex-wife just because he finally came to grips with his sexual orientation, but had divorced her because of her erratic behavior that was often unpredictable and violent. The courts, however, left the child with a sick mother who was not caring for him instead of placing him with a loving father who wanted to take care of him. The solution finally came when the mother's wealthy family stepped in and hired a nanny for the baby rather than grant custody to a gay man who loved his child.

Gay marriage and allowing gay people to live as themselves will save many heterosexuals from going through the kind of turmoil and feelings of betrayal that occur when they find out that their marriage to a gay or transgender person was a sham. Even if it is not intended as a sham, living a lie, regardless of the reason, is still a sham. Hopefully, Gay marriage will legitimize family, and society will begin to recognize that a child should be raised by loving parents, gay or straight, rather than be left in an abusive or neglectful situation.

In those days, however, society considered any man who was not a macho, heterosexual male to be half a man and unworthy of privileges that other men take for granted. It seems some want to take us back there because they haven't yet realized that Gay marriage is also good for straight marriage. It can prevent the kind of heartache that heterosexual people face when the Gay person they are married to finally gets honest with themselves. In the past, gay men were considered to be half a man versus being *"real men."* Perhaps many in society still believe that. I don't know that I wrote this poem about any particular person, but I wrote it about the idea of being half a man; half in one life, and half in another. I think I wrote it before I dated or had a relationship with a man. Maybe I wrote it about what could have been my fate. I certainly tried to turn myself into a heterosexual. I tried to play the role for a very long time. I dated several girls, had sex with girls, and for many years tried to fit myself into society's mold, but thank God, I never married a woman. Thank God the story in this poem never happened to me.

HALF A MAN

The day breaks, silent.
There is a warm and flowing,
Sweet and mellow
Crystal dawn.

He wakes to another day,
To heartache and pain
That he hides so well,
Another day of fear
And tragic thoughts
Of hell.

He turns and sees her
Lying there, sleeping,
Soft and gentle,
Smooth,
Breathing slowly

Like gentle waves on the sea.

He's told himself
A thousand times
That he loves her,
And he does.
He's told himself
A million times
That he can make it
If he tries,
And he has
Desperately
Tried.
Still, he does not love her,
Not the way she thinks.

He has a life that seems wonderful,
Wife and kids,
Smiling faces,
Comfort,
Warm and loving friends,
And still, he feels
Empty inside,
Alone.

On Saturdays,
He meets his lover
So he can, for a time, be himself.
On Saturdays,
He's half a man
With half a man,
His lover,
Secretly lying by his side.

His wife is loving,
Warm and sweet,
Wholesome,
Affectionate,
Complete.
She's maternal,
Sexy,
Pretty
And nice,
But he does not love her,
Not the way she thinks.

His children are a part of him,
His soul,
His life,
His blood.
His children
Present his only love
That stands true
And right,
The only ones
That keep him
Trying and trying and trying,
Both day and night,
To be something that he's not.

Yet, sometimes, he thinks
That he would
Risk it all,
His respect,
His honor,
His family,
Church,

And career
To live the life
He needs,
But he can't,
And never will.

He's tried to love her,
All these years,
Tried to love her
Like he knows she deserves,
And for all she knows,
He does.
He's told himself
Ten million times,
"Someday, I'll change
And love her that way."

Yet, on Saturdays,
He meets his lover
And builds greater
Worry and torment
Deep inside.
On Saturdays,
He's half a man
With the half a man he loves
Lying secretly by his side.
Together, they love,
But together, they fear,
How much longer can they hide?

Poem Introduction – FREAKING OUT

It is pretty difficult to go through traumatic experiences without developing anxiety that can sometimes be extremely intense to the point of panic. It is a phenomenon of an abusive childhood that a child develops trepidation and hypervigilance, learning to listen to every footstep in the house. For instance, I have a friend who used to work for "*Psychic Friends Network.*" Younger readers may have to Google that. She once made a comment that I thought was very interesting. She said, "I had to become psychic out of self-defense because my father had schizoaffective disorder, and you never knew what he was going to do." My thought was that she did not become psychic; she became so hypervigilant that she would notice the tiniest nuance of micro-expression on her father's face or the tiniest inflection of tone in his voice that would indicate he was about to become violent. Learning those skills of hypervigilance protected her, to a point, when she was a child, but also made her very attuned to reading people's micro-expressions and the hidden essence in their voices. This allowed her to focus on and usually name the concerns they were dealing with. They then thought she had amazing powers because she could read them so well. Yet, there was a downside. She was so sensitive to anger that the slightest expression of frustration could throw her into panic and have her desperately trying to fix an essentially insignificant disappointment. Then, she made irrational and illogical decisions. Anxiety is often the result of hypervigilance, and my friend certainly had her share of that.

Anxiety is a normal emotion, but it can become an abnormal problem for people who have experienced trauma. It is the emotion that is produced when we are in overt danger. It is natural and normal when we are in certain dangerous situations, and not so normal when it kicks up at times when no real danger is present. If, for instance, you happened to be visiting the zoo and a tiger got out of the cage, anxiety would kick in. Your body would route energy out of things like digestion or other bodily functions that would not benefit your escape from the tiger. The brain would divert that energy into the parts of your body that would help you escape: your arms, legs, and heart. Your brain would kick into hypervigilance, and you would be looking for any tree to climb or hiding place to keep from being mauled by the tiger. That is normal anxiety. A slight uneasiness at a job interview or meeting a new person is normal anxiety. A panic attack is abnormal anxiety. One of the reasons people tremble during panic attacks, for instance, is that there is an intense urge to run, but there is no logical reason to run. Yet, the energy has to go somewhere. So, it goes into trembling, a pounding heart, and hyperventilation. Believing the thought of being mauled by the tiger has potency just as the actual threat of being mauled by the tiger. The subconscious mind cannot tell the difference between reality and imagination unless trained to discern.

Humans have very complicated brains capable of memory and creating thoughts and images. Also, everything we think has an emotional effect. Therefore, when we have a fearful thought, even one that we don't think we think, anxiety kicks in as though we need to run from the tiger when there is no real danger. That fear thought could be triggered by something that is only remotely similar to something that occurred during a time when we were being traumatized. It could be a smell, a sound, someone who looks like our perpetrator, or just about anything else. We may not even recognize the actual trigger at the time the anxiety kicks in, but it is something that our subconscious reads and reacts to without our conscious awareness. It could also be based on worry, a form of fear. Because the body diverts energy away from things like digestion during times of panic, those who chronically worry and have anxiety usually also have chronic digestive problems. The digestive system doesn't work properly because energy is diverted to places necessary to help us flee and our digestive system doesn't have enough energy to work properly. The body is supposed to return to normal functioning after the danger has passed, but human imagination can cause the body to respond as though the danger has never passed.

Fear is a fantasy that something bad is about to happen, and anxiety is the emotion that is produced by that fantasy. It does not matter whether the fantasy is based on something that did happen; it is still a fantasy. It does not matter if we have generalized and assumed that because something happened in the past, it will happen again; it is still a fantasy. The good news is that we can change our fantasies. However, we are not likely to realize that we have any control over our thinking in the middle of a panic attack, and perhaps then is when we have the least control over our thinking. Still, we can learn to control our thinking even during a panic attack and implement logical interventions such as mindfulness or distraction.

I am grateful that I have only had a few total panic attacks, but I have had some. One that I remember occurred when I had just started graduate school and had not accepted my sexual orientation yet. A repairman came to my apartment and, before leaving, proceeded to come onto me. He was attractive, but the invitation for sex threw me into terror. I had barely dabbled in sexual contact with men before that but never comfortably, and there was something about him that triggered me. I couldn't put my finger on it, but when I couldn't breathe and was shaking like a leaf, he excused himself and left. My panic attack prevented him from acting on his intentions. Before accepting myself, there was a terror that acting on any thoughts of attraction would be overwhelmingly wrong. These were the dregs of having grown up in an authoritarian religion.

It would be a couple of more years before I could become comfortable with myself and my sexual orientation enough to permit myself to consummate a sexual encounter. Oddly enough, my journey toward self-acceptance and the cessation of trying to fit this square peg into a round hole came from straight people. Except for the friend who accompanied me to my first gay bar and encouraged me that it was okay, not one gay person had previously contributed to my freedom. It was straight people all along. When, a couple of years later, I was in therapy with a heterosexual male psychologist, I continued to have difficulty accepting myself. He convinced me to enter a therapy group that was made up of all straight men. For weeks, I said little or nothing about myself and offered feedback to other group members. One day, this big, burly guy (the kind I was terrified of) said, "You have been coming in here for weeks, and you haven't talked about your problem. I want to know what is going on with you."

That triggered another panic attack. After all, having been told that I was worse than a murderer and having been abused by men, I feared the hatred of any straight White male. I was terrified of men in general. After trembling and trying to gain my composure, I said, "I don't think I can."

He said, "Try."

Finally, I was able to get out, "I think I might be bisexual." That wasn't true, only close to the truth, and it was still an effort to protect myself because if they thought I might have some attraction to women, they might go easier on me. I was that frightened of them.

After I said that, he smiled and asked compassionately, "What's wrong with that?"

Then, the rest of the men began to affirm me and affirm that they didn't think less of me because of my attraction to men. It took several times before the door could finally be opened to accepting myself and engaging in genuine self-love. Later, I came out to my father, who did not respond well initially, but after my stepmother talked with him, he came around and apologized for his initial response. Then he talked about how queer people were treated very badly in his generation and how he had fears for me, given that being queer set me up for hate and potential violence. I had those fears myself.

Over time, I gained more and more control over my anxiety and learned to fit meditation into my regular daily routine. I learned how to manage panic attacks, utilize mindfulness, ground myself back in the present moment, examine the fear behind the panic attack, and redirect my thinking.

Often, it is helpful to sit down as soon as the panic attack passes and write down anything you can recall that was going on in the few minutes before the panic attack started. What were you seeing, hearing, smelling, tasting, feeling in your body, or thinking just before the panic attack started? This may help reduce the frequency and severity of panic attacks because it helps to begin identifying triggers and start making sense of them. Still, it is not a substitute for seeking professional help.

Grounding yourself and practicing physical mindfulness during a panic attack is helpful. Touch things, hold onto a counter, put a piece of ice to your forehead, stick your head in a freezer, take deep breaths of cold air, look at something to the left, and try to take a deep breath. Look at something to the right and pull as much air into your lungs as you can. Look down at something, perhaps your feet, and draw as much air as possible. Look up to the ceiling or sky and take a deep breath. If you can't take a full, slow breath, breathe as much air as possible and try again. Start naming things around you. "I see a table. (take a breath) I see a chair. (take a breath) I see a television set. (take a breath) I see the floor. (take a breath) I see the ceiling ... etc."

Also, if there are thoughts of fear, redirect them to something else. Ask yourself, "What can I do about that right now?" It is important to put it in the form of a question. Ask yourself the question and make your mind answer it. Your mind knows the answer. If the answer is 'nothing,' as it almost always is, the next question becomes, "What deserves my attention now?" If I can't do anything about it *right now*, no matter how important it may be, it is not a priority and does not deserve my attention. It only deserves my attention when I can do something about it. If it is a fantasy and is not happening right now, I have to decide if I like the effects of that fantasy. Is it a positive or negative fantasy? Does it bring a smile to my face or a frown? The good news is that, although we may have to practice it like any other skill, we can train ourselves to pick better fantasies. The truth is, positive thinking will never hurt you, but negative thinking will.

This is a poem, obviously, about having had a panic attack.

FREAKING OUT

I'm freaking out!
I want to shout!
Fear!
Fear!
Fear!
What if?

Oh no!
Fear!
Fear!
Fear!
I'm freaking out!
I'm going to shout!
Every cell in my body
Is vibrating!
Every muscle in my body
Is shaking and tense!
I'm freaking out!
Why?
Why?
Why?
If only I …
If only I …
Could stop
And breathe!
I can't breathe!
I can't breathe!
I'm panting like a dog!
Shout!
Damn it!
Shout!
Damn it!
BREATHE!
Damn it!
Just Breathe …

Poem Introduction – CRAZY MAN

I was raped once when I was in my twenties. I didn't realize that it was rape at the time. I realized that I had anxiety and that I was trying to resist, but I didn't realize it was rape until the next day. I had a date with a man larger than me, at least 4-5 inches taller and not overweight, but heavier and stronger. He was very attractive, and I brought him to my apartment after having been together for dinner. I had gone to bed with him willingly. I wanted to have sex with him. However, it took a turn. He wanted to do something I didn't want to, and he would not take 'no' for an answer. He kept pushing me until he overpowered me and did what he wanted. I had mixed feelings about it. I wanted and was attracted to him but didn't want what he did.

That night, after my date left, I thought that it had been just a bad liaison, merely a date gone wrong, even though I was filled with a numb tension that nagged at me, a heaviness in my chest, and I felt like I needed to cry but couldn't. Overnight, I had a dream of being back on the farm. My uncle was drunk and insisted on driving my car. I told him he couldn't drive it, but he took my car anyway. I saw him drive off, and although I had tried to stop him from taking my car, I had been unable to stop him. Then, he was suddenly standing right in front of me, grabbed my ass with both hands and forcefully slammed his pelvis into mine. I woke up, realizing, from the symbolism of the dream, that what had happened to me that night was rape. If anyone is forced into any sexual encounter that they don't choose, that's rape. The damage may not always be overt, but it negatively impacts the victim of the rape.

In dream symbolism, a car usually represents our body, the vehicle that carries us around. The fact that my uncle was taking my car without my permission meant symbolically that he was using my body without my permission, and when he slammed his crotch into me, that was an overt sexual assault. My uncle had been the one who had done things to me during my childhood without my permission. By abusing me, he took away my choice over my own body. When I woke up from that dream, I realized that my date had been with an abuser, like my uncle. Even though he didn't hurt me or beat me, he still forced me into something that I didn't want to do. He drove my car without my permission. Although it did not appear the way one envisions a rape to be, he had raped me, nonetheless. I realized that part of the reason was that I was afraid to set boundaries with him. He was bigger than I was, and subconsciously, I had reverted to my childhood when I had no power to fend off my perpetrator.

Of course, no report was ever made, and no charges were ever filed. Rapes occur all the time to both women and men, straight and gay, in which the victim justifies it, blames themselves, or doesn't consciously realize that their rights and boundaries were violated. I experienced date rape, and many women have to endure that without having any recourse legally as I also had no legal recourse. Too often, others assume it is okay to manipulate or force others into doing things they don't want. Too often, too many people don't listen when they are told 'no.'

Often, if not usually, people who have been abused and traumatized, especially in childhood, either don't realize where their boundaries are or that they even have a right to boundaries. Those who have survived abuse often get abused again as adults simply because they don't know how to define their boundaries or even realize that they can define their boundaries. They may also violate the boundaries of others. When children's boundaries are violated, they are trained to believe that violating boundaries is okay. Therefore, childhood victims of things like sexual abuse often perpetrate on other children. This is not because they are bad kids; it's because they are given unspoken permission by their abuser to do to others what was done to them.

As a metaphor, there is a story about circus elephants that, when they are babies, they are chained around one leg to a steak in the ground. The baby elephant can only go in a circle to the distance at the end of the chain and then is restrained from going further. After having this conditioning as a baby, an adult elephant can be tied to a steak by a rope and could easily pull up the steak or break the rope, but it does not break free because it was conditioned only to go as far as the length of the tether. Our conditioning from abuse leads us to assume that there are limits to our choices and rights, that we are not allowed to set boundaries, or that it is not possible to set boundaries. This becomes an opportunity for those who exploit to take advantage of us, and therefore, abuse may repeat when we are adults. Healing means learning our boundaries, that it is okay to have boundaries, how to set and maintain them, and that we have a right to them. It also means learning that others have a right to their boundaries.

If that night I was raped, I had gotten up and told him to get out, or I would call the police; he probably would have left, and I wouldn't have been raped, but like so many who have been abused, I didn't realize at the time that I even could set those boundaries. I didn't know how he would react and like so many who have been abused, I avoided conflict. His size intimidated me the way I had been intimidated as a child. I don't know if he might have become violent if I had put my foot down. I didn't realize that I could put my foot down. We have a right to set boundaries, and we are not "crazy" just because we decide to set and maintain our boundaries or because we do not give in to the manipulations of those who seek to take advantage of us. They may call us crazy, and they may use all kinds of manipulations to get us to allow them their will over our bodies, but we own our bodies. Your body belongs to you, and no one has a right to do anything with your body that you do not permit them to do. Those who are victimized often blame themselves, but you are never at fault when you either had no control or didn't realize you had control.

This is a poem about being violated and left feeling shame, blaming myself for something that was done to me and not chosen by me.

CRAZY MAN

Crazy, man!
Crazy, man!
Don't you know,
That's crazy, man?
I don't want to do that.
Don't you know that's crazy ...
Man?
Don't you know that's ...
Man, don't, you know ...
Crazy, man!
Man?
Man?
Man?
Don't you ...
Don't you know that's crazy?
Man, don't you ...
Man, don't!
Don't, man!
Don't!
Man, don't!
Don't, man!
Don't!
Don't!
Don't!
Don't!
Don't!
Don't!

What just happened?
I must be crazy, man.

Poem Introduction – WINTER LOVE

Thankfully, most of my involvements were not abusive, even though most were dysfunctional and unsustainable. There were those glimmers of hope when love and liaison became joyful and beautiful. This is a poem about one of those times. This is a poem about a relationship with a man I came to know right after graduating college. The relationship was never sexual, and he was heterosexual and married, though he was having problems in his marriage. Even if he had not been married and gay, I would have had difficulty permitting myself to be sexual with him, but the fact that he was married put up yet another barrier to any sexual involvement. When he came to visit, we would cuddle on the couch together and talk until it was time for him to go home. He never offered sexual interaction, and I never asked for it. I would have been too frightened to have even considered sex with him, and I had continued dating girls and trying to press myself into a heterosexual mold. Coming to grips with my sexual orientation would not come for several more years. I assume, like the upperclassman I met in college, this man was another heterosexual man who was openly affectionate. Since he was having problems in his marriage, maybe affection and discussion without attachment and expectations of sex were what he needed at the time. I, most assuredly, needed male affection, and this was one of the few times, before coming out, that I allowed myself the luxury of it.

WINTER LOVE

We didn't make love that night.
There were no stars that fell from the sky.
In the soft lamp light,
There was only you and I.

We didn't move mountains
Or explode in ecstasy
Yet, each moment was beautiful,
Each time you touched me.

Holding you,
I felt as though
Our lives had merged.
I felt we shared
Eternity
With all wrongs
And misgivings
Purged.

When you left,
An emptiness was cast.
I walked to the frost-framed window,
And watched you drive away.
There I stood,
A sentential to the dark.
I watched and watched
Until red tail lights
Winked
And were gone.

Poem Introduction – TOO MUCH

I learned to enjoy my attraction, to love and be attracted to someone while knowing that anything more than loving them and sharing their friendship was impossible. I learned to step back and experience the relationship on their terms to be around them and spend time with them. I learned to control myself and my desires. I had to. I learned that I would rather allow a relationship to be what it is without trying to change or manipulate it than risk losing it. I learned to love people as they are without trying to change them, regardless of my attractions or desires. I learned to revel in and be grateful for my desires, even if there would never be any opportunity to act on them. I learned to live within the boundaries of a relationship and enjoy the relationship within those boundaries. I, therefore, have no regrets of ever having loved or desired anyone.

TOO MUCH

What can I say of you?
That you are strong, gentle, and loving?
That you are more than 'just' a man?
That you are my lifetime of hope?

Why should I care what you are?
Why should I categorize you?
Shouldn't I merely accept you as you are,
As my friend?

I have not loved so much in a very long time.
Will I break?
Will I falter?
Will I become greedy for you?
I hope not.
I don't want to scare you away.

Yet, it is not possible
To get enough of you.
My feelings seem rather strange,
Too romantic,
Or something not meant to be.
Should I love 'just a friend' as much as I love you?
I do
But,
'Just' is such a small word.
No friend,
If a true friend,
Is ever 'just a friend'.
The words to describe you
Are anything but small.
So I can't say them out loud.
I keep it to myself.
If it were to be too much,
It might scare you away.
So, I don't dare say
That I love you,
But I do.

Poem Introduction - FATHER

I longed for my father throughout my childhood. Having lost my mother and having no male figure worthy of being called a 'father figure,' I banked on the hope that I would one day meet my dad. I think I may have had unrealistic expectations of that, but what I received when I met him was far superior to what it could have been. Given distance and time, he did what he could to be the father I deserved and that he knew I needed.

After a while, it became evident that meeting my dad was not going to miraculously heal the wounds buried deep in my heart. Having him take me in and love me as his own was wonderful, but it didn't undo the damage that had been done throughout my childhood. I would have to do that myself.

I don't know when I wrote this or how old I was, but it was in my record book where I wrote poetry when I was young, so it must have been written before age twenty-five. Nonetheless, this poem is about my feelings toward my father at that time.

FATHER

I skip a stone across a stream.
The sunlight reflects on the water and gleams.
The breezes blow through treetops, green,
And I alone know what I think.

For too many years, I felt alone
Now, I stand and skip a stone.
Too many years have all now gone.
You were not there. I stood alone.

I played alone from fall to fall,
Played in winter snow beneath oak trees, tall.
In summer, I went swimming and heard the birds call,

But you were not there to share it at all.

When I met you, it was too late
To recapture my childhood. That was my fate.
I had not known you, your smile, your face.
I had no love from you, not even a trace.

A small boy needs a strong, guiding hand,
Someone to lift him up to stand,
Someone to hold him close when he feels bad.
A little boy needs a loving dad.

You did your best to make up for lost time.
You called me your son and made me part of your life.
You gave me the father that I so needed as mine.
You loved me and tried to heal my years of strife.

But here I am, grown and free.
Remembering the day when you met me.
Yet, an emptiness remains that no one can see.
Still alone, I skip a stone across the stream.

Poem Introduction – FEAR OF FEELING

Of course, I was afraid of feeling. Most of what I felt, I dared not show or say, or it was a torment that I never wanted to feel in the first place. I learned that the only emotions I was allowed to have were anger, resentment, rage, or humor, but I had very little humor in those days. However, many men grow up being taught that the only emotions they are allowed are either anger or humor. Often, men fall into one extreme or the other. What people don't realize is that anger is never the real emotion. It is always driven by vulnerability, disappointment, fear, sadness, or hurt—*the hurt dog bites*. So, men who feel those vulnerable feelings respond with anger because they have been taught that it is better to be pissed off than to cry. For most men of my day, the only time they were allowed to cry was at funerals, and it is amazing how much of that unrealistic and ignorant mentality has been handed down to younger generations today.

There was a therapy concept back in the 1990s that the three primary rules for children who grew up in dysfunctional families are, "*1. Don't talk. 2. Don't trust. 3. Don't feel.*" I remember, as do many others, the stupid demand of an abusive parent to a tearful child, "You better shut that up, or I'll give you something to cry about!" There was more than, "*Big boys, don't cry.*" For me, it was not only my sadness, hurt, and tears that I had to hide but my attraction and feelings of affection, as well. My attractions especially had to be hidden. The first time I ever confessed having those feelings to anyone was when I told the upperclassman in college that I had fallen in love with him. It had taken a tanker truck full of courage to admit that to him, and I was excessively lucky in 1974 that he accepted and honored my feelings even when he could not return them. He also did not spread rumors around campus or out to me at a time when that would have been overwhelming and devastating for me.

It took a while for me to learn that it is okay to have feelings, that feelings are natural and normal, and that, unless one is a sociopath, we all have them. Yet, even sociopaths have feelings of jealousy and rage. As I gradually began to get in touch with and accept my feelings, I became aware that others would hide their feelings. Sometimes, we must withhold our feelings, and we all do, to a certain degree. We pull it together to go to the store and don't break down in the middle of the grocery when we are grieving or sad. We wait for an appropriate place and time to cry. We don't share our feelings of attraction with every person we are attracted to because of respect for their boundaries and maybe respect for the boundaries of spouses, either theirs or ours. However, we can still acknowledge, to ourselves at least, that we have feelings and permit ourselves to have them even if we don't express or act on them. The key is to permit ourselves to have the feelings instead of trying to suppress or eliminate them. Whether we express them or not, we can permit ourselves to have our feelings. Rather than forcing ourselves to extinguish feelings, even the ones we don't express, we can still honor them, learn to sit with them, and know that feelings are natural and normal and do not require actions.

FEAR OF FEELING

What's so frightening?
What is it that you're afraid to feel?
I once feared, too, just like you.
I have that fear no more,
But I'm still not sure
What I was afraid of, then.
Seems we all fear our feelings.
Is there something wrong with feeling?
No, indeed.
Every feeling has its merit, has its value,
From the faintest sigh
To the loudest laughter or a grief-filled deluge.
We'll never know the value of feeling
If we don't let ourselves try,
Just as we'll never see the sunrise
If we never open our eyes.

Poem Introduction - PAIN

One of the characteristics of many who grow up in abusive situations is a strong sense of sympathy, often too much. Because of our awareness of our pain, we are often very sensitive to, and sometimes overly compassionate with, the pain of others. Learning to back away and allow others to have their pain is a very important component of trauma and abuse recovery. It is, of course, easier said than done, and in the beginning, it means that we have to resist the urge to entangle ourselves in the feelings and problems of others despite our overwhelming sympathy for them.

There is a concept in the Al-Anon program called *"loving detachment."* This means that we continue to love a person and have compassion while letting them have their pain without trying to fix it. Another saying from the Al-Anon program is, *"I didn't cause it, I can't control it, and I can't cure it."* Co-dependents who gained that title by having grown up in alcoholic, drugging, or abusive homes feel responsible for the emotions of others. Often, we are told that the angst of an abusive parent is our fault, and this begins making us think that we are responsible for the feelings of others. The abuse also doesn't have to be overt but may be covert in the form of a parent who places emotional dependency on a child or when parents place children in an emotional tug of war between them. Because small children are egocentric, they tend to assume that they are the cause of anguish in others. My abusive uncle and grandfather didn't mind letting me know that their lives would have been better if I had never come along. Yet, my uncle still would have been an alcoholic, dependent on his parents, engaged in an ongoing battle with Grandpa, and engulfed with vehement self-loathing, even if I had never existed. Grandpa would still have been selfish and controlling.

Children tend to believe what adults tell them. A child does not know the difference between nectar and poison when fed by any adult. Although general temperament may be the result of genetics, children come into the world pretty much as blank slates onto which are written their culture, family attitudes, racial attitudes, religion, etc. They may go through life having never questioned the validity of things they were taught as children.

They may still stand by erroneous beliefs even throughout life. If we never question our indoctrination, we get to keep it, especially if we defend it. When we give ourselves permission to question the beliefs we developed in childhood and begin to recognize that there is another way of looking at the world, we begin to experience a freedom that we may have thought was impossible. It can be a very painful and internally conflicting process when we begin to question our ingrained beliefs and consider alternative views. We end up with war between our ears for a while, but the good news is that while a closed mind can never be filled, an open mind is eventually filled with truth. So, if we keep our minds open, it's a war we cannot lose.

What is very important to understand is that detachment is not cruel. We are not harming others by protecting our hearts and emotions from their hurt and their issues or hurtful behavior. We are not responsible for their feelings, and we don't have to get caught up with their neediness or hurt just because they want us to. Some people want to be rescued and don't believe in their ability to take care of themselves, while some need to rescue others because they think they have to take responsibility that does not belong to them. The difference between caregiving and caretaking is that caregiving provides help to someone incapable of helping themselves. Caretaking is taking responsibility that belongs to someone else when they are capable of self-care but are not engaging in it. When others are dependent and seeking a rescuer, we can teach them what we know while allowing them to feel what they feel and struggle with their pain. Either they will choose to learn what we have learned, or they will go on with their previous attitudes and beliefs. It is, in fact, often detrimental when we attempt to fix and rescue another person. When we rescue and enable others, we send the unspoken message that they are incapable of fixing themselves and don't have to put in the discipline it takes to engage in recovery. Observing their pain and struggle while detaching from it and encouraging their strength to overcome it is possible and preferable.

One of the amazing people I met when I was in college was a young man who was a seventeen-year-old sophomore with a double major in music and psychology. He could play piano, trumpet, and organ beautifully and had a 4.0 GPA. Mind you, when I first met him, it was during my first semester of college when I was an eighteen-year-old freshman who was frantically struggling to keep a 2.0 GPA. The fact that he had the grades, the double major, and could play all those instruments at seventeen was not the most amazing thing about him. The amazing thing was that he had been born with birth defects. His left arm was about half the length of the average arm and had two little fingers on it. His right arm was normal in length but had no thumb and essentially only three fingers because his index and middle finger were fused at the bone and could not be separated. One day, I told him how amazing I thought he was and asked him how he could do all he did, especially with his handicap. He said, "When I was a little boy, first learning to feed myself, if I dropped my fork on the floor, my parents would sit there and say, 'Pick it up. You can do it.'"

What loving parent, seeing their handicapped child struggling on the floor to pick up a fork and feed himself, would not be tempted to take over and do it for him or even start feeding him instead of requiring him to feed himself? Yet, his parents knew that life would be tough for him and that he would need to step up to the plate if he was going to make it. They loved him so much they believed in him. It was, perhaps, the most difficult way to love. So, instead of rescuing him from his pain and struggle, they encouraged him to work through it, and he did. If they had rescued him, they would have created an invalid and probably a very angry one. The last time I talked to him was while I was almost finished with my Master's degree. I ran into him at a bar and discovered that he was finishing his PhD in psychology, and I'm sure he became an exceptional psychologist. He succeeded because he was taught to succeed. He succeeded because he was not rescued when he could do things for himself. He succeeded because his parents believed in him instead of enabling or abusing him.

Those of us who are empaths must learn how to train our empathy. We have to learn how to tame it and know the difference between empathy and sympathy because most of the time, when we think we are being empathic, we are feeling sorry for another person. The truth is that it is possible to have a great deal of compassion for someone and for the pain they are going through without acting on our urges to intervene and rescue. It is possible to express our compassion without attempting to fix something that is not ours to fix. It is characteristic of most of us who have suffered trauma that we don't want others to suffer the way that we suffered. However, it is important to understand that we never control another person's feelings or choices. No matter how much compassion we may have for them or how much it hurts to see them mess up repeatedly, we must remember that it is their pain to feel and their life journey, which they must learn to navigate. Not acting on our pity and sympathy is part of learning to walk our life journey. It prevents entanglements while allowing us to be appropriately charitable to the needs of those incapable of maintaining their self-care.

This is a poem about pain and empathy.

PAIN

I felt a pain …
Somewhere …
I'm not sure where or why.
It was like burning …
Like losing …
Like dying, inside …
I heard the words spoken,
I think.
Words like recordings played slowly.
I really didn't want to hear.
I really didn't want to know.

I felt like crying, but my face was dry
Like a desert scorched by an unrelenting sky.
I needed to cry,
I wanted to cry,

But my face …
Was dry.

On and on, I let it go.
I let it go on and on and on.
On and on, I let it be.
I let it be …
and tried to think.
It's not my pain; it's not for me.
It's not my life, it's your life.
Your pain, your problem,
Your strife.

Yet, somewhere …
There is a pain in me.
I felt it just now,
Like burning,
Like losing,
Like dying, somehow …
I felt it just now,
That pain in me.
I felt it deep …
As you began to speak.

Poem Introduction – THE DOOR

These are the lyrics of a song that I wrote when I was in college. I learned to play guitar after sitting and admiring the guys who would congregate in the evenings on the tall steps of our dormitory, playing guitars and singing. They agreed to teach me to play, so I bought a pawn shop guitar, sat on the steps with them, and began learning chords. Since I had written poetry for most of my life, I also fell into writing songs.

This song was written after I met Marcy (my mentor), and she began teaching me to let go of resentments from my past. When she met me, I was filled with hatred for my uncle, for my childhood, and myself. She began to teach me that, by holding onto that resentment and hate, I was feeding the same monster that had created it in the first place. Our resentments and hate can be like a contagious disease that spreads to others or gets handed down from generation to generation. When we are abused and tormented, one of the things that can happen is that we come out swinging, not necessarily at those who hurt us, but at life itself. We can distrust almost everyone, resent the slightest infraction, and frequently feel victimized, jealous, critical, judgemental, and vengeful.

It was an eye-opening awareness when I realized that by engaging in my hatred and resentment, I was being like my abusive uncle and grandfather. I was not drawing a line and letting go of the past; I was carrying the past with me and projecting that same vengeance onto others. I wrote this song upon realizing that the past is gone. Whatever happened is what happened. Done is done and can never be undone. That includes my mistakes as well as the mistakes of others. What they did to me is what they did to me. By resenting it and hating them, I was mentally and continually doing to myself what they did to me. By hating and resenting them, I allowed them to hurt me repeatedly in my mind. When I let go of the past and dedicated myself to healing and love, my life improved. I began to feel better, and most of it was a simple matter of letting go. We may think that clinging to our resentment is something we need or want to do, but it feels better to let go. Forgiveness does not absolve them; it frees us. For instance, we can grip and cling tightly to even a soft pillow, and the tension will begin to hurt our fingers, but when we let go, it feels better. Whether we cling to anything in our past or let it go is up to us. We may have to practice letting go over and over, but it is in letting go that our freedom is found.

This song is about my early efforts to let go of my past.

THE DOOR

Oh, they branded you with guilty eyes
And trampled on your dreams.
Then, they salted you with simple lies
That fall between the seams.
They told you that the love you have
Is only make-believe.
Then, they cruelly broke the heart you wore
Extended on your sleeve.

So, you've given up on early dawn
For something down the road,
But you failed to be an ending to the lies,
Because you've taken all the hate they held as their reality,
And you've let it burn the truth out of your eyes.

You've got a right to feel the hurt
And nurture it with care,
And you've got a right to anger with
The pain that was placed there,
But revenge is just a word they use
To propagate the pain
So, the players of the madness game
Can have their way again.

Now, you're wild about a paying back

For long-lost miseries,
And you're panting with a rage that bends
A strong man to his knees.
You're fighting for a way to say
You can't stand it anymore,
But the hands of time already move
The closing of that door.

You held the pain, you let it grow,
A weed out of control.
So, the past that crushed your will to love
Still beacons at your door.
You know that hatred multiplies,
But love can do the same.
It's the one you feed the most, my friend
That wins this crazy game.

Yes, you've given up on early dawn
For something down the road,
But you failed to be an ending to the lies
Because you've taken all the hate they held as their reality,
And you've let it burn the truth out of your eyes.

Now, you're wild about a paying back
For long-lost miseries
And you're panting with a rage that bends
A strong man to his knees.
While you're fighting for a way to say
That you can't stand it anymore,
The hands of time have already moved
The closing of that door.

Love and Lovers

Segment Introduction

The poetry in this section is about my adult experiences of finding my way in love and relationships. It primarily concerns my relationships beyond those of first love in the previous section. It is about the relationships I had after I permitted myself to have gay encounters and after I accepted that who I am is who I am and that I deserve to live and express who I am as much as any other person. Most of this poetry was written when I was in or beyond my forties. So, there is a little more maturity in these, but still a tender heart.

Poem Introduction – IN LOVE

What does the phrase *"in love"* mean to you? We spend much of our time with and do social things with people we love. That includes friends and family, but we are not *"in love"* with mothers, fathers, children, grandparents or buddies, are we? We love them, but it seems to be a different kind of love than being *"in love."* Being in love with someone is not required to enjoy time with them. However, being *"in love"* seems to have a different flavor than the love we experience in general. That doesn't mean that it is a stronger love.

I've heard it said that you need to marry your best friend because, when you are elderly and the sex is gone, what will you have left? When the sex is gone, are you still *"in love?"* I have said that love is like a cake, and sex is like icing on the cake. The cake tastes good, but icing makes it taste sweeter. Most of our loving relationships are cake without icing, but some people indulge themselves with too much icing and not enough cake, or only the icing and no cake. Nothing but the icing can become overpowering and unsatisfying because there is no base or substance to sustain it, leaving us with a queasy feeling. Sex doesn't have anything to do with being *"in love,"* and love certainly is not a requirement for having sex. So, being *"in love"* is not just about attraction or sexual engagement.

Some spiritual practices teach that there is only one type of love and that we have different contracts in our relationships. Most of those contracts (unspoken contracts) do not involve sex. Most of the time, the contract that involves sex is to establish marriage and family, but doesn't someone love their parents, their children, or best friends as much as they love their spouse, even though they may be *"in love"* with their spouse? Isn't it also possible to care about someone and have an ongoing sexual relationship with them without being in love? If there is only one love, there is no such thing as being *"in love."* So, what makes being *"in love"* different? To many people, being *"in love"* means being infatuated, which, if you think about it, really isn't love at all. Being infatuated doesn't have anything to do with making a relationship work. In fact, it may have more to do with the demise of relationships because infatuation means idolizing someone. The problem is that idols are easily toppled because it is very easy for them to fall off the pedestal that we placed them on. They are, like all of us, fallible human beings. Infatuation is not love, and often, breakups and divorces occur because one or both of those in the relationship started with infatuation and do not really know what love is, how to express it, or don't really care.

Selfishness is the number one culprit in the destruction of relationships. When we love someone, we want them to be happy, fulfilled, and have the best possible life. That is the opposite of selfishness. We may have desires and hopes for what they might give us in return, but love does not focus on that and does not require it. However, when we get so focused on what the other person is supposed to be doing for us or how much we are doing for them that they are not returning, it creates a problem, a vacuum of sorts that really cannot be filled as long as we maintain selfish expectations. The flip side of that coin is having someone have selfish expectations of us and, in the worst relationships, selfish expectations of each other. As I said earlier, love is not quid pro quo. If either or both parties in a relationship are selfish and self-serving, the relationship will not work. Yet, those who genuinely love each other can have huge problems that do not diminish the quality and commitment of their relationship. When the marriage vows say, *"for better or for worse,"* that is not a contractual obligation. However, when you truly love someone, you want to love them for better or worse. You want to care for them when they need it. When couples go through hard times, there are basically two choices. You can take it out on each other or help each other through it. Those who help each other through it find that they have an even stronger bond with one another once the difficulty has passed.

So, maybe being *"in love"* is that feeling you get in your heart when you know that the person you are with is the one you are meant to be with and want to be with. Maybe being *"in love"* is missing them when they are at work or wanting to do something nice for them, just because. Maybe it is looking forward to seeing each other at the end of the day or lying down with them at night simply knowing they are sleeping by your side. Maybe it is a desire to see them through hard times and stand by them without selfishness when there are struggles. Maybe it is reveling in their successes, encouraging them, and supporting them in accomplishing their dreams. Maybe it is letting them care for you when you are not feeling well and caring for them when they don't feel well. Maybe it is that peck on the lips each morning before heading to work. Maybe it is sweet affirmations, cuddling, and giggling. Maybe it is looking forward to the future, trusting that the one you are with will share it with you. Maybe it is opening up to each other, being honest, and being vulnerable. Maybe the sex is nice, but you don't really care if it is there or not because that is not the real reason you are sharing your life as intimate partners, and being intimate partners is really what it is all about. Some people think that sex is intimacy, but it isn't. Intimacy is a bond of trust built between two people over time, and sex can be merely one way of expressing that intimacy. Intimacy is knowing that you have each other's backs, no matter what. It is having complete trust and honoring that trust without expectations or demands. Perhaps that is the actual definition of being "in love."

IN LOVE

We don't have to be in love
To go out for dinner and a movie.
We don't have to be in love
For a night out on the town.
We don't have to be in love
To sit in a coffee shop,
And have a long and meaningful conversation.
We don't have to be in love
To sip wine and nibble on appetizers.
We don't have to be in love
To cuddle on the couch and watch TV.

We don't have to be in love
To be attracted to each other.
We don't have to be in love
To have passionate sex.
We don't have to be in love
To linger in the sensuality of intimate moments.
We don't have to be in love
To sleep all night enfolded in each other.
We don't have to be in love
To enjoy the morning with coffee and toast.
We don't have to be in love
To do anything we want to do, anywhere, at any time.
We can enjoy everything together
And love will never be required.
We don't have to be in love to do any of this,
But all of it is so much sweeter, still,
When we are in love.

Poem Introduction - ENOUGH

This is for all the times I have given my heart permission because when you truly love someone, you will never unlove them, no matter what. Love does not come and go. If it can go, it was never there in the first place. It most assuredly does not flip back and forth between love and hatred. We cherish those we love. We give kindness and compassion to those we love. What we never do is try to harm them. It must have been something else you were feeling, perhaps infatuation or need if your love flips back and forth. Someone you love may hurt you to the point that you must let go of the relationship, but that doesn't mean you stop loving them, and true love has no regrets. It may indicate that they didn't really love you, and if that is the case, then the best possible option is to let them go.

ENOUGH

Shall I regret that I have loved you
when winter tints my aged head?
Shall I look up from the nursing's pillow
And wish for other memories instead?
I think not.
For you gave me more than love,
You gave me fortitude.
You taught me the value of solitude.
Should I regret that?
You ask me again if I regret.
How can I regret love?
It was better to have known you,
To have had too little of you,
Better to say,
"Not enough,"
Than to say,
"I had nothing at all."

Poem Introduction – THE COURAGEOUS HEART

I certainly know the pain of betrayal, and I understand when people decide it hurts too much to try again. I have had my fair share of betrayal when others were not as committed to the relationship as I was. Grieving is not just for when people die; it is also for the times when they reject us or break our trust. A quote I love is attributed to Queen Elizabeth II: *"Grief is the price we pay for love."* That is so true of any love, whether it is a romantic commitment or the loss of friends, family, or pets. The question is not whether we will experience grief or hurt because we will. All relationships come to an end one way or another. Forever is a concept, not a reality. If we spend a lifetime together, most often, one will pass before the other. Even the best relationships are painful sometimes. Some disappointments must be worked through, and rough edges must be smoothed down. The question is not whether a relationship will involve hurt. The question is whether the love is worth the pain, and if it is real love, not abuse, it always is.

THE COURAGEOUS HEART

Trusting love is not an easy thing to do.
The wounded heart retreats within the soul,
Hides and dares not look out.
The wounded heart shudders with fear
At the mere prospect of letting anyone get close again.
The wounded heart protects itself,
Lashes out, withdraws, hides, and lashes out again.

How dare you come close!
How dare you love me!
How dare you invite me to love again!
How dare you show tenderness and mercy!
How dare you be patient!
How dare you coax me from behind my pain.

The wounded heart is frightened,
And great courage is needed
Even to muster a little peek
From behind the veil.

The courageous heart steps forward,
Cautiously and carefully,
But steps forward, nonetheless.
The courageous heart allows another chance,
And another, or another,
If necessary.

The courageous heart knows
That even a moment
In the bliss of genuine redeeming love
Is always worth the pain.

Poem Introduction – MOON OVER SAN FRANCISCO

My friend, Larry, was one of the first to contract HIV and AIDS during the AIDS crisis of the 1980s. He had had symptoms as far back as 1978. He lived in Dallas and would come home to visit his parents in Arkansas and then end up in the hospital with rare pneumonia that his doctors couldn't make sense of, especially since he was in his early twenties. That happened a couple of times, and his doctors were baffled. His friends diagnosed him in 1982, but the doctors didn't give him the diagnosis of AIDS until 1985. I had a friend living with me in 1982 who had been a friend of Larry's in high school. We were sitting together watching the evening news when Tom Brokaw announced a new disease affecting primarily gay men and identified the symptoms. My friend and I turned to each other simultaneously and said, "Larry." We knew long before the doctors confirmed it.

Very little was known about HIV and AIDS then. At the time, they didn't know what was causing it or how it was transmitted. It was a terrifying time and became very terrifying for me. I suppose one of the reasons I'm still here is that I was practicing safe sex before anyone ever coined the term. The only time I was promiscuous was during the first several months after I permitted myself to be with men when I was about twenty-five. At that time, I was like a kid in a candy store for a little while, but it didn't take me long to identify that I didn't want to sleep with strangers over and over without having a committed relationship. I wanted someone to spend my life with, and if not that, I wanted to be with someone I knew and liked, not some random stranger. However, after Tom Brokaw's broadcast in 1982, I became grievously terrified of getting AIDS, especially as I witnessed what was physically happening to Larry and others. I had a horrible case of *AFRAIDS*. Larry died in 1987, and my *AFRAIDS* went into a frenzy at that time. That lasted until the Spring of 1989 when I was driving down Green Hills Drive in Nashville, ruminating about dying a horrible death from AIDS. Suddenly, a voice in my mind said, "What the hell difference does it make what you die of or when? Everybody has to do it." Just as suddenly, I was at peace. I had not just admitted that I would die someday; I accepted death. Peace and freedom are found in acceptance and permeate the rest of life when it occurs. Acceptance means freedom because we stop worrying about dying and get on with living.

Like many gay men of the day, Larry had been promiscuous, but there was one time when he had fallen in love. He briefly moved to San Francisco to be with his man but discovered it would not work out. In 1986, when he was hospitalized, I had come from Nashville to Little Rock to visit with him and other friends. At the time, I stayed in his apartment while he was in the hospital. He had an enormous poster of the moon over San Francisco on his bedroom wall. I knew he continued to love the man he met in San Francisco, and one afternoon, I sat at the foot of his bed with my guitar under my arm and wrote a song about his one love. Later, his parents asked me to sing it at his memorial service. These are the lyrics.

MOON OVER SAN FRANCISCO

I saw the moon over San Francisco,
Several years ago.
I looked out on the lights of the city,
And felt a light in my soul.
I fell in love
In San Francisco,
Gave my heart to the night.
I saw the moon over San Francisco,
And in those days, I smiled.

Now, the boats float across the bay,
And the seagulls cry.
I'm standing here in a sea of emotion
Waiting for the tide.
I see your face
In my mind,

See love flood your eyes.
I see the moon over San Francisco,
And I'm starting to cry.

I saw the years go slipping by
Like silk rides the wind.
We never quite step into the future
Living the past again.
I hold your memory just one more moment,
Surrender it to the night.
I see the moon over San Francisco
And wipe the tears from my eyes.

I see the moon over San Francisco
And through my tears
Comes a smile.

Poem Introduction – LOVE IS A WORD

Love is one of the most common words in our language. People drop it like a dollar in a tip jar, say it as a social ritual, say it without meaning it, say it as a manipulation, say it without knowing what it really means, and say it while thinking that it means something other than what it actually is. It certainly took me a long while to get past the idea of love as a need. It took me a long time to understand what love is, and I think many if not most, people don't know what love is. It gets confused with so many things, including neediness, fear, control, idolatry, passion, romance, and lust. Yet, genuine love is none of those things. Love in its truest form is wanting the greatest and highest good for someone, whether with or without you.

LOVE IS A WORD

Love is a word
Tossed about like a tennis ball in a laundry load
Bouncing off this, then that,
Only occasionally tangled
And released to bounce around again.

Love is a word so often said
Because it is something we want
Instead of something we are willing to give.

"I love you" is a phrase that,
Means …
To many,
"I need you. Take care of me.
Lick my emotional wounds
Because I am too scared to believe
That I could be alone
And love myself first."

"I love you" is a phrase that causes
In many,
The need to bolt and run.
Too often, it is used as an excuse
To take rather than give,
Frightening those who have been
Taken as emotional hostages
Instead of truly being loved.
Too often, it is used as a temporary solace
In the blinding storm of life
Instead of being the beacon
That guides our way through the storm.

Love is a word that few understand
And few really mean when they say it.
It is a word cajoled and fished for,
Suckled like the breast of a she-wolf that feeds,
Only to turn and bite.

Few there are in this world
Who can separate love from neediness.
Few there are who recognize
That real love is a desire to give
With no expectation of return.
Love is like the sun.
It only shines.

Few understand that love
Expects nothing
But seeks the highest good
For anyone who is loved.
Even fewer recognize

That the most genuine love
Is eternal love that sees no sin,
That accounts for no wrong,
That never controls nor forces anyone,
That is pure forgiveness,
That separates no one from another,
That sees no greater value in one
Than any other,
That eternally shines even when we hide from it,
And
Patiently—patiently waits
For the prodigal to come home.

Poem Introduction – LET GO

Over forty years later, I wrote this poem about the upperclassman I had fallen in love with in college. At the time, I had idolized him. He was a strikingly handsome man, and he lamented to me once that no one really loved him for who he was but that all they were interested in was his looks. He certainly had many girls who showed great interest in him when he was young. Although he accepted my attraction to him, he could never believe that I loved him rather than just being attracted to him. I told him that if he were mutilated in a terrible accident, I would still love him, but he didn't believe it. I meant it. I loved him; his looks were secondary, but he could never accept that. What had meant the most to me was our relationship and his affection. Still, you can never convince someone of a truth they aren't willing to accept. Perhaps his poor relationship with his father caused him to mistrust the expression of love from anyone. Years on, I finally accepted that he could neither receive nor return my love, and I let go.

A couple of years after writing this poem, I accidentally stumbled upon an obituary indicating that he had died, perhaps around the time I wrote this. There was a deep sadness but no tears. I still love him and will always be grateful for the experience. I also feel a sadness that perhaps due to mental illness, his life became hollow and lonely while I was learning to fulfill my own.

LET GO

I ached for you to want me.
I ached for every chance to be in your presence,
And every touch was like a drug
Leaving me intoxicated,
Craving
More, more, more.
I ached for you to love me,

Desire me,
Be with me
Live with me,
Make love to me,
But you could not.
The greatest ache
Was wanting
What I knew I could never have.
In time, my idolatry
Was replaced with the recognition
Of just how flawed
And human You are;
That it could never have been
Even if you had wanted a life with me.

Still,
After all this time,
I ache for you.
Forty-plus years on
And still,
I ache for you.
I have no idea where you are
Or what you have become.
I only know an emptiness
In my heart where only you belong,
An emptiness that will never be filled.

I have moved on,
Fallen in love again,
And I am in love with someone else,
Even now.
I have loved others over the years,

Deeply and intensely,
But
Never have I felt the soul clenching
Longing that I had for you.
Perhaps the strongest longing
Is for the one we can never have.
Perhaps young love is made more potent
By need,
And mature love is tempered by
Hard-fought wisdom.
If you were here now,
Even today,
I would not hesitate to tell you
How much I dearly love you
And then,
I would let you go.

Poem Introduction - OAISIS

The term *"friend with benefits"* annoys me a little. For one thing, it seems to imply, to most, that your sexual friend, to whom you are not committed but with whom you spend regular time, is just for the convenience of sex, a go-to if you can't find someone else. I have not looked at it that way. I have had these no-strings-attached relationships a couple of times, and neither was about convenience. For one thing, I had a genuine affection for both of them, and they occurred many years apart, each lasting for several years. It was just that we enjoyed one another's company. Still, in both cases, it was a situation in which committing to a long-term relationship wasn't an option. One of them was with a younger single bisexual man who was about 80-90% straight and maybe 10-20% gay. He was attracted to men but didn't want a life-long relationship with a man. He wanted his long-term partnership to be with a woman. We enjoyed our time together while it lasted. We didn't see each other that frequently, but when we did spend time together, that often included sex. For both of us, it was an affectionate and enjoyable time together. Previous to that relationship, there was a man who came by almost every Sunday afternoon for about three years, and we would spend the entire afternoon together, being physically intimate but often not having sex. We would lie together, caress, talk, and hold each other. Sometimes, an orgasm occurred, but often, it did not. When I became involved with my first long-term partner, that involvement ended. I am still friends with the younger bisexual man almost twenty years later. However, we have had no sexual contact since 2005. The other man was quite a few years older than me, and I lost touch with him.

This is a poem about these relationships, perhaps about these types of relationships.

OASIS

You were an oasis in the desert of my life,
A brief stop along my journey.

You were an oasis where I could drink of your attention,
And be refreshed.

It was not love, at least not what they tell us love should be.
We both knew and accepted that it was temporary.

I required nothing of you.
You asked nothing of me.
There were no demands,
No selfish fits about being deprived of each other.
Instead, we let it be.

Instead,
We enjoyed our time together until it passed.
And when it passed, there were no tears,
No gnashing or grieving.
When it passed, there was only gratitude
For a time spent together
In the comfort of one another
Without expectation or demand.

Perhaps then, it was more like real love
Than what they tell us love should be.

Now, as I look back, I do not mourn.
I do not feel a sense of loss.
I only feel gratitude.
For a time,
That my soul languished
In the oasis of your arms.

Poem Introduction - SHINE

Not every relationship is an oasis. Some take on very different meanings for very different reasons. Not everyone can handle an oasis type of relationship or any other kind of romantic involvement, for that matter. I certainly understand the fear of letting someone get close, the fear of getting hurt, and, for some gay men, the fear of accepting themselves. When we truly love someone, however, there are no expectations. That was difficult to learn, and I know it is difficult for others to learn, especially when they think love is quid pro quo. Love is like the sun; it only shines. Some are so afraid of letting themselves be loved that they sabotage the opportunity. This is a poem about such a person.

SHINE

You think yourself unworthy of love.
I love you anyway.
You sabotage your chances for love.
I overlook the times that you have hurt me.
You cannot bring yourself to trust.
And I have given you every reason to trust.
You push me away when I get close.
I wait patiently.
You feel guilty when I give to you,
And think you owe me in return,
But a gift requires no payment.
You cannot bring yourself to believe
That love has no expectations,
Yet there is nothing that I expect from you,
Not even that you love me in return.
I will shine, like the sun, only as much as you will let me,
But if you choose to hide from the rays of my love,
I will not follow you into the darkness.

Poem Introduction – TEARDROP YOU WON'T LET FALL

Not long after I first permitted myself to be with men, I met a guy at an afternoon gay men's party who introduced himself to me by walking up and kissing me. He then pushed me down the hall of this stranger's house, into the back wall of the hallway, and proceeded to kiss and fondle me. I didn't know what to do or how to take that, but I was attracted to him and only fought it momentarily out of embarrassment and shock. Because I had been raised with my boundaries being violated and not knowing what was or was not acceptable behavior in many situations, including gay culture, I stopped putting up resistance shortly after the initial intrusion. In retrospect, he forced himself on me, but I submitted as one of my first sexual encounters. I don't think I had even really noticed him before that point, but I later discovered that he had bet with one of his friends that he could do what he did, and I would submit. He had probably witnessed how shy and subdued I was at that party. He won his bet. Besides, after having never really had the option up to that point, I was intrigued by the idea that men would actually come onto me or want to sleep with me. I didn't know any rules about how that was supposed to happen. I didn't feel attractive and didn't feel like I had much to offer in the sexual department.

As was usually the case in those days, I felt and behaved rather shyly. I am not generally a shy person, and I'm not an introvert, but my abuse and upbringing had me questioning whether I had any social skills. I was there at the invitation of someone I had met, who I didn't really know, and I didn't know anyone else there. I don't even remember who he was or how I met him, but I had been given an invitation by the guy who was throwing the party. I had no idea what to expect and found myself wondering what etiquette should be applied, hoping that I wouldn't screw up and be ridiculed or laughed at. I knew nothing about being around other gay men, and I had continued having my insecurities after college. Becoming involved with gay culture presented an entirely new set of insecurities. It didn't matter who I was around; I still felt like I didn't fit in.

After this man pushed me to the end of the hall, he took my hand and led me to an adjacent bedroom. We lay down on the bed and began to talk. He knew the owner of the house. He introduced himself to me formally, and we began to date. We did not have sex at that first meeting. I was not about to have sex with a man I had just met in some stranger's house on some stranger's bed with a party going on outside the door. That's where I drew the line. Yet, after a short period, I moved in with him. It was far too quick, but young desperation does not take time to get to know someone first. That was the first time that I tried committing myself to a relationship. I was in my mid-twenties, and it didn't last long—only a few months. I, therefore, never counted it as a long-term relationship. Besides, he was never committed to me. To him, I was a convenience if he couldn't find sex somewhere else. I didn't want to be a convenience, so I ended the relationship shortly. As Dolly Parton once said, "*I don't play second fiddle in nobody's band.*"

After moving in with him, I learned that he had problems, and although I believed in monogamy and committed myself, I soon became aware that he did not believe in commitment. It became quickly obvious that he intended my role to be his stand-by in case he was not able to score sex somewhere else. He was a bartender and would stop by peep shows with his tips before coming home, often not arriving until 4:00 or 5:00 a.m. In retrospect, I'm damn lucky that I didn't contract an STD from him, God forbid AIDS.

He came onto other guys in front of me and cruised the parks looking for "*tricks.*" He pressured me to have orgies with other couples and manipulated me when I refused. He was a sex addict, drank too much, and used drugs. He had problems that he couldn't seem to face, and it became quickly apparent that committing himself to me or any relationship would not happen. When someone extends so much energy into trying to avoid and run from their problems rather than facing themselves and letting themselves feel, it is not conducive to stable relationships. Addiction is often about running from some inner turmoil or deep-seated pain that people don't want to face. Often, that pain seeps out around the edges of addictive behavior and becomes evident.

At the time, I had started going to Al-Anon meetings with the recommendation of my graduate field supervisor when she learned that I had grown up with an alcoholic abuser (my uncle). So, I began learning skills of detachment and began withdrawing from trying to get him to pay attention to me. I stopped focusing on his behavior and stopped trying to change him into the monogamous partner I wanted and needed. After that, his behavior escalated into angry fits when he could no longer manipulate me, and I soon moved out.

I had been writing songs, more than poetry, for a while, and following are the lyrics to a song I wrote about observing him when I had finally begun to learn the Al-Anon concept of 'loving detachment.' This is the only poem in this segment that I wrote when I was still in my twenties and the discovery phase. I was once offered a contract on it by a producer in Nashville, but on the advice of another songwriter who told me they would take my rights and shelve it, I turned down the contract. Now, I wonder … what if?

TEARDROP YOU WON'T LET FALL

I know it's hard, I've seen you try,
I've seen those sad memories well up in your eyes,
A time or two,
When you didn't know I was
Watching you,
And so, you see
I understand more
Than you think I do,
But it's your pain to feel.

You know you can't hide it,
But you give it your all.

You must know I see it,
That teardrop that you won't let fall.

You've kept it in a thousand times
When I've seen emotions rising in your mind,
You fought it off,
And tried not to show me
That you could cry like anyone
Who had so much pain
Down in his heart
I'd hoped you might see.

You know you can't hide it,
But you give it your all.
You must know I see it,
That teardrop that you won't let fall.

Poem Introduction – BROKEN

My first long-term relationship lasted eleven years, although ten years existed between that and the person described above. Five of those years were spent dating no one while I tried to figure myself out and get my shit together. I didn't want to make another mistake, even though that is precisely what I did, but it was a different mistake. I took those five years off from dating to figure myself out because I noticed a pattern in which I kept dating one alcoholic or addict after another. I decided that my man picker was broken and had to be fixed. So, instead of dating, I went to Co-Dependents Anonymous groups, Adult Survivors of Abuse groups, and Adult Children of Alcoholics groups. I read self-help books and continued therapy. Still, when I finally decided to date again. I ended up going out with several men who were obviously like my first attempt at having a partner. One of them, actually a blind date set up by friends, drank six mixed drinks over the course of dinner and could not wait to smoke between the salad and the entre. He was a police officer and a very handsome man, but not someone I was willing to see again, especially after witnessing his drinking and smoking habits.

I tried so hard to be careful but made a mistake anyway. Although I didn't pick another addict, in the end, I picked someone so broken that he was addicted to withdrawal and perfectionism. Too late, I learned that his childhood had wounded him far more than mine had wounded me. He constantly cleaned and could not tolerate the most minute things, such as a drop of wine spilled on the kitchen counter. Cleaning was his way of avoiding and pushing back the anguish of his childhood, and it permeated his behavior. One day, I was making a stew for dinner and had a ladle that I used to stir periodically. I turned around and couldn't find my ladle. I went to the drawer to get something else to stir my stew, and there was the ladle. He had washed and dried it and had put it back in the drawer before I could pick it up to stir the stew again. I gave him orders to stay out of the kitchen when I was cooking.

He didn't smoke or drink, was very congenial and friendly, appeared comfortable in social situations (even though he would quickly withdraw), was considerate and kind, and loved cats. Also, some signs and coincidences (belief in magic) caused me to think that we were meant to be together, and maybe we were. All relationships teach us something.

He was a Vietnam-era veteran but had remained stateside, where his duties had more to do with the Cold War with Russia than the War with Vietnam. In retrospect, I realize we were meant to be together, but not for the reasons I thought. He presented yet another lesson that I was to learn. Perhaps we are meant to have every relationship that we have because, if they don't teach us through wisdom, understanding, and love, they teach us through their brokenness, in whatever way their particular brokenness manifests, and how it may clash with our own brokenness. This is a poem about my first long-term partner.

BROKEN

I don't know what I was thinking,
Believing in magic,
I guess.
There it was
The sign!
It had to be a sign!
We had the exact same birthday,
Exactly five years apart,
Our first, middle, and last names,
All had the exact same number of letters.
Was it a sign? Numerology?
Should I believe in magic?
It had to be a sign,
But. . .
Apparently not.

You were too broken,
But at first,
I did not know how broken you were.
At first, you put on a very good show,
Not just for me but for everyone.
Your smiling congeniality,
Friendliness and charm
Hid the fact that you were broken,
Inside.

You had a childhood worse than mine,
A torment, indeed,
But you weren't like me.
Unlike me, you avoided
Rather than confronted.
Unlike me, you buried yourself
In your obsession to be perfect.
Unlike me, you hid your brokenness
So that it could not be healed.
You put on a mask for the world
So that no one would see your brokenness,
Lest they
Break you even more.
Unlike me, you suffered in silence
Until the emotional boil erupted,
And then you returned
Again, to your silence
And your ongoing
Passive
rejection.

Come here, go away.
Come here, go away.

Come here, go away.
Go away,
Go away,
Go away.

I was not sympathetic enough,
Perhaps.
I pushed you too much,
Perhaps,
But enticing and entreating you
Did not work.
Empathy and understanding
Did not work.
You would not budge.
You would not come out from
Your hiding place
which imprisoned you
And tortured you
While it deprived me.

You could trust no one,
Could trust no love,
Could trust no affection,
Could trust no bond,
And as you pushed me further
And further away,
You sank into your loneliness
And sadness.
You drowned in your uncertainty.
Then,
Finally …
Finally …

I could try no more.
Your well was dry
And there was no use in
Dipping another bucket in it.
You would not come out
From behind that wall,
The fortress you had built
Around your heart and soul.
Then,
Finally,
I surrendered you
To your torment
To your self-imposed prison,
And moved on with my life.

Poem Introduction – FIRST MEETING

He sat in a khaki hat across the gazebo where *"Naked Karaoke"* took place. He looked nervous and somewhat forlorn, and like myself, he had opted out of going naked. He was cute, and I dared to walk over and talk to him.

The previous years had not been good, with 2003 becoming the worst. I lost Granny in April 2002, Marcy died in June 2003, and in December 2003, I finally walked away from my first long-term relationship. For two years after that, I had done nothing. I didn't date. What options could there be when I lived in a small town of 12,000 after moving back to the Ozarks in 1997 to care for Granny? Since it was during the years before dating apps, or at least my exposure to them, I didn't meet anyone, but I was lonely. Then, I heard about a gay men's retreat center about an hour's drive away. A gay male couple had purchased a farm in the Ozarks and turned it into a campground for gay men. This included cabins and set-up areas for tents. *Okay*, I thought. *I could at least give it a try.*

Mind you, I didn't like to be around a bunch of gay men. Parties and collections of gay men, in my opinion, got out of hand with sexual innuendo, shadiness, and teasing, and maybe I tended to take it too seriously. Also, I'm not too fond of camping. I considered that growing up in a four-room house with no running water constituted all the camping I should need for a lifetime. However, I wanted to be in a relationship or at least maybe meet someone who might be another oasis. So, even though I was hesitant about going, in 2005, I decided to book a weekend there before the 4th of July. I would be off that Monday, the 4th, anyway, and it seemed like a good time to go. I purchased camping equipment just for the event that I never used again and went. After arriving, I set up my tent and went to *"Naked Karoki."* I was not about to take my clothes off in any public or semi-public setting, even though I don't judge if others do. In fact, I often enjoy that they do. I suppose there are dregs of growing up in a fundamentalist church that will always be a part of my psyche. Since he also had not disrobed, I thought we might share some sensibilities.

I asked him to help me pick a song since I had forgotten my reading glasses at the tent. After a brief conversation, he put his hand on my knee and said, "You're hot." That began my second long-term relationship. Although we never lived together, we spent weekends and vacations together for seven years. Either he came to my house, or I went to his. He cared for his elderly mother in a small town also about an hour's drive away and had an apartment in a converted chicken coup on their small family farm. I felt like I had a lot in common with another country boy. We understood farm life. We did things together and shared much about our love of plants, gardening, and flea markets. So, we enjoyed a lot of activities. He frequently did sweet and thoughtful things for me, and the one thing that I cherished most was when he would lie down on the bed in his apartment, turn away from me, and wave his hand for me to join him for a nap. Saturday afternoons were often spent napping.

Since I cared for Granny, I understood his need to care for his mom, but during the last few months of our relationship, he began to change and made excuses not to spend the weekend with me. His personality seemed to change during that time. He was nearing fifty, his doctor had placed him on testosterone, and he began listening to music by artists like Lady Gaga and Katy Perry instead of the country music he had always preferred. I loved the transition in his music preferences, but maybe I blindly ignored that these were unusual and fairly sudden changes. The warning signs were there, including frequently questioning whether I was being faithful to him, but my heart couldn't see the signs. I had no reason not to be faithful to him and reassured him instead of recognizing that the one who is accusing infidelity is often the one committing it.

Soon after our trip to Chicago for our seventh anniversary, he sat me down and told me he wanted to break up because "We don't really have much in common." It was out of the blue and a total shock to me. I couldn't understand why he would do that, but I would not cling. I never want to be with someone who doesn't want to be with me. So, I accepted. Previously, I had expected that we would move in together after his mother passed and continue to make a life together. However, before that month was over, and we separated our phone bills, he called to tell me that the bill might be a little higher that month because he had been "sharing some dick pics." Then, I knew the real reason for the break-up. He had gotten bored.

Getting over it was significantly more difficult for me. It took me ten months of grieving before I was even close to ready to consider dating again. By that time, I had dating apps and tried to date, but it seemed like I encountered one fiasco after another. So, after a couple of months of bad experiences, I stopped dating entirely.

So many things about that relationship were meaningful to me, especially our naps together. I dreamed about him for a long time after the breakup. Finally, I had the last dream: I got off a city bus at a bus stop. He was lying on a bench and waving for me to come nap with him. Yet, although I had cherished that part of our relationship, I left him there and walked away. I had finally let go.

This is a poem about our first meeting.

FIRST MEETING

When I first saw you sitting there,
Lonely, sad.
I felt it, too.
Lost souls praying silently,
For a miracle of connection.

I dared approach,
And you dared rest your hand upon my knee.
Frightened need became bond,
Became love.
Joy exuded from you
Along with tears.

Little gifts you brought
Touched my heart.

I became entangled.

Years passed.
Joy reached crescendo
Like an orchestra
Playing in my heart.
Then my heart fell
Like a vase on tile,
And shattered into cutting shards.

Many times, I had seen you fumble,
But in the end, you did not drop it,
You threw it down.

Now, years since,
I think of you often
And wonder why?
I will never understand.
I can't.
How could I understand
That you would rather throw me away
For one-night stands, than have my love?

Sometimes.
My mind calls up the vision of you
At that first meeting,
I see you there,
Sitting alone,

Sadness beneath a khaki hat.
You were just as lonely as I.

Then I wonder—
Would I do it again?

My heart answers
Too soon
For a reason
To pull it back.

Poem Introduction – YOU DID NOT DIE

When I met my second long-term partner in 2005, at fifty, I thought I was too old to find someone again. The previous partner of eleven years had a midlife crisis and was five years older than me. That relationship ended when, at fifty, he thought he had fallen in love with a younger man who was only playing him. That guy saw it as a game and had no intention of committing to him. He would do things like come on to me in front of him before I knew they were seeing each other. My partner would stay up late talking to that guy who would lead him on and tease him but would never have sex with him. My partner lied to me about where he was when it became apparent that he was with the other man, and he would back out of our dates with friends at the last minute to be with the guy who was playing him. Even though it was obvious that their relationship would never work, it also became apparent that our relationship could not overcome that breach of trust. That was in 2003. Then, in 2005, when I finally decided to date again, I met a sweet but insecure man seven years younger than me. I also lost him to his midlife crisis as he was nearing fifty. His personality changed, and he decided he didn't want me anymore. Since I tend to be very loyal, the mid-life crisis never happened to me, although I did start trying to date again at fifty after the breakup with my first long-term partner. Yet, I was devastated by the losses when it happened to both my first and second life partners.

This was written after my second life partner informed me, with no warning, that he wanted to end it. I didn't see it coming. The suddenness of it made it seem as though he had died to me. He suddenly withdrew and left me to pick up the pieces of my grief.

YOU DID NOT DIE

If you had died, the message would have hit me
Like a bullet through my soul.
I would have fallen to my knees, wailing, "God, please no!"
But you did not die.

If you had died, our loved ones would have gathered
Soulfully by my side.
They would have rocked me in gentle comfort
Offering sympathy as I cried,
But you did not die.

If you had died,
There would have been memorials held in your name,
And I would not have been the only one with a heart
So crushed and maimed.
But you did not die.

If you had died, the cut would have been final and clean.
The memories of you loving me
Would have carried me so sweetly
Through my tortured grief,
But you did not die.

You did not die.
Instead, you killed our love.
You took away a precious thing
That, for me, was all and enough.
You shattered our connection,
And coldly walked away.
All the years we shared together,
You heartlessly betrayed.

You did not die,
But you crushed my very soul.
You left me torn and empty,
And helplessly alone.

There are a few who comfort me,
And some who understand
That love forsaken can be a lonelier pain
Than a love that simply ends.

Poem Introduction – ONE LAST CHANCE

When my second long-term partner left me in 2012, I believed that in the gay man's world, fifty-eight might as well be ninety-nine. I had given up on dating entirely. I decided never to date again and that I would give up on the idea of a committed relationship with anyone. I concluded that I might sleep with someone here or there if I got the chance, but I didn't consider that for several months after I stopped trying to date. I was fifty-nine by that time. After that, I was amazed that young, handsome men in their twenties were attracted to me and coming on to me, not wanting a sugar daddy but wanting only to spend time with me. There were two who were very nice, but I would consider neither for a committed relationship nor did they consider a committed relationship with me. A young man who was twenty-seven and identified as straight contacted me and asked if I would be willing to "experiment sexually." I was completely surprised by that because I had never seen him show any sexual interest in men. Since I had decided that I didn't care anymore, I knew him and liked him, and since I had no further interest in finding another life partner, I allowed that to happen for a time and enjoyed the attention and affection.

Then, I set about moving to a warmer climate when I could no longer take the Missouri cold, and both of those guys moved to other cities, too. I thought my second partner had taken my last chance to find love. I thought he was the last and that I would never find love again, but I had thought that at fifty when I met him. When he left, I was most angry with him because it meant I would have to date again if I ever wanted to find someone, and I didn't think that anyone would ever want me at my age. Dating, most assuredly, sucked, but when I let go and stopped thinking about finding a life partner, I discovered that I was still sexually attractive to many, and when my God-Child kept telling me, "Age is just a number, don't worry about it," I decided I might give it another chance, but still had no real intention of dating, just occasionally sleeping with someone if I got to know them and liked them. When I moved to The Coastal Bend of Texas, I was sixty years old and saw no reason to even try for another committed relationship.

This is a poem about my fears when my second partner left me. For two more years, I would think that I would never have another chance at love.

ONE LAST CHANCE

People say I look young for my age.
I smile and say, "Thank you."
Still, I am old.
My last birthday told me so.

It brings only slight comfort
knowing that I look younger than I actually am.
Still, my heart lives within a desert wilderness.
It always has.
Despite a wealth of loving friends,
The majority of my life has been spent alone,
And age only makes
Any chance of escape
From my wilderness
Even less likely.

There has been the occasional oasis,
A brief time when I was allowed to drink
Nectar from love's cup,
But the nectar dried up.
It always does.
It has been my heart's tragedy
To fall in love with a liar,
And my soul has been repeatedly
Forsaken by those who cannot commit.

As age begins to crawl across my face
Like a spider weaving a web
That traps my youth within,
I find it difficult not to despair.
Each grey strand of hair
Leaves me feeling
Even more helpless.
I am trapped within my wilderness.

I should be used to it by now.
But I'm not.
Like a child at Christmas
I dared to hope
That you would be my wished-for gift.
Yet, Christmas has come and gone.
My age moves on,
And the older I get
The more I despair
That instead,
You were …
My…
One …
Last …
Chance.

Poem Introduction – WORTH IT

After my second partner left, as noted in the introduction of the last poem, I gave up. I stopped trying to find love. That did not mean that I wasn't grateful for the love I had experienced. I have always come to a point of gratitude after all my relationships and all my losses, including losing loved ones and pets to death. I agree with Queen Elizabeth II that *"grief is the price we pay for love."* Yet, if, at least, our love is real, it is always worth it.

On September 16, 2015, when I was sixty years old, two weeks after I moved to The Coastal Bend, I met my husband, not expecting that we would ever be a couple. It was a meeting, simply a meeting, nothing more. I still thought I would sleep with someone if I liked him, but I would have no expectations of anything else. He and God had other plans (see *And He Prayed*-next). This is a poem about the transition from one relationship to the other.

WORTH IT

I don't exactly know when I fell in love.
There was no marker,
No switch,
No sign saying, "This is it!"
I did not experience
Bells and whistles,
Thrills or gongs.
Instead, it crept upon me
Like a morning fog,
Gentle, soft, and cool.
I settled in,
Kicked off my fears,
Relaxed in the moment of embrace,
And let it be.

Year after year,
It went on,
And I knew
I was in love.
I felt it in my soul.
I felt love's smooth caress
Upon my heart.
I languished in trust
That this,
Despite the occasional disagreement,
Would always be.
I took each day as it came
With gratitude.
I cherished each moment
Of laughter, togetherness,
Tenderness, intimacy, and comfort.
I saw my life unfolding,
Just you and I together
For as long as life endures.
I trusted that you felt the same.
I saw no evidence to the contrary.
Then, you told me one day,
"No more."
You gave no reason,
No explanation that I could understand,
Just, "No more."
Had you been acting for all those years?
If so,
Either you deserve an Academy Award,
Or I had no awareness at all,
And buried my head in denial,
Believing,
Truly believing,

That you loved me.
You said you loved me.
You cried.
We cried together,
Shared tender moments,
Consoled each other,
And enjoyed each other.
Then, suddenly,
It was over.

The creeping fog
Became solid ice.
Your farewell
Shattered it into shards,
Sharp and cutting.
I thought I could never
Heal from those cold lacerations.
For months, I isolated,
Hid in the cave of my mind
And licked my emotional wounds.

No matter how I tried,
I couldn't understand.
I made up reasons,
Tried to justify,
But I could find no justification.

A year went by.
I tried to emerge,
Tried to find love again,
But no one I found
Was you.
Do you have any idea how much courage it took

For me to even try to trust again?
Dating is a minefield that I never wanted to cross again,
But my choice was to isolate or try.
You forced me into that choice.
I questioned if it was even worth it,
Worth the risk of having my heart
Shattered again.
My soul called back,
"Yes, try again.
Yes, trust again."

And so, I have come to this place
With someone else who is
Totally different from you.
I have my fears, my caution.
I have my misgivings and hesitation.
Still, I am allowing it.
Still, I am letting go.
Finally, I am feeling again.
The gentle stealth of love
Is upon my soul.
I am taking a chance
On being shattered again.
If that day comes,
So be it!
Every precious moment
Between trust and torment
Is worth it.
Just as every moment
I spent
With you
Was worth it.

Poem Introduction - AND HE PRAYED

Two weeks after I moved to The Coastal Bend, I met my husband. To me, it was just a prelude to maybe having sex, just a meeting. After committing myself for life twice and having my heart torn apart each time, I didn't care anymore. It wasn't that I had sworn off love or was afraid to love again; I didn't care. I was too old to care anymore. Why bother establishing a relationship if all I will get is dumped? Still, there was a reservoir of hope within me.

We met at a pier and went for a walk. We stopped at a beachside bar and had margaritas, then continued to walk along the shoreline, and we talked a lot about a lot. After spending a couple of hours together, I asked him if he could give me a lift back to my apartment even though it was just across the street. I could have walked it easily, but I asked him for a lift. I don't know why. He drove me home, let me out at my apartment parking lot, and went on. I enjoyed our visit but didn't expect much. I knew I would see him again, but I continued my usual activities.

I didn't know that, after that first meeting, my husband had stopped his car a few blocks from my apartment and prayed that he could spend his life with me. He and God had other plans. I had multiple hesitations about getting involved with him or anyone else and continued to go out with other men after we met. For one thing, at the age of sixty, I was twenty-three years older than him, yet my God-child's voice rang in the back of my head, "Age is just a number." At age twenty-five, she married a man who was fifty-two, so I guess she meant it. When it came to just sleeping around, I didn't care about age as long as someone was at least in their twenties, but I was a little more concerned about a committed partner. Being of Hispanic-Mexican descent, my husband was from an almost completely different culture, and I knew far too little about it. He was also coming, far too freshly, out of an abusive relationship in which his last partner had not only been physically and mentally abusive but had cheated on him, stolen from him, and grossly deceived him. That man, incidentally, was a preacher in an authoritarian church. It was two more months before I gave in to exclusively dating him, and after that, he told me that he had prayed for us to be together.

AND HE PRAYED

How could I know that you prayed to be with me?
We walked along the bay,
Had margaritas at a beach bar,
And that's all it took for you to decide
That you wanted to spend your life with me?
There was no comment, no commitment, no promise,
And no reason to decide so soon,
But, so quick, you decided I was the one?
Why?
I'm an old man.
Who would want me now?
Little did I know that you get what you want,
That whatever you pray for comes to be,
Or so it seems.
Little did I know that you had stopped your car
A few blocks from my apartment,
And committed to God
That you wanted to spend your life
With me.

I had given up on love.
I thought it was impossible,
Again,
At my age.
I resisted ever getting involved again,
Continued to go out with others,
And yet, you calmly waited

For your prayer to manifest.
I resisted,
Held back,
But in the end,
You got what you asked for.
Be careful what you ask for.
You might get me.

Now, years have passed,
And here we are.
Yet, I did not intend to fall in love.
I refused to fall in love.
I had given up.
All I wanted was some fun,
To live the rest of my life
As comfortably as I could,
Alone.
Love had often been taken from me.
Why would I expect to love again?
Why would I want to?
I thought that I was the only one capable of committing,
And I had given up on committing.
I was wrong.
I'm not the only one.
How was I to know
That you prayed to be with me?
How was I to resist divine intervention?
How was I to know that anyone
Could love me that much
And commit to spending life with me?
Did you know what you were getting into?
No, you didn't, but here you are.

All these years later
Despite my frustrations
And moody ways,
Despite all my resistance
And refusal,
You prayed for me
And made me love,
Again.

Poem Introduction – COBALT BLUE

I have long taken to nature during stressful times. I learned it from Granny and Marcy. I call it rocking in the arms of Mother Nature, and I have found that Mother Nature will always solace and comfort me. In graduate school, I used to go to Pinnacle Mountain State Park outside of Little Rock and go off the trail. The signs say not to do that, but I'm a country boy. Through the woods, I found a huge cliff overlooking the Arkansas River where I could watch the eagles sail around on the air currents and see the tugboats going up and down the river. I would sit there for a few hours away from all the other visitors, away from school and stress, and then drive home refreshed.

When I first moved to The Coastal Bend, it was an extremely stressful and lonely experience. So, I took to nature again. I would cross the street to a small, somewhat hidden beach where I would sit on a stone by the water watching the waves and sea birds or walk around looking for sea glass. I know that blue is one of the rarest sea glass finds, especially cobalt blue, and to this day, even as I write this, I still have not found one myself. After my husband and I first started dating, he would join me in my search for sea glass, and we would spend wonderful evenings together on that small, somewhat secluded beach, roaming up and down near the water's edge, looking for these jewels of the ocean.

COBALT BLUE

Clear sea glass
Hides amid the sand, gravel, and bits of shell,
Hardest to see,
But most plentiful.
Green and brown pieces
Are plentiful, as well.
Yet, Cobalt blue is the color
I have most prized.

Still,
I have never found one.

We dance back from the water's edge,
Laughing,
Protecting new tennis shoes
From ocean's soaking.
Bent over, I gaze at bits of shell,
But you distract me.

"Oh, look, honey!"

You point to sea-worn glass
Of cobalt blue.
There it sits, alone atop the sand.
"It's the one you wanted!"

Excited,
you hand it to me
Like a baby for a blessing.
I accept,
And coo, "Thank you."

Soon,
On the same day,
On the very same
Day,
You find a red piece,
Even more rare.
You present it, as well.
Again, I smile,
"Thank you."

I never tell you
That I am jealous,
Jealous
That I did not find it,
Myself.
I wanted to find it,
Myself.
You took that from me
With your tender, loving gift.

If I had found it,
I would have kept it.
Unlike you,
I'm selfish that way.
Yet, you are anything
But selfish.

Cobalt blue is the sea glass
I have most prized,
Yet, I have never found one.

Still …
I did find you.

Poem Introduction – I AM CONTENT

When my husband and I got our house together, I would open the garage door on cool and sunny autumn days, get out my easel, and paint at the edge of the drive. Even though I am an untrained and primitive artist, I love to paint and draw. Of course, part of that time was spent painting a few things to hang on the walls of our bare, new house. Nonetheless, I love to paint just for the sake of painting. I find it to be a relaxing and pleasing meditation. As you will see in this poem, my husband is a thoughtful and wonderful man.

I AM CONTENT

Evening shadows fall over the garage,
My makeshift studio.
The painting is coming along nicely.

You take the parrot from the cage
And place him on my shoulder.
"He likes to be outside."

You fetch me a glass of wine
And kiss me, not once, but three times,
Gently and sensually.

Is this happiness,
This simple comfort taken at the end of the day?

I mix acrylic and smear it on canvas.
My professional artist friend used to say,
"Art is anything you can get away with."
Can I get away with this?
All I know is that it makes me happy to paint.

I cannot—not express.
In some form, some way,
It has got to come out of me.
Sometimes, the wrong things
Come out of me.
Often, the things I say are blunt and truthful,
Not intended to offend,
But they offend, anyway.
Sometimes, I express too much.
Often, I feel there is so much in me
It can never all come out.

I don't have time.

If I were to say it all,
Do it all,
Paint it all,
Photograph it all,
Invent it all,
It would take more lifetimes
Than I have available.

All I know is that
In this moment,
Brush in my hand,
Bird on my shoulder,
A glass of wine nearby,
And the sensation of your kiss
Yet, lingering on my lips,
I am content.

Poem Introduction – YOU STAY

After having been through three failed relationships with men incapable of or unwilling to commit to a real relationship, including the first short-term involvement, I was surprised to find how loving and attentive my husband can be. He proves himself repeatedly, and as time passes, we become more and more comfortable with each other. I never thought anyone would stay, and I had to challenge my fears repeatedly, but he has stayed.

YOU STAY

Although, with a tender touch,
Your love is professed,
My heart resists.
Although longing years
May yet culminate
At last, in connection,
My heart resists.
Tender wounds
From heartaches past
Still haunt,
And wait to heal.
Your love seeks to be
A balm,
And yet,
My heart hides
Behind my caution.
I am too old to trust eternity
Or believe in fairy tales,
Or that anything
Of this world
Will be
Forever,
And yet,
I am comforted that you stay.

Poem Introduction – SOUL TO SOUL

Intimacy is not sex or affection, although most people think of it that way, and intimacy can certainly be expressed through sex and affection. However, intimacy is a bond of trust built between two people over time. Sex and affection are merely a couple of the many ways that intimacy can be expressed. The therapy term for expressing intimacy is our *Love Language*, which may vary from person to person. Intimacy is knowing that you have the other person's back, no matter what, and they have yours. It means you fully trust them, and they trust you. It manifests in all types of relationships. Romantic involvements may include the expression of intimacy through sex, but it isn't necessary because intimacy can be expressed in so many other ways. When we are in a marriage, we commit to each other to build true intimacy that will see us through conflicts and difficulties. We dedicate our lives to one another and make our bond closer. Granted, there are times when, regardless of the legal papers, one person is married, but the other is not. One person has committed to the development of intimacy, and the other either can't or won't commit or didn't consider what they were getting into in the first place. When trust and bonding are there, intimacy develops. The deeper the intimacy, the more connected and committed the couple feels. It may take a while to build intimacy, but as it grows, so grows the bond of the relationship. You can be guaranteed in any relationship that no matter how close you are to each other, problems and conflicts will arise. As time passes, those conflicts become less significant and more easily resolved. When a couple doesn't have intimacy and they go through a rough spot, they take it out on each other. When they have intimacy and go through a rough spot, they help each other through the problem because they know, soul to soul, they are in it for their relationship and their commitment to each other.

SOUL TO SOUL

My soul lingers in your soul,
In the sweet essence of communion.
Whether here or there,

Together or apart,
My soul lingers in your soul,
And yours in mine.

I resisted, you know,
I tried not to feel this,
Dared not to trust again,
But I simply let it be.
We lingered with each other
Fought with each other
Laughed with each other,
Cherished each other.
You cherished me until
I cherished you in return.

My soul lingers in your soul.
Two become one, yet
Totally unlike the other.
We grate on one another,
Irritate each other, yet
We take care of each other.
We know each other
And each day,
Get to know each other more.
We sacrifice for each other,
Encourage each other
And linger together in tender repose.

My soul lingers in your soul.
Deep water flowing through ravines,
Splashing up against the stones
Wearing away the hard edges,

Making them smooth so that
We flow together diversified
But unified.
Hungry but fulfilled,
We thirst, always,
For one another,
Always filling up,
Showing up,
Consistent and devoted.

My soul lingers in your soul
And yours in mine.
Rising up, we linger in one another.
Time after time.
Your head on my shoulder,
Your arm across my waist,
Your consistent kisses are remembered
To get me through each day,
And a thousand years on
I will still know that
My soul lingers in your soul
And yours in mine.

Poem Introduction – PATCHWORK HEART

Maybe I am a *"hopeless romantic,"* whatever that actually means. I have always wanted the relationship and the commitment more than I wanted simple sexual interaction. I have a lot of sexual energy and very much enjoy sex, but it has always been bonding and love that I have wanted most, and I certainly don't want to have sex with someone I don't like. For years, I tried to establish and maintain loving relationships. Sometimes, they were the Oasis in the desert, a passing and temporary refreshing solace. Several times, I fell in love. My heart has been broken and torn many times, and I have repeatedly found myself picking up the pieces and patching it back together. I have saved the memory scraps from those lost relationships and cherished the beauty within them. I cherish all my experiences, and the memories are now collected into a kind of patchwork within my mind.

Where I came from, there was a long tradition of quilting. Women of our family collected scraps of old clothing from years back to make patchwork quilts, and even though they were made from discards, those quilts were greatly valued. I inherited many of them from my mother, grandmother, and great-grandmother. The quilts gave a second purpose to previously discarded, outgrown, or damaged things. I have patched together my memories of love, and that way, like a warm quilt, I have created my patchwork heart. By the way, this poem was written several years before I met my husband.

PATCHWORK HEART

My patchwork heart is made of pieces
Tattered and torn by life.
There are shreds of romance once worn
Like a soothing cloak,
Then taken,
Tossed in a closet,
Forgotten,
And eaten away by the moth of time.

My patchwork heart is made of memories,
Joyful moments of my history
When love was,
For a brief span of time,
Good to me.
Yet love,
Once colorful, new, and delightful
Faded in the wash of loyalty.

My patchwork heart is made of ecstasy,
Born of nervous discovery
When youth still found love to be an adventure.
I once perceived that first trembling touch
To be far beyond what might ever be granted to me.

Then, I reveled in lovemaking and sensuality.
Yet time has caused the thread to bare
On this, my treasured memory.
There is not one piece without some despair
Within this antique treasury.

My patchwork heart is sewn together by strength,
Hard-won through love's regrets.
Once nothing more than discarded scraps,
From scattered pieces, I have made it.
I have stitched together the patches and patterns
That I have managed to collect.

I have hope that, as I age,
In moments of cold loneliness,
My patchwork heart may become
Warm cover.

Spirituality and Everything Else

Photo by Kathi de Fontaine

Segment Introduction

Most of the poetry in this section is about spirituality, worthiness, and mindfulness. Some are about my years of not only my own experience of suffering and recovery but also witnessing the suffering of others with a new awareness after my climb toward healing. Some are just observations or responses to something that touched me.

Regarding spirituality, I grew up being taught that there was only one true religion and that ours was it. There was denial among the practitioners that the church's denomination had begun with an American preacher in the early eighteen-hundreds. No, it was taught; ours was the only true religion prescribed by and practiced by Christ himself, even though our church seemed to contain little of the love that Christ encouraged. I, therefore, grew up terrified that I was going to go to hell because if this is the one true religion, and the preacher says that being who I am is worse than being a murderer, I must, therefore, be destined for hell. Somehow, my loving heart, ethics, and compassion, or how good I might otherwise be, didn't seem to matter. The only thing that mattered was that If I was gay, I was condemned to hell.

Even though I was told that I would go to hell for accepting a scholarship to a Presbyterian college, going to that college ended up being the best thing that had ever happened to me. It awakened me to ideas other than those instilled in me during my upbringing. It led me to an exploration of spirituality rather than blind acceptance. It led me to recognize that the ones who say you are not allowed to question are the ones who need to be questioned most. It led me to the realization that all religions are valid, and it gave me a hunger to learn more. Still, relinquishing the ideas I had grown up with took a great deal of anguish, self-searching, and, more than anything else, courage.

Over the years, I have studied multiple different religions. I briefly worked for the Nashville Jewish Community Center in the 1980s and began developing a better understanding of Judaism. Probably the religion I know the least about is Hinduism, but I know quite a few things about that religion, as well. Buddhism is a religion; if it can be classified as one, that makes the most sense to me. However, I have also studied Hinduism, Islam, the Tao, Wicca, and Native American spiritual beliefs and have always retained my Christian roots. I have learned that religion is a tool to help us develop our spirituality. It is not a tool to impose on someone else. Their tools may be just as effective as ours; if not, they have the right to choose which tool they will use or whether they want one. It is a myth to think that a belief in God is required for the development of ethics and morality. Many, perhaps most atheists and agnostics maintain a strong moral and ethical compass without a belief in religion.

A tool serves a purpose but can be used for things other than the intended purpose. A hammer, for instance, can be used to drive a nail, but a hammer can also be used as a murder weapon. The decision and intent of the person using the tool determines how the tool will be used. Religion can be used to help practitioners develop their spirituality, or it can be used for the accumulation of wealth and power, as a tool for subjugating others, or as an excuse to kill. Misusing the tool does not mean it is defective, but it is important to remember that no religion is perfect. No religion should ever be worshiped as though the religion is God instead of a tool to help us understand God. It is just as possible to make religion into an idol as anything else.

I taught a college sociology class for a time, and one of the segments in the textbook was about religion. Religion, despite what some might think, is a sociological phenomenon. For that class segment, I would draw a diagram on the board, a kind of bell curve with authoritarian religions on one end and mystic religions on the other. Most religions fall somewhere between the two and have elements of both. On the authoritarian end, the concept is that you must follow the rules. It's all about the rules. If you do not follow the rules, you will not receive a reward in the afterlife and will be severely punished (go to hell). When a religion is extremely authoritarian, not only do they believe that they have the right, but in fact, they believe that they are obligated to impose their religion and rules on others. This is why there are theocracies and religious states.

No religious state or theocracy is ever based on a mystical religion because, to them, it is not about the rules but about developing spirituality, enhancing the awareness of divine love, learning to live a good and happy life, having compassion, and learning about how to gain the mystical experience in which they feel a connection with God and with all of creation.

If you want to learn, they will teach you, but never try to force anyone into their beliefs because they understand that there are many roads to the same city and different tools to accomplish the same task. Whatever tool you use is up to you. How you use it is up to you. Mystics do not impose themselves on others and tend to be compassionate and understanding. There is no need for a sales pitch because they practice their spirituality for themselves, not for accumulating wealth, trying to influence, or subjugating others. Besides, if a religion has to advertise, it is not a religion; it's a business. "*A good tree cannot bring forth evil fruit; neither can a corrupt tree bring forth good fruit.* "*Wherefore by their fruits, ye shall know them.*" (*Matt. 7:15–20.*) Those who become too focused on the letter of the law may be missing the whole point. "*You blind guides, straining out a gnat and swallowing a camel!*" (*Matthew 23:24*) Throughout history, much evil has been perpetrated by authoritarian religions that focus on the letter of the law. We know the good or the bad by what they produce. Mystics focus on the point of the law. They don't strain at the letter of the law. They don't judge or try to impose their beliefs on others. They know the law is for them to practice, not for them to impose on anyone. As a result, mystic religions (Christian or otherwise) tend to stay out of government. There doesn't have to be a separation of church and state with mystics because they have already separated themselves from the state.

In Islam, for instance, you have the Shiites and the Suni on the fundamentalist or authoritarian end of the spectrum, with jihadists being the most extreme. Then, you have the Sufi on the opposite, mystical end of the spectrum. Many people have never heard of the Sufi because the Sufi don't get up in other people's business. They don't try to control or establish an Islamic state. There has never been a Sufi theocracy. They don't advertise or indoctrinate. You can either follow the way or not follow the way; the choice is yours. Sufism started in Turkey. It developed after the death of Mohammed in 632 A. D. but did not develop into an order until the 12th century. Some people have heard of the *Whirling Dervish*, and these are, in fact, Sufi practitioners who whirl in a kind of meditative dance to increase their spiritual awareness. The mystics are all about their relationship with

God and the development of their spirituality. Part of that awareness is that they know they have no business defining the way for others who may find their way by utilizing their own tools. As with the Twelve Steps programs, mystic religions multiply by attraction rather than promotion and certainly not by forced indoctrination.

In Sufism, like in Buddhism, there is a master teacher who works with novices to teach them about the tools of the religion and how to utilize them to increase their ability to access the spiritual experience. When I visited Istanbul in 2011, I loved our tour guide's story about a Sufi master and his novice. The master noted that three Imams were sitting in a row studying the Quran. The master said to his novice, "Go and slap each one and tell me which one is a master." The novice did as he was instructed. He slapped the first Imam, who slammed his Quaran shut, stood up, and slapped him back. The novice slapped the second Imam, who immediately became angry but collected himself and returned to studying the Quran. He slapped the third Imam, and that one did not respond at all. He didn't even look up from his study but continued to study the Quran. The novice returned to his master and said, "The first one thinks he is learning the way, but he is not learning the way. He continues to be trapped in his attachments and anger and does not know the way. The second one is learning the way and is beginning to practice the way, but he still has much to learn. The third one is the master, for he knows that all things come from Allah."

I love that story, and it fits wonderfully with what I began to surmise from spiritual studies, which included my initiation to understanding spirituality through my Presbyterian college, Unity Church, the Twelve-Step programs, A Course in Miracles, and studies of various religions worldwide. I have also read several Buddhist books and developed a new understanding of Christianity. In time, I understood that Heaven and Hell are constructs, symbolic of the experiences we put ourselves through with our mental states. When we separate ourselves from love and live in a state of fear, anger, attachment, and selfishness, we place ourselves into a mental state of hell, and our experience in the world often mirrors externally what is going on internally. On the other hand, if we point ourselves in the direction of love and practice loving thoughts of kindness, acceptance, humility, forgiveness, compassion, gratitude, and caring, we place ourselves in a heavenly mental state, and our external experiences also mirror what is going on with our internal experiences. I will explain the true definition of humility in my poem, *A Single Step*.

I now know that nobody gets it all right all the time. We all make mistakes and slip in and out of a loving state of consciousness. *A Course in Miracles* states that, at any given moment, we are either moving toward love or away from it, and we have a choice to correct our course away from fear and back toward love or experience the consequences that fear produces. When we move in the direction of love, we also move into a state of happiness, which is the inevitable outcome of keeping our minds aligned with love. In that state, like the Imam, who was a master of the way, we realize that all things come from God. Most of us (self-included) are not likely to experience that level of enlightenment. However, they don't call it a spiritual journey for nothing. There is always further to go and more to learn. Spiritual arrival is usually not experienced, and those who think they have arrived spiritually have arrived at their egos rather than genuine spiritual awareness. An old Buddhist saying is, *"He who thinks he knows does not know. He who knows that he does not know knows all."* In other words. The one who is humble and open to learning and continuing on *his/her/their* spiritual journey is the one who understands the journey. The one who demands that *he/she/they* has the answers comes from an ego state rather than spirituality.

I learned from the Twelve-Step program that I could change my understanding of God. The first three steps are: 1. *"We admitted we were powerless over (you name it) and that our lives had become unmanageable."* 2. *"Came to believe that a power greater than ourselves could restore us to sanity."* 3. *"We made a decision to turn our will and our life over to God as we understood Him."* Now, I had grown up, whether consciously or not, pretty much thinking that God is an asshole, a vindictive S.O.B. who will torment you for eternity if you don't do exactly what 'He' says. The unspoken mixed messages of the church were, *"God loves you, but He's gonna get you if you don't watch out."* And *"Sex is dirty, so save it for the one you love."* As a consequence of growing up in an authoritarian religion, I was not about to turn my will and my life over to an asshole, and if I was going to burn in hell anyway, why bother? But then, it occurred to me that Step 3 invited me to change my understanding of God. If I think of God as a loving, compassionate, and benevolent force that wants nothing more than my greatest good and happiness, I can turn my will and life over to that. It also occurred to me that despite my resistance, my screw-ups, and my anger, something had certainly taken care of me and had guided my way throughout my life. Then, I wondered, "What might happen if I cooperate?"

As my spirituality developed, my anxiety and fear began to fade away. I began to be able to handle things that had once frustrated me and caused me to be sullen and resentful. Sometimes, I still become angry, but I have learned to work through it quickly rather than letting it roll over into resentment. As I meditated, I began to become calm. I still struggle with dregs of adverse thought habits that developed during my childhood, but I have much better control of those than I used to have. Nonetheless, some stresses test the system. Moving to The Coastal Bend of Texas was one of those stresses.

On the one hand, I needed to live someplace warmer and more hospitable to the cold-sensitive neuropathy I had developed, and Missouri winters had begun to torment me physically. On the other hand, when I moved to Texas, there were the challenges of being lied to about the apartment I rented online without ever seeing it. I trusted that a legitimate management company would not mislead me. However, instead of being a nice "renovated" one-bedroom apartment described to me, it was a filthy rat-infested mess with all kinds of problems. It had been semi-renovated with a new (cheap) stove and refrigerator, but that was about it. I had been sent misleading photos, and when I got to The Coastal Bend, my choice was either to go ahead and move into that apartment or put my things in storage and move into a hotel while I tried to find something else. A hotel can be expensive; I would not have a place for my cats, and the lease had already been signed. Initially, I didn't realize all the problems. Since I was already overstressed, I decided to go ahead and move in. The landlord did precious little to address the problems, including leaks, windows where the rain blew in around the sills, mold, broken kitchen tiles, broken hinges, plumbing problems, rats running along the window sills and leaving droppings in my kitchen that were the diameter of a quarter, and a four-foot pile of trash that had been left on the landing. I was also paying $300.00 a month more for that apartment than the mortgage on my four-bedroom house in Missouri, which had not yet been sold. In addition to paying the mortgage on the Missouri house, I also had to pay for lawn care and maintenance. So, I was a bit strained financially, among other things. Even though I had grown up in a four-room house with no running water, it was clean, and we didn't deal with things like the rain blowing in or rats. My Texas apartment was the worst place I ever lived.

My spirituality, as usual, saved me during that extremely stressful time. The good thing about the apartment was that it was across the street from a public beach. My spirituality was practiced by visiting that little beach and looking for sea glass, taking my camera to photograph the gulls, or merely walking the shoreline. It was practiced by taking walks, meditating, and maintaining my affirmations even amid the nagging doubts and the fear that I had made a colossal mistake that would be almost impossible to fix. During those walks near the ocean, I noticed the gulls seemed to be laughing. They seemed to have no care or worry at all, and I began to focus on the laughter of the gulls to bring a smile to my face and help me transcend my slip away from love into fear. The gulls helped me return to love and reminded me to let go and let God be God in my life. They reminded me of the present moment and the importance of bringing my attention back to the moment in mindfulness instead of allowing myself all the mental anguish and anger that came with the move.

Although I am a spiritual eclectic, I have never given up on Christianity. There are verses of the Bible that I grew up with that take on an entirely different meaning for me now. Rather than looking at the Bible as entirely literal, I now see that the Bible has symbolic meaning. One of the things I learned in a folklore class at Lyon College is that wisdom was passed down through storytelling before the invention of writing and that storytelling was usually symbolic. The stories were memorized and told repeatedly, with slight variations throughout the generations. The stories were for teaching wisdom and spirituality through symbolic meaning. When humankind learned to write, one of the first things they did was write down the stories passed down from the centuries before. I realized that the Bible is no different, and one of the verses I recall from childhood was *Matthew 23:24, 'Ye blind guides, which strain out a gnat, and swallow a camel.'* I now interpret that to mean that when you strain at the letter of the law, you will likely miss the point of the law. Another verse I commonly recall is Matthew 22, 34-40, *'Jesus said unto him, Thou shalt love the Lord thy God with all thy heart, soul, and mind. [38] This is the first and great commandment. [39] And the second is like unto it, Thou shalt love thy neighbor as thyself.'* In other words, it's all about love. Love is the foundation of every major religion; we have nothing if we don't have that. *1 Corinthians 13:* "*If I speak in the tongues of men and of angels, but have not love, I am only a resounding gong or a clanging cymbal.*" I once heard a Unity minister quote a version of The Golden Rule from every major world religion. They all admonish us to treat others as we want to be treated and love as we want to be loved.

I learned in early Bible school that the term *neighbor* referred to everyone, even though the church itself didn't seem to get that fully. The verse says you shall (or will) love everyone as yourself. I thought of *'as yourself'* as including yourself, and the verse meant you would love everyone, *including* yourself. My study of spirituality led me back home to my roots but with a different understanding of those roots. It made me aware that the rules are not as important as love. According to the Bible, *'On these two commandments hang all the law and the prophets.'* So, love God and other people. In other words, love God and others because love is the bottom line, not authoritarian condemnation.

Some of the following poems are not directly about spirituality but have spirituality tied into them, even though they are simply observations and awareness. Many of them were written after I moved to The Coastal Bend and once again had to utilize my spirituality to find comfort and peace. Now that Granny, Marcy, and other mentors are gone, My spirituality has become my anchor in the storm.

Poem Introduction – DIAMOND

Let's talk about wound care. If you get a little cut or a nick, it will probably heal in a week or two without much effort. You might not have to put a Band-Aid on it or medicate it. However, a different process must occur if the cut goes deep. For one thing, you can't seal it over. If you do, it closes off air to the deeper portions of the wound and creates a breeding ground for infection. Instead, the wound must be opened and heal from the inside out. Early in healing, it has to be treated and packed daily, if not more often. Each time the gauze packing has to be removed, it is very painful. Yet, it is necessary for the gauze to be removed and for the wound to be cleaned and regularly medicated if it is to heal. Eventually, the wound heals, but it always leaves a scar. That scar may be tender, but the longer it goes without reinjuring, the less painful it becomes. After a while, it becomes only a reminder of the wound that once occurred, and although the wound is no longer painful, the scar is evidence that it occurred. Remember, I referred to my own scar during the introduction of *The Hurt Dog Bites?* That scar is an important reminder of a valuable life lesson.

Emotional wounds are very similar. If there is a slight affront to your ego or someone says something that hurts your feelings, you will probably be over that in a day or two, a week max. It could indicate a bigger problem, a deeper wound beneath the surface if you are not getting over it. For instance, when someone experiences trauma, especially childhood trauma or repeated severe trauma such as domestic violence, sexual assault, or combat, the wound is too deep to just heal by itself. It has to heal slowly and with great care. Until it heals, it is very tender, and even the slightest affront can seem overwhelming. It is not likely to heal if you tell yourself that you can handle it by yourself and that you need to *"embrace the suck"* and get over it. Just like being physically cut deeply, you need professional help when the emotional wound cuts to your soul, at least the help of support groups or the guidance of someone who has gone through their own healing. When you get help and start opening that wound, of course, it will hurt. Initially, your pain reactions could worsen, but when you are willing to do the wound care and let others help you, the wound begins to heal. Yet, even when it heals, there is always a scar, which may sometimes be a little sensitive. Yet, it can never be as sensitive and painful as the initial traumatic wound.

One of the things I tell people is that you have to understand that trauma is a liar. Trauma takes an insane situation or a series of insane situations and tells you that all your life will always be like that. The lies of trauma are that you can never be safe again, and therefore, no one or no situation can be trusted, and you are worth less as a human being, weak or ineffective because you were unable to control the trauma or were treated as worthless by the trauma. Especially in childhood, when we are treated as worthless, we begin to believe that we are worthless. A child does not know how to discern nectar from poison and so believes the lies displayed in the words and behavior of their abusers. Many had terrible childhoods that pushed them to the very edge of a traumatic breakdown. Then, after ending up in military combat situations or experiencing further trauma as an adult, they were pushed over the edge of a traumatic breakdown. Some had childhoods that pushed them over the edge before they had a chance to grow up. Some had adult trauma so severe and dehumanizing that it pushed them over the edge.

What is most important in recovery is to keep yourself reminded to confront the lies of trauma. The truth is that most of the time, most of us are safe in most places and most situations. The truth is that there are people who can be trusted, and the most important truth is that your worth as a human being is identical to every other human being. Your worth is never determined by what happened to you. Your worth is never determined by your experiences or the mistakes you might have made. Your worth is never determined by whether you are among the "have" or the "have not." The creator of all creation determined your worth before you were born, which is the same measure as everyone. True self-esteem is the recognition (not the wish or belief) that it is impossible for any human being to be more valuable or less valuable than any other and that we are all as valuable as everyone else, no matter who they are or what they think.

When we know this, affirm this, and recognize that this means we deserve happiness and healing as much as anyone, we begin to take better care of ourselves and heal.

I was very lucky. I did not experience additional extreme trauma as an adult. When I was raped, I had enough awareness and healing under my belt that I could understand and resolve that rather quickly. I was lucky to have a loving mentor and guide (Granny) through my childhood, one of the most critical times for a connection. Granny was my anchor in the storm of my childhood. She held me steady through it. Studies show that if children have an anchor, someone who they know loves them no matter what, then they are more likely to survive and heal from childhood trauma and less likely to attempt or commit suicide.

As an adult, I met loving mentors and guides when I went to college, but it didn't stop there. I have had guides throughout my journey. I also had the guidance to seek therapy as soon as I got away from my abusers. My high school counselor gave me that without even realizing that he had. Because of having mentors and guides, I had it a whole lot easier than many who suffered trauma. It means that I started healing earlier than many. Still, it took me a long time to heal and trust, and at first, I only trusted women. Later, I discovered that there are women who are just as bullying and abusive as my tormentors. Later, I trusted men and received wonderful spiritual guidance from many male mentors. More than anything, it took me a very long time to recognize that my worth as a human being is equal to everyone. However, it is important to learn from my recovery that even if you didn't have mentors and guides like I was blessed with, they still exist, and you can still find help.

I can tell you that I had some really good therapists and a couple who were really bad. If you think you are not making progress, it is important that you first talk with your therapist about that, and then, if it still can't be worked out, consider a different therapist. Unfortunately, there is a shortage of mental health providers, and many people can't afford the services. Also, some mental health providers have not tackled or are not tackling their own personal healing. Therefore, it is important to understand that other options exist to assist recovery, such as Twelve-Steps recovery and other support groups. Some of the best help I received was from Unity church ministers, who, unlike the authoritarian preachers of my past, loved and accepted me and guided me toward the love of myself. Regardless of your experience, plant the idea within yourself that your worth is equal to everyone, and then nurture that with every ounce of your being. Affirm to yourself, repeatedly, "*My worth is equal to everyone. I am as good as anyone, but I am better than no one. I deserve to be happy.*"

DIAMOND

Tears drip,
One upon one,
 to the floor
And soak into the carpet.
He sits
Slumped over,
Hands folded,
Face down.
I see nothing but hair,
Hands,
And tears.

He suffers
As I have seen so many suffer,
As I have suffered, myself,
Not from wounds of the body,
But wounds of the soul.

Scars from slash marks adorn his bare arms,
A history of anguish
Because the sight of blood

"Calms me," ... he says.
He would rather feel the pain
Of physical wounds
Than face his
Wounded spirit.

I pray
Silently to myself,
"God help me reach him."

I can't undo the
Mental and moral torment
Of his childhood
Where he first learned
To devalue himself.
I can't undo the atrocities
Of additional trauma
That cut those existing wounds
Down to his psychic bone.
I can't make his choices
For him.
However,
I can pray
That caring for him
Opens a tiny sliver in the darkness
So, a little light
Might shine in.

I cannot heal him.
I can only reach out to him,
And let him know that I value him.
I can only affirm that his worth

Is equal to all.
After all,
A diamond thrown into the trash
Is still a diamond,
And its worth remains as much as it ever was.
Discarding it does not change
The value.

I can only affirm to him
That those who hurt him
Were wrong.
Those who mistreated him
Were mistaken
Just as he was mistaken
When he accepted their lies,
And mistreated himself
And others.

Those in pain
Lash out.
It's what they do
Until
At last,
When backed into an ethereal corner,
They stop for a moment
To lick emotional wounds.

That is when
Someone needs to sit with them,
Comforting,
Teaching,
Praying to be let in

Just enough
To value them,
And be fair with them,
Be real with them
Until they can be fair
And real with themselves.

Until they are able
To love themselves,
To realize that
They are
Not only worthy of love,
They deserve it,
Someone need only sit with them ... and care.

You can throw a diamond in the trash,
But it does not change the value of the diamond.
You can throw your life away,
But it is still a life worth saving.

Poem Introduction – A SINGLE STEP

I've talked quite a bit about growing up in an authoritarian church and mentioned before that one of my uncles told me I would go to hell for attending a Presbyterian college. Perhaps the underlying reason for that admonishment was the fear that I might learn the truth and overturn my indoctrination. That I did. At that college, I began to question spirituality and consider that there could be other ways of understanding. I opened my mind. At eighteen, it started one day when I was spouting off about something being a sin. I was repeating what I had been taught, judging as I had been taught to judge. A Presbyterian pre-ministerial student asked me, "Why do you believe that?"

I said, "Because the Bible says so."

He asked, "Where does it say that in the Bible?"

I quoted the verse.

He asked, "How do you know that's what it means?"

I said, "Because the preacher says so."

He asked, "How do you know the preacher is right?"

I said, "Because he is ordained by God."

He asked, "How do you know he is ordained by God?"

He backed me into a corner without ever challenging or confronting me. All he did was ask questions that I could not answer. However, the message was clear: *Don't just swallow what they feed you. Think for yourself.* When he asked me how I knew the preacher was ordained by God, I was furious because he proved me wrong without even citing any evidence to the contrary. However, the message was received, and I proceeded to work on thinking for myself and learning to question.

After that, I met Marcy, who guided me further toward realizing that there is another way of spiritual understanding. Later, I began to consider other spiritual ideas and study other religions. Eventually, I stumbled onto *A Course in Miracles*, which, at first, tore me up emotionally because it began to address the instilled guilt of my childhood and help me understand worth and worthiness. Then, I began to feel more secure in my spirituality.

I moved to Nashville in 1984, where I first encountered *A Course in Miracles*. After studying it for a couple of years, I traveled home to visit my grandparents. I brought my *ACIM* book with me and kept it in my bedroom. At some point, I decided to go for a walk out on the farm. When I returned to the house, Grandpa, who had snooped in my bedroom while I was gone, yelled at me, "Come here!" He pointed to the footstool at the base of his chair and said, "Sit down!"

I sat on the footstool below him and said, "Yes, sir?"

He leaned over and literally shook his finger in my face. He said, "I want you to know something! That stuff you are studying back there is gonna send you straight to hell!"

I smiled and said, "Grandpa, if there is anything I have learned from the stuff I'm studying back there, it's that neither you nor anyone else has the right or the authority to condemn anyone to hell."

He sat back in his chair, seeming stunned, and said nothing. After a moment, I asked, "Is there anything else?"

He said, "I guess not."

Then, I went on about my business. At that time, I had graduated from graduate school and had been independent since I was twenty-one. Yet, he still thought he could command and intimidate me like a little boy.

On another trip home, a year or so later, I was reading *Peace is Every Step* by Thich Nhat Hanh. Grandpa would certainly have considered reading the work of a Buddhist monk would send me to hell, but he never confronted me again. The book had instructions for a walking meditation, which was very simple. The only instruction was, "Walk as slowly as you can." I decided to try it.

One thing to understand about where my grandparents lived and where I grew up is that it was far into the country. They lived on a dirt road lane between two other dirt roads, and barely one or two cars a day went through that lane if that. So, I went out onto the dirt road and began to practice walking as slowly as possible. This took quite a bit of concentration. I soon realized that I needed to hold my arms out for balance. I placed my foot down, heel to toe, moving it as slowly as possible, and then shifted my weight to lift the other foot and place it down the same way. A single step could take up to thirty seconds or more to complete. I have no idea how long I was out there, but I didn't get far from the house. However, I was gone long enough that Granny got worried and came looking for me. Before she arrived to end my walk, I was lost in the meditation, and something amazing happened. As I was placing my foot down very slowly, I saw a pebble displaced from under the front of my shoe. At that moment, I realized that this one step had permanently changed the world. I could never put that stone back in precisely the same place as it was before the step, and even if I could calibrate that, it would be an additional change, not an undoing of the change that had occurred. What happened could never be undone; as small as it was, it had forever altered the universe. I understood at that moment that every step I had ever taken, every action, created an irreversible change in the universe. I affirmed to myself that I had just changed the world and asked, "How important does that make me?" The answer was infinitely important. I realized that I not only have the power to change the world, but it is impossible for me *not* to change the world. My very existence changed the world. Then, I realized that every step that anyone has ever taken has permanently changed the world, and every step that anyone will ever take will permanently change the world. I asked myself, "How important does that make them?" The answer, of course, is infinitely important. That one single step ended years of self-doubt and feelings of unworthiness. It made me realize that my value is beyond measure but can't be any greater or lesser than anyone. This not only defines true self-esteem but defines true humility.

A SINGLE STEP

A single step changed me forever.
A single step created
Epiphany,
Awakening,
Awareness.
Understanding,
Peace,
And finally,
After so many years
Of feeling like
I didn't deserve to be here,
Self-love and belonging.

A single step made me realize
That I am here for a reason.
We are all here for a reason.
We all belong
Because we are all meant
To be here.
There are no exceptions!

A single step,
Not only changed me forever,
But changed the world forever.
It changed the universe forever.
It made me realize
That no one is expendable
Because we are all co-creators
With the creator of all things,
With existence itself,

And our mission is to
Become aware
Of our eternal unity.

In a single step
Recognition came
That I cannot be insignificant,
That no one can be insignificant,
That there is no such thing
As unworthy or undeserving.
A genuine humility came,
An understanding that
I cannot be more important
Than anyone else in the world
And no one else
Can be more important than me.
My worth,
Our worth
Is equal to all worth.
I was humbled by a single step
And that humility was the greatest thing
That ever happened to me
Because …
Not only was I humbled,
I was exalted.

A single step caused me to realize
The intrinsic value of all creation
Including myself.
No more would I believe
That I have no value.
No more would I look upon another

And fail to see a child of God.
My foot came down in a single step
And the pebble moved from
Beneath my shoe.
I would never be able to put it back again.
I would never be able to undo that single step.
As insignificant as it might seem,
That single step
Altered me and the universe forever.
That single step powerfully proved
That every action anyone ever takes
Creates a permanent change in the universe.

In fact,
Every step I have ever taken
Changed the world forever,
And every step I will ever take
Alters the world forever.
Every step that anyone ever takes
Alters the universe forever.
Every action,
Every breath,
Every thought,
Alters the universe forever.
At last, I understood
How important I am,
How important we all are,
And how every action
Of everyone
Every day
Alters the universe forever.

We are unaware of most actions,
But what if
We all became aware of
How infinitely powerful we are?
What if
We all became aware of
The cause and effect of
Intent and how every action
Of anyone affects the life
Of everyone?
What if we take responsibility
For our intent and our conscious actions?
Because ....
Whatever we do
to anything or anyone
We also do
To ourselves.
This is why we cannot sew
Anything that we will not also reap.

In that one step, I realized
That I have work to do.
I have love to teach
For I experienced
The most profound love
In that moment,
And it must be shared.
Because ...
If I can understand love
In a single step,
So can everyone else.
Anyone can

Realize, as I did,
In a single step,
How powerful they are,
Yet, how humble they are,
Equal to all,
And each one
Can realize
Their immeasurable value,
Knowing it is the same
As the immeasurable value
Of everyone else.
If that happens, then…
We will create
A world of peace
With no malicious thoughts
No arrogance or selfishness.
We will create
What we are all here to create.
For, learning our true value,
And recognizing that it is
Equal to all,
Is the foundation
Of eternal love.

Poem Introduction – BATTLE CRY

When I moved back home to the Ozarks in 1997, I eventually bought and renovated a hundred-year-old Victorian farmhouse on a hillside about a mile from downtown and the county courthouse. There had been a Civil War battle in that little town, and the county courthouse had been burned.

One day, years after owning the property, I was walking through my backyard and happened to look down. A brass button from a Union soldier's uniform was lying in the grass, which had parted just enough for me to see it. It had some deterioration but was still intact. When I asked others about this later, I was told that troops often camped on a hillside because they could view the lower ground, and my house was on a hillside. I have no way of knowing whether fighting occurred on that property, but likely it did because the property was so close to downtown. When I found the button, my mind began contemplating its history, inspiring me to write this poem.

BATTLE CRY

I found an old brass button in my backyard.
It once adorned a Union soldier's uniform,
And lay among the blades of grass almost
A hundred and fifty years.
It waited patiently, finally to be discovered.
How many times had I stepped over it,
Or mowed past it, never to notice?

I had lived on that property for ten years,
And there it lay the whole time,
But there it lay for all the previous years combined.
I picked it up to see the eagle
Still proudly spreading its wings

Beneath the clustered bits of dirt,
And realized I may have been the first to touch it
Since the soldier,
Whose uniform it once embellished
Last pushed it into the buttonhole.
Likely, he had camped on this ground.
Perhaps he had fought on this ground.

My house, over a hundred years old,
Was not standing then.
This hillside was likely pasture
Rolling up above the county courthouse.

They had burned this tiny town to the ground,
Left it in ruins,
And left anguished survivors to rebuild and try again.

My mind envisioned the battle,
Gray and blue uniforms soaked in dark red blood,
Fierce screaming rage, gunshots echoing among the oaks,
And bayonets stabbing.

America's bloodiest war
Left almost seven hundred thousand dead,
And those who died were
Brothers and friends, family and neighbors.

Many sacrificed so that others might have freedom
Which had been previously deprived.
Could this soldier have lived to face another day,
Or did he die on the ground where I was standing?
Did his blood saturate this sod,

And marry the red clay deep beneath my feet?
Was this button ripped off his jacket
As his corpse was dragged away,
Or did it merely fall unnoticed from thread worn thin?

If he survived,
What wounds did he carry from this place,
Wounds that others could not see?
Did fitful nightmares of battle cries
Make him sweat through cotton sheets?
Did he startle, half from his skin,
At the snap of a twig?
Did he sit alone and weep with guilt and remorse
For those he loved who fell beside him,
Or did he grieve for those, once his countrymen,
Whom he had killed?

Did someone weep for him
While watching his silent torment,
Or weep because he never came home?

Only a guess is possible now.

As I held the button in my hand,
I could not help but wonder,
Who last touched it?
What was he like?
Where did he come from,
And where did he go?

Whoever he was,
He swayed my heart and made me think.

Without knowing I would ever live,
Much less come to stand in this place,
He touched me.

Whoever he was, he honored me
That I could hold this small button in my hand,
And wipe the years of bitter dirt away
So it could shine again.

Poem Introduction – BEHOLD

Sometimes, I write what I see and experience. I practiced mindfulness as soon as I first learned it. My friend Marcy taught me to stop, take in the nature around me, and behold the beauty in every moment of every day. Granny had taught me mindfulness without even realizing she was doing it. As I mentioned earlier in the introduction of *I Am a Stone*, Granny would leave the house when she got angry and have peace when she returned. She told me she would go and walk the fence row of our 160-acre farm. Without calling it that or realizing it, she practiced mindfulness and brought her attention back to the moment instead of allowing it to wallow in anger.

I now know that the same brain regions affected by memory are affected by imagining the future. Therefore, it becomes easy to imagine that the past will be like the future, even though no moment ever repeats itself. For trauma survivors, this is particularly important because their brain keeps casting past trauma over into future imaginings to keep them in a state of distress and turmoil. Mindfulness is one of the best remedies for this. When those who have experienced trauma learn to practice mindfulness meditation, they begin to quiet these trauma-related ramblings of the brain and begin to feel a greater sense of peace and contentment.

The simplest form of mindfulness is to take a moment several times a day and focus on your surroundings. This might only be for a few seconds to check in. You might even set a reminder on your phone to periodically focus on the here and now. Fully notice the moment, not the perceived threat of danger, not the twangs of grief, guilt, regret, fear, worry, or the burning of resentment, but the actual moment. Take in and truly see shadows, reflections, colors, shapes, patterns, and textures for that moment. Truly look at what is around you. Listen to the *"sounds of silence."* Notice the tick of a clock, the buzz of a fan, traffic passing, or a dog barking up the street. Wherever you are, stop and listen to whatever is actually there. Notice your body, feel your feet in your shoes, the touch of your clothes on your skin, the sensation of taking a deep, slow breath and feeling your chest rise and fall as you breathe, or the feeling of the air in your nostrils. Don't just notice it; examine it, and if for only a moment, lock your attention on *now* instead of hurtful memories of the past or trepidation about the future. Simply be aware of *now*.

I wrote this one day while living in Nashville after staring up into the autumn sky.

BEHOLD

Clouds swim
Like white fish
In a classic
Autumn blue sky.

I stand on the earth
In perfect awe.

The wind sings.
The leaves dance
In chilly, fragrant air.

I behold this artistry.

Love is in the sky
Dressed in blue
And white.

Love is in the trees
Wearing red, gold
And green.

Love is in the wind

Singing crystal
harmonies.

Love must be in me
That I behold
Such things.

Poem Introduction – BLOOM

I watched one of my young proteges, who shall remain unnamed, as she grew up, so beautiful, intelligent, and talented while she deteriorated into self-loathing as a teen. There were many factors at play there, but one of them was the betrayal by her best friend when she was thirteen years old and the bullying of snooty little girls who tried to disguise their own self-loathing by projecting it onto her. She was called demeaning names, and that, combined with other tragedies that occurred around the same time, caused her to believe that she was *"fat, ugly, and stupid,"* and she was thrown into anorexia. She was anything but fat, ugly, or stupid, but she would believe no affirmation to the contrary.

One of the greatest tragedies of the mind is that once a belief has become set in place, the only person who can change it is the one who believes it. Our ego defends what we believe, not necessarily the truth. It looks for whatever fits with the belief and counts that as *"evidence,"* while it denies whatever does not fit with the belief, even if that is the truth, and nothing can convince us of a truth we are not willing or ready to accept. If we believe that we are unworthy and unacceptable, no amount of convincing can, therefore, change our minds. We have to come to that within ourselves. Meanwhile, those who love us look on in sadness, hoping that we might be able to see what they see in us, and yet, we deny it. Only when we consider that there could be another way of looking at something, a different perception, can we see it. For instance, we might look for something on the shelf and can't find it when someone says, "It's right there." Until they show us, we don't see it, but to see it, we first have to consider that they do.

I wrote this poem for my young friend.

BLOOM

Little one,
How profane is your self-loathing
That you cannot find within yourself
One thing
To compliment if it does not match with vanity's illusion?
It has never matched.

How I ache
When I see such beauty and talent
Within you
That you will not acknowledge,
Much less praise.
How I ache further
When you accuse my compliment
Of only being offered to make you feel better.

So often you proclaim me a liar
When I dare to share with you
The truth that I know,
Yet you will not believe.

You are the bud of a flower
Refusing to bloom.

You could be,
Will be,
The most beautiful flower in the garden
If you would only open yourself to the light.

You could unfold with awe
If you would only once realize
The marvelous gift that you contain.

Oh, how I yearn
That you
Might, one day,
Turn your face to the sun

And bloom.

Poem Introduction – DANCERS IN THE FOREST

These are lyrics to a song I wrote on a whim in my thirties when visiting my grandparents for a few days. Sometimes, things like this would just come out of the blue, and the song or poem would be written in just a few minutes. The words would flow instantly out of me; all I had to do was write them down. I have no idea where this came from, but I was still working on my spirituality and still trying to accept and love myself as a gay man. I permitted myself to sleep with men long before I came to a genuine self-love. Full acceptance of myself took a very long time. Maybe this is a metaphor for me, my spiritual seeking, and my self-discovery, but sometimes, music, lyrics, poetry, and words appear and beg to be written.

DANCERS IN THE FOREST

There are dancers in the forest
With their arms outstretched to sky
Reaching out to touch the spirit
And they never question why.
Rings in their noses
Striking their poses
They beckon gods of night.

There are questions left unanswered
Deep, the spirit seeks to find
Little passages of wonder
In the corners of your mind.
Driving a sports car
Cruising a gay bar
In this, you search the world for light.

Is it here?
No, no, no.

Is it there?
No, no, no.
Is it anywhere?

Underneath the mask of ego
Lies a timid bit of love
Hiding from the mass bravado
In the bottom of your cup.
Daring to give it,
Feeling so stingy,
Do you know what you've done?

Is it here?
No, no, no.
Is it there?
No, no, no.
Is it anywhere?

Daring to give it
Feeling so stingy
Still, you search the world for light.

Poem Introduction – THE ALLIGATOR

"Big boys don't cry." That is one of the most ridiculous and harmful assertions ever perpetrated against men. Of course, boys cry, men cry, and everyone cries if they are normal human beings. Nobody stops to think that there is a natural reason for tears. They don't exist for nothing. We are supposed to have them, we are supposed to release them, and unless they are deliberately generated as a manipulation, there is a perfectly natural and logical reason for them. Simply put, they help to wash away the pain. When we allow ourselves to grieve our losses and grieve the traumas that we have experienced, we begin to heal. We accentuate our healing when we give ourselves a moment of vulnerability with loving and trusted others. Our mind begins to put things in perspective and define the difference between now and then. We find ourselves healing when we allow ourselves to grieve and allow the grief to come through us instead of getting stuck in us.

This poem is about witnessing a man stuck in his pain, unwilling to let his tears flow.

THE ALLIGATOR

His tears peak out
Like the eyes of an alligator
Floating just beneath
The surface of his grief.
He would not let them come
Lest they,
Like the alligator,
Leap out
Uncontrolled
And devour him.

Men hold their pain because they fear it.
Men hold their pain because they think

Suffering makes them more of a man,
And releasing it makes them weak.
Men hold their pain because
They are taught the lie
That one ceases to be a man,
Ceases to exist
If the tears come.
Men hold their pain
In defiance of their humanity
Having been taught
That being a real man
Means being something more than human.

I watch him
As the eyes of the alligator
Drop below the surface of his grief.
It doesn't matter
That I have told him it's okay to cry.
It doesn't matter
That I have affirmed that crying
Is strength, not weakness.
It doesn't matter that I have assured him
He will not stop thinking.
He will not stop being a man,
If he cries.
It doesn't matter
That I have declared
That he will not be defenseless.
Hell!
You still think, even if you're crying.
You still do what you need to do.
Crying does not remove your power to choose.

It doesn't matter.
He doesn't believe me.

The alligator sinks below the surface
Of his grief.
I watch as tears are hidden away,
Covered over with a skim
Of mundane congeniality and a forced smile.
I wish I could,
With love, like a father,
Enfold him in my arms
And let him weep.
Instead,
I sit three feet away
And allow his choice.
I sit three feet away
And love him anyway.
I sit three feet away
And pray for his healing,
Silently, to myself.
I sit three feet away
As he chooses again
To wrestle the monster alone.
I sit three feet away
And let go.

Poem Introduction - LIGHT

I wrote this in the 1990s after seeing the film *The Doors*, which is about the life of Jim Morrison and stars Val Kilmer. At the time, I was trying to break into the music industry in Nashville, an attempt I voluntarily relinquished. I was chosen out of fifty male vocalists nationally to audition for *Star Search* in 1989, but I messed up a song I had written and had been singing for years. I drove away from the audition, asking myself why I had done that. The answer was, "Maybe you don't want to be a star." There are a lot of sacrifices for fame, and many don't understand how demanding that can be. The *Star Search* team had asked me to come back and audition the following year, but I never returned. Maybe I didn't want to face those kinds of demands. Now, I think about all the young and wonderfully talented stars who have burned themselves out and died before their time: Marilyn Monroe, Jim Morrison, River Phoenix, Heath Ledger, Amy Winehouse, George Michael, and Prince … The names go on. They seem to shoot to the top of stardom, shine brightly, burn out, and fall from the sky. Elton John almost went that way but, thankfully, lived into old age with hard-earned wisdom. See the film, *Rocket Man* about the life of Elton John.

I realize that I may never be a star—likely won't—and I don't think I want that much fame, even if I could. However, I realize that even if I don't light up the sky, I still have a purpose, as we all do. I can still make a difference, make my mark, and do whatever I can to teach at least a few people some skills to improve their lives. I can at least share the skills that I have learned.

This poem is my desire to bring more light into the world.

LIGHT

Some people burn like candles,
Lingering and slow.
Some people burn like fireworks,

In a flash, they're gone.

Should I have been a rocket,
Bursting colors in the sky,
Dancing fancy on a breath of wind,
Glittered bits before the eyes?

Would I have been remembered,
When in brief, the show was through;
A feast of chatter on delighted tongues
That try to tell what eyes have viewed?

I am but a candle
Burning carefully and slow;
No glittered grandeur, my destiny,
No sky-lit rocket show.

I am but a slow fire,
A flicker and a glow.
A small light, but steady,
Hidden and unknown.

Perhaps there'll be no memory
Of this small but worthy flame.

Perhaps there'll be no epitaph
Carved beside my name.

Yet, for a while, I'll linger,
And try with all my might
To spread the weary darkness
With one tiny, faithful light.

Poem Introduction – OBLIVIOUS

While coming back to the office after lunch one day, I saw a bird hopping around on a fence, and I began to think about all the crap that continually goes on in the world and how that bird, unaware, enjoyed the moment. I suspected that the bird was only mindful of its existence, living for no other reason than to experience life. The bird was oblivious to all the things contained in my mind. It simply lived joyfully in the moment, relishing the moment's experience.

OBLIVIOUS

A bird stands on a fence near where I work.
I walk by, and the bird takes note of me,
But does not fly away.
It stands contentedly experiencing the eternal now,
Observing with neither malice nor desire.

I realize there must be trillions of birds all over the world
Sitting on fences, wires, or tree limbs right now,
Each one oblivious to anything
Other than this very brief moment in time.
Each one is oblivious that anything other
Than this eternal now could possibly exist.

Every bird, on every perch, in every place all over the world
Is completely oblivious to the human ego,
The need to be right,
The need to dominate, even to the point of killing.

Not one bird realizes that the world is at war.
Not one bird realizes how billionaires profit

From the manufacture of expensive weapons
Which must be used so more can be made,
Or the war industry will fail.

Not one bird realizes
Those "rich bastards" would cease to benefit
From destroying the lives of both the guilty
And the innocent
If war were to cease to exist.

That bird, sitting on the fence,
Knows nothing of agony,
Racism,
Hatred
Or greed.
It knows nothing of abuse,
Malicious intent
Or the perverted desire to rape.

It knows nothing of children
Who suffer tremendous pain and heartache
Because of unbridled abuse and selfishness
Perpetrated by those who call themselves ...
Human.
That bird cannot even comprehend malice.

It need not ever exclaim,
"Forgive them, for they know not what they do."
Forgiveness is unnecessary to the oblivious spirit.

That bird sits contented beneath the blue sky
Basking in the morning sun.

It is completely oblivious to anything
But peace.

As I walk by,
How I wish that I
Could be
That bird.

Poem Introduction - ONE

We have the illusion of separation in the world, but there can be no separation of spirit. Considering only energy and space exist, there can be no separation of anything in reality. Energy merely takes one form or another. It cannot be destroyed, and it cannot cease. When you set a log on fire, it does not cease to exist. It merely ceases to exist in its current form. It transitions into smoke, ash, and heat, but all those things are already contained within it. We are all made of the same elements. Many carry their ideas of separation into their concepts of the afterlife. Yet, even in our illusion of separation, we are more alike than most would want to admit, and it is not just that our bodies are all made of the same elements.

I think about a song, *Russians*, that Sting wrote during the Cold War. The lyrics are, "*I hope the Russians love their children too.*" Deep down, we all want the same thing. Unless completely disconnected, deeply wounded, and out of touch, we all want happiness for our loved ones. That includes all children. We might prefer sports over the opera, but we both want to be entertained. We might have sexual attraction to different genders, but we both want love and family. We might have different races, religions, or political views, but we want to be free and comfortable. We all want to be treated with respect, honor, and dignity, even if we don't treat ourselves that way. We are all certified members of the human race, no matter the differences we may perceive or the separation we may condone.

This is a poem about how much we are alike.

ONE

Do you see me?
Not my face, my clothes, or my figure.
Do you see ...
Me?

Do you look beyond the external persona

And ever try to view into my soul,
Or do you look only at your perception
Of my external presentation,
Your judgment of me?

Can you see the little glimpses
Of the real me
Behind these eyes?
Can you feel the hidden distress
That my persona tries to hide?

Do you see me only through your perception,
Your own beliefs, judgment, and prejudice,
Can you see me as I am
When your judgment is stripped away,
And I trust you enough to lower the mask of ego
That protects me?

Can you feel the wound in my heart,
The one that has been there
From the first time I was shamed,
The one that worsened every time I was shamed,
Especially when I shamed myself.

Can you understand how much we are alike,
You and I?

We may seem very different on the surface,
Different bodies,
Different age,
Different looks,
Different race,

Different culture,
Different gender,
Different vocations,
Different countries,
Different families,
Different friends,
Different politics,
Different attitudes,
Different religion,
Different sexual orientation,
Different life experiences,
And yet,
We are more alike than all our differences combined.

We long for the same love,
The same respect,
The same understanding,
The same appreciation,
The same happiness,
The same comfort,
The same compassion,
And the same peace.

Deep down, we all want the same things.

What a shame that we think
We have to deprive or deny another
To get what we want.
We all want,
And need,
Genuine love.
Yet, we seldom trust each other enough

To receive it,
Much less give it.

We all want freedom and happiness,
But seldom seem to understand how to achieve it.
We don't seem to understand
That we must give what we most desire
In order to receive it
And when we deprive any other,
We are ultimately depriving ourselves.

So,
Can you truly see me when the time comes
That you take a look?
When you truly see me,
It will be like looking into a mirror
Because I am you.

Your body may be over there
And my body may be over here,
But that is only the illusion
That we are different.

In truth, I am you.
You are me.
There is no us versus them,
I versus you.
There is no separation.
There is only—we,
And we are forever and always
Eternally the same,
One heart,

One soul,
One child of one eternal creator,
One eternal self,
You,
me,
One.

Do you see me?

Poem Introduction - PEONIES

One day, after a hard May rain, I saw that the peonies in my front flower beds were beaten down to the ground. Their petals were drooped, but the pink blooms were still intact and beautiful. I realized the sun was coming out, and the leaves and petals would soon dry. When sufficiently dried, the stems would rise again, bringing the flowers back to the top. They would return to their beauty and their place in the sun.

I love peonies and grew up with them blooming in Granny's front yard. It was a beautiful presentation outside that covered the violence and heartache inside. They are a common flower in the Ozarks and around the South, and I wondered how many families had them beautifying the yard of a home where violence was hidden within. They are delicate but strong and, to me, a symbol of strength.

PEONIES

I love good old Southern peonies,
Although hard May rains
Often come and beat them down
The way some abusive Southern men
Beat their wives.

Even face down on the wet grass
They maintain a certain dignity,
A stoic beauty
That cannot be diminished by their bruises.

Like the country women who grow them,
They are strong.
Even when petals fall
Like bloody teeth
Knocked across a linoleum floor,

Their fortitude is a barrier
Far stronger
Than a wadded fist.

They do not need fist and muscle,
The illusion of power
Wielded by weak and insecure men.

They do not need control of men
As men so need of them.
All they need is control of themselves.

There is wisdom in knowing when to remain face down
And when to stand.

Wisdom realizes that the sun will shine again,
And some rain falls gentle
Caressing those same bruised petals
That others have beaten.

Poem Introduction – SOUL ENCOUNTERS

I believe in soul encounters. I call my novels *The Soul Encounters Series* even though it is not a true series. One story does not lead into another, following the same characters through an epic. Instead, a character in each novel goes on to tell his/her/their story in a different novel. Each novel is a different story with different characters, so it's not a true series. The only connection is the soul encounter that the protagonist of one novel has with the protagonist of a previous novel. They meet, and the meeting impacts both, but they have a completely different story to tell. I based the idea on knowing there are times when our souls meet, and we connect with someone, often briefly. Then, that experience passes, and we may never see that person again. Yet, the encounter has left an indelible mark on our spirit and memory. Often, these soul encounters are only one meeting, which is a coincidence and perhaps seems insignificant. Yet, it doesn't feel insignificant or like a coincidence. Sometimes, the encounter can last only a few minutes. Sometimes, it lasts a little longer, but it generally ends with an awareness that we had not previously perceived or a feeling in our hearts that we had not noticed. Sometimes, it leaves us simply feeling gratitude for having had the encounter. It could be a brief discussion with a stranger in the produce section at the grocery. It might last longer than that and be an interaction over a few days or weeks, but it is not an extended involvement. Technically, every encounter is a soul encounter, but what I call *soul encounters* happen to be something significant that latches on to the heart and mind, which is a gift to the spirit. Those are generally brief.

One of my soul encounters occurred when I was in high school, and I met an elderly Russian woman living in an old abandoned store in Oxford, Arkansas, of all places, a tiny town with a population of only a little over six hundred. So, let me digress a little here. I said in the introduction how closely my family resembled *The Beverly Hillbillies*. In *The Beverly Hillbillies* movie, the joke was when Granny said Jethro was educated at Oxford, and everyone thinks she means Oxford University. Then, the truck drives by the Oxford, Arkansas, population sign, which correctly identifies the actual population of the town as around six hundred. So, now I'll continue. My encounter with this Russian lady living in Oxford only lasted a few visits. Her name was Olga, and she told me she had left Russia during the Bolshevik Revolution. She told me stories about playing piano for the Tzar's troops as a girl. However, there was no piano playing when I met her. She was well into her nineties in 1972, and arthritis had twisted her fingers to the point that they were almost unusable. I was fascinated and visited her a few times but lost contact with her after leaving for college. Having grown up in what I call "the butt-crack of nowhere," I was amazed to meet such a fascinating person. I don't remember how she ended up in Oxford, Arkansas, but I do remember the impact she made on me.

I have had the opportunity to meet several genuinely amazing people in my life time, including in the late 1980s when I worked for the Nashville Jewish Community Center. I met an elderly Jewish man who survived the death march from Auschwitz into Germany at the end of World War II when the Russian army was pressing into Poland. Fifty-six thousand prisoners, mostly Jews, were marched thirty-five miles in frigid weather, and anyone who lagged or fell was shot. Fifteen thousand died on the way. This man had been about fourteen years old at the time and had lost his entire family during that march. He immigrated to America after the war. I saw the number tattooed on the inside of his left arm with a European-style seven and at first questioned whether I was actually in the presence of someone who had been through the Nazi atrocities. I didn't initially mention anything to him but asked his son-in-law, who informed me that talking with him about it was okay. Later, I brought it up to him, and he tapped the tattooed number on the inside of his left arm and said, "That's a blessing to me." I asked him how that could possibly be a blessing, and he told me that whenever he felt down or felt like things were not going the way he wanted, he could look down at that number and realize how bad it could be. I will never forget him or his story and try to remind myself of the lesson he taught me during that soul encounter. It could always be worse if we feel ungrateful, especially for trivial things.

Also, in Nashville, I met Hideko Tamura Snider, who wrote the book *One Sunny Day*. She was from Hiroshima and was twelve years old when the Americans dropped the nuclear bomb on Hiroshima. Her father was away in the Japanese military then, and she was home with her family. The book tells of her experience on the ground during the blast, obviously far enough away that she lived through it, but she still experienced the aftermath. She also immigrated to the United States after the war, became a social worker, and married a Jewish man. We maintained email contact for a couple of years before I lost contact with her. It was fascinating to me, after knowing my own father's experience as a POW in Japan, to meet someone who experienced WWII in Japan from a different perspective. Her book is excellent, and I highly recommend it. Of course, my father was also a remarkable person to have survived the entire length of WWII in Japanese POW camps.

What was most impressive to me about all the above soul encounters, including my relationship with my father, was the empowerment of these people, how they had survived such incredible and horrible tragedies and traumas but came out of it on top. They not only survived, they thrived. They say the best revenge is to live well, and I think they did. I don't know how well Olga lived other than she escaped what could have been her fate as a young girl in Russia. She did not live as a wealthy or privileged person in America but appeared happy and contented. She felt safe to be in America and to have escaped what Russia had become.

Often, a soul encounter is just a happenstance meeting with a stranger containing a deeper meaning than just the surface experience of the moment. It can be a much shorter experience. Maybe it means something to us, but the others barely notice or remember. That happened to me right after I graduated college at twenty-one. I had worked in a town where I didn't know anyone. I missed my friends at college and was terribly lonely. I couldn't seem to make friends and had little in common with many of the people I had met there. I was also continuing to go through my turmoil between my sexual orientation and the authoritarian church, which had a powerful influence on that town. As I had done since childhood, I turned to nature for my comfort.

Where I lived, there was a pasture on the other side of the road opposite my garage apartment, and a tree line was just on the other side of that pasture. One day, I decided to take a walk in those woods. I crossed the road, went over the fence, crossed the pasture, and discovered a pond hidden amid the trees on the opposite side. I had sat on the pond bank for a while, tossing bits of gravel into the water and watching the ripples, when I heard the sound of a tractor motor. I came out of the trees and stood on the pasture's edge. On the opposite side, near my apartment, I saw a young man on a tractor, and he was plowing the field from the outside edge into the middle, which is an odd approach to plowing. I stood there and watched him bring the plow around the edge of the field. Then, he stopped right before me and asked, "Need a lift?"

I could easily have walked back across the pasture, and he knew it, but he offered the ride anyway. I said, "Sure."

He motioned for me to climb on. I got up on the tractor behind him with my hands on his shoulders, and he plowed slowly around the other edge of the field. When he returned to the side near the road by my apartment, he stopped as though he knew where I lived. I got off, said, "Thank you for the lift," and never saw him again.

There had been no conversation as he plowed around the opposite edge of the field. I stood behind him on that tractor with my hands on his shoulders, experiencing and appreciating the physical contact. I was grateful to have that one little ray of sunshine in the darkness of my loneliness. It was as good as a hug.

Wherever he is today, he may not remember or know how much that meant to me. However, it was a cool drink to a thirsting heart, and I will forever be grateful for that soul encounter and a short ride plowing around the edge of a field just as I am grateful for that and other soul encounters as well as those that are yet to come. Technically, all our relationships are soul encounters, whether lengthy or brief. I think of the lyrics to George Michael's song *A Different Corner* which is one of my all-time favorites, "*Turn a different corner and we never would have met.*" You can think of everything as a coincidence, or you can think of everything as a miracle. I think of everything as a miracle, and I think of an *ACIM* statement that every encounter is holy, for in each one, we meet the son (child) of God. However, some, often brief, maintain a lasting impact.

Below is a poem about another soul encounter after moving to Texas. This was very brief, but for a moment, there was a connection that didn't feel like it was only a friendly chat. This did not occur in a gay bar, but in a small community bar in an inland small town.

SOUL ENCOUNTERS

The insecurity flows from him
Like an open faucet over a sink.
He is talkative and friendly.
Yet, even in his congeniality
His fear glistens behind the effort.
He makes small talk at the urinals
In a bar bathroom.
Yet, he turns away, angling the stream
Lest his example of manhood be seen.
He is small in stature,
Likely having had to fight for recognition
Among those who would bully
Smaller people.
His intoxicated friendliness
Lasts no longer than it takes for his bladder to empty.
He flips his zipper back into place,
And disappears into the crowded bar.

He disappears into his universe,
His existence,
Back to whatever he deems to be reality.
Soon, I will return to mine.
Obviously, he made an impression on me
Or the memory would not be planted.
There is a lingering essence of a lesson there.
Love who you are.
Be proud.

Washing my hands,
I see my face in the dim mirror
And smile.

Poem Introduction – THROUGH FORGIVING EYES

I received as much of my healing from being counseled by Unity ministers as I have from therapists, as much from reading books on spirituality as from self-help books. If you think about it, understanding true spirituality is the ultimate self-help because you cannot understand it without loving yourself.

In 1989, I had an opportunity to perform for an event at First Church Unity of Nashville and thought about writing a spiritual song for the occasion. However, I had a problem: resentment that I didn't want to face or release. I had recently ended a relationship with someone who had repeatedly violated my physical boundaries when I had repeatedly asked her to stop. One thing I am extremely intolerant of is someone pinching my ass, even a close friend, especially when I have repeatedly asked them to stop. If someone asks permission, I might say 'yes.' However, intrusion without my permission is forgetting that my body belongs to me, and I have the right to determine who is allowed to touch it, when, where, how, and for how long. My anger with this friend finally built to the point that I cut her out of my life completely. Even then, she showed up at my door one night unannounced when I had guests. I reminded her I had told her I wanted nothing more to do with her. After all, the rule is, *"Treat me right, or you won't treat me at all."* I had given her repeated chances to respect my boundaries, so enough was enough. Showing up at my house without an invitation or even a call to ask was yet another violation of boundaries. I had been clear with her. What I am never going to do is ghost someone with whom I have had a genuine friendship. I will be honest enough to explain my concern and allow someone to rectify the difficulty. However, that will also be clearly explained when I have had enough. In those days, I found it particularly difficult to let go of my resentments, and maybe I didn't understand yet that it is possible to forgive someone and still maintain the previously set boundaries. Forgiving someone without further interaction is possible, especially when they have shown you that they have no intention of offering the respect you deserve.

For the event at church, I decided to get an idea for a song by pulling cards from a stack with quotes from *A Course in Miracles*. I intended to pull a card randomly and then write about whatever theme was identified on the card. The first card I pulled was about forgiveness. When I pulled the card, I recognized that I continued to cling to resentment. So, I did not want to write a song about forgiveness. I couldn't write about what I was not willing to choose. I returned that card and pulled another card; the theme was forgiveness. I pulled another and another, and they all seemed to be about forgiveness. Finally, in frustration, I said, "God, give me something else. I'm still pissed off. I am not ready to forgive her and don't want to write about forgiveness!" The next card I drew said, "*Nothing can convince you of a truth that you do not want.*" Busted! I knew then that I had to write a song about forgiveness and that I had to let go of my resentment. I understood that resentment is its own kind of tyranny, mainly toward the person who retains it. These are the lyrics of the song I wrote, which has been the most appreciated and requested of all the songs I have ever written. Yes, I have forgiven that woman for violating my boundaries and many others who have violated my boundaries or have otherwise hurt me. I still didn't let her back into my life. I think it is important to understand that just because you forgive someone does not absolve them of responsibility, and it does not mean that you have to continue to expose yourself to their toxicity if they are unwilling to change. Witnessing them with love does not mean continuing to allow them to hurt you.

I now, almost daily, pray this prayer: *Thank you, Holy Spirit, for teaching and helping me relinquish all judgment, resentment, and unforgiveness toward anyone for anything so that I may know myself and all others as sinless, holy, and innocent.*

THROUGH FORGIVING EYES

What kind of world would I see through forgiving eyes?
What kind of world would it be?
I'd like to know
What a world of only love is like,
But I guess it starts right here with me.

Gonna learn to say "I'm sorry" and start to be more kind.
Gonna stop and start all over
There's no better time.
Gonna start to be more loving
And change this life of mine.
Gonna start to see my world
Through forgiving eyes.

There's nothing wrong with feeling a little scared.
Don't you know,
We all have stumbled in the dark.
But there's a light that shines through forgiving eyes,
And it lights the way for troubled hearts.

Gonna learn to say "I'm sorry" and start to be more kind.
Gonna stop and start all over
There's no better time.
Gonna start to be more loving
And change this life of mine.
Gonna start to see my world
Through forgiving eyes.

Gonna start to see my world
Through forgiving eyes.

Poem Introduction – LITTLE TEXAS TOWN

After moving to the Texas Coastal Bend, I discovered little inland towns. My husband is from one of those little towns. There is a difference between these little towns in Texas and the small towns I have experienced in states like Tennessee, Missouri, and Arkansas. The fact that there is a huge Hispanic population in South Texas is not the least of that. There are many similarities between one town and another, hence the description of cookie-cutter in the poem. There may be cookie-cutter towns in other states. However, one tends not to find these types of cookies outside of Texas. The culture is different. For one thing, Texas has its own culture. It may be a bit arrogant since I don't see any other states making state-shaped cast-iron frying pans, cake pans, etc., but southern Texas is a bit different from the rest of the state. For one thing, bar life differs from other types of bars elsewhere. There is, of course, that blue-collar ethic that can be found in country bars all over America, but in small-town Texas, there is a variety of people and an eclectic presentation. The music may range from traditional country music to Tex/Mex Tejano, Cumbia, Plena, pop, or rap. The towns lay as if they sprouted amid fields of corn and cotton as though they had grown from the soil itself. Like any other Texas weed, they seem to pop up here and there, and it is not as though you would miss one if you blinked. It is as though you might not even notice if you didn't pay attention. Yet, when you pay attention, there is so much to pay attention to and a fascinating blend of cultures.

This is a poem about one of those little towns.

LITTLE TEXAS TOWN

It's a cookie-cutter little Texas town
Formed in a historic Texas mold
The streets are flat.
The land is flat.
Summer heat hangs on it like a heavy coat.

It's quiet, yet violent.
Wholesome, yet profane.
A river runs through it
And floods again and again.

Signs in Spanish hang,
Worn and abandoned.
It used to be grand,
But there is not much to it now.
They shot a film there once,
A claim to fame.
Tejano music plays in the bars
Mixed with country and modern dance.
The bar crowd is a mix of Texas circumstance.

It's a cookie-cutter little Texas town.
Towns like this scatter around
Among the mesquite and rattlesnakes.
These little towns pop up from place to place
Amid the vastness of the Texas south.
They reek of Texas pride,
Perhaps a little Texas doubt.
What will this little Texas town become?
Probably not more than it is right now.

Poem Introduction – GRANDIOSITY

The Twelve-Step programs teach about the importance of humility, probably because arrogance can be a thin veil over a wounded heart and gross insecurity. Narcissism, for instance, is excessive compensation for extreme insecurity. Alcoholics Anonymous coined the term *"King Baby,"* which means someone who wants to be king but acts like a baby and has a narcissistic sense of special entitlement. Yet, grandiosity can also lean in a negative direction. The opposite of arrogance is thinking of yourself as the worst of the worst, the most pathetic victim and emphasizing the importance of being terribly unimportant. It's still ego grandiosity, just on the flip side of the ego coin. Most of the time, we don't even realize we are being grandiose, especially when that is negative grandiosity, and we see ourselves as victims of life and humanity. We like to think that we are the only ones who suffer, that life, instead of being lived, is something being done to us, something that we must endure unless we decide to check out before our time is up. Tragically, some do.

On the other hand, we like to pump up our importance and stare down our noses at those "poor bastards" who don't appear to be cut from the swath of quality we think we came from. We want to be so important, and in seeking such, we fail to recognize just how important and unimportant we are at the same time. We are all cut from the same fabric of the same universe, all co-creators with God in this process that we call life. We can't even take a step without permanently changing the universe and existence itself (as noted in the poem *A Single Step*). It is impossible for us *not* to change the world; therefore, we are all grand. Yet, in knowing that, there is humility because it makes us no more or no less important than anyone or anything else. We all change the world, and all have, therefore, equal importance, equal value, and equal inheritance. It means that we are here because we are meant to be here. We exist because existence exists. Every life has meaning and matters, regardless of who it belongs to. There is a reason why one of the commandments, one that has been repeatedly broken since the dawn of humanity, is *"Thou shalt not kill."* Unless it is an accident or self-defense in a life-threatening situation, the only way that it is possible to kill another human being is to assume that their value is less than your own, to dehumanize them. Yet, mentally dehumanizing them does not change their value as a human being.

Often, we set about killing someone's spirit while their body still lives. This is what abuse does, and it is also impossible to abuse anyone or anything unless you assume their value is less than your own or you want to try to diminish their value to what you perceive to be less than your own. Hate does the same thing. Those who are confident have nothing to prove. Therefore, those confident in their human worth have no reason for hate or abuse. No matter who you are, you are alive because you are meant by the universe to be alive. Even if that life is but a micron in the expanse of the universe and its entirety, it is still important but never more important than anyone else's life. Some keys to humility are learning to honor yourself without dishonoring others, to love yourself so that you can love others, and to respect others as much as you want to be respected. Again, I revert to my Christian roots: *"In everything, do to others as you would have them do to you, for this is the Law and the Prophets." Matthew 7:12*

This is a poem about putting yourself in perspective.

GRANDIOSITY

We think we are so important,
We humans.
Yet, we are individually, only one
Among billions of other human beings.
Yet, we are only one among
Trillions of species inhabiting a ball in space
That, although it seems grand and vast to us,
Is merely a pale blue dot,
Even within our own solar system,
Much less the universe.

Further away, this blue dot becomes
A speck that can only be seen
Like a virus in an electron microscope.
We are merely the tiniest portion of existence,
Within the tiniest portion of existence.
Our time is limited
To less than a nanosecond
Within the lifespan of the universe.
It is as though the instant we are born,
Poof! We die.
Still, we aggrandize ourselves
As though we are the center of the universe itself,
Even if that is to ridicule and condemn ourselves,
See ourselves as victims, or the worst of the worst.
Even in our self-condemnation,
We are grandiose,
Tiny creatures roaring at
An expanse
That doesn't even notice us.
Yet, we remain
An integral part of
Existence, itself.

Poem Introduction - LISTEN

Those who have survived abuse and trauma may check out and be wrapped up in mental activity while their bodies run on autopilot. They may repeatedly disconnect from the present moment. They walk through life unaware, not paying attention or noticing what is happening around them. The flip side is being hypervigilant and acutely aware of everything and everyone around them, but this is not mindfulness. It's anxiety. Mindfulness is a different kind of awareness. It is an awareness of the simplicity of the moment rather than being hyper-focused on the possibility of danger.

This is another mindfulness poem about the importance of connecting to and being aware of the moment that is currently present.

LISTEN

Have you ever stopped to listen,
Truly listen?
There is more to hear
Than the music playing overhead
At the grocery store
Which we more often ignore
Than perceive.
There is more to hear than
The moan of cars on a busy street.
There is more to hear
Than the clink and bloop of a video game,
Or the noise of a shouting commercial.
There is more to hear
Than blaring music or
The tinnitus causing ringing
Constantly in our ears.
Have you ever stopped to listen
To the subtle sound that the breeze makes

When it dances with the leaves?
Have you ever stopped to listen
To birds calling from those trees?
Can you hear the still, small voice
Of silence?
There is no true silence.
The world is constantly speaking,
But we do not hear the most important message.
We ignore all but our noise.
People have become so accustomed
To drowning out the true voice of the world
That they never hear the message of silence.
Stop ...
Listen ...
And you will hear
The still, small voice
Of peace.

Poem Introduction – DUSK

This is another mindfulness poem. Often, I sit on my deck watching the hummingbirds until the last one comes to the feeder and dusk has begun to steal the light. I find a great deal of peace simply sitting, often with a glass of wine, watching the nightfall.

DUSK

There she is,
The lingering dusk
After the sun
Has dipped
Below the horizon.
The night bugs call,
A song of peace
Gently crooning to the darkness.
There she is,
The gentle drift
As day sinks into night.
The hummingbirds gather
For one last feast
Before the darkness
Settles onto the world.
Here, I am engrossed
In this peace
Watching the day give in.
She settles, so still
Like a receptive lover
Waiting for night
To enter in.
Here in the moment,
I feel so still,

So peaceful and content.
Here, at this moment,
I surrender as well
And let the darkness
Soothe me.

Poem Introduction – THE LUCKY ONE

For most of my life, I thought I was poor. Granny and Grandpa had raised children during The Great Depression, and I don't know what Grandpa may have been like before struggling through it, but I suspect The Depression did something to him. I used to say he could pinch blood out of a penny, but he had much more than he let on. Still, I grew up in a four-room house with no running water until I was about fourteen when a new well was dug, and the back porch was enclosed to give me a bedroom of my own. Before that, I slept in a twin bed shoved to a wall in Grandma and Grandpa's room. Even after the porch was enclosed, my bed was shoved into one end beside the chest-type deep freeze, and anyone entering or exiting the house through the back or going to the bathroom went through my room because the rinky-dink bathroom that Grandpa installed was on the other end of the porch. Even that was not as bad as my first apartment in The Coastal Bend. I am grateful that my life is much better now.

There were many reasons why I thought I was poor, but Grandpa's attitude was one of the most significant. When I was in the ninth grade, the school took agriculture and home economics students to the state fair in Little Rock. That was the only year I took an FFA agriculture class. Besides, I never wanted to be a farmer and couldn't wait until I got out of there. It was, again, one of those things I did because that's what boys are "supposed to do." I know *Future Farmers of America* still exists. However, I imagine it is likely found only in rural schools. So, when the trip was planned, and I was in the ninth grade, the school sent home a memo saying that a minimum of ten dollars was recommended for the day. Grandpa reached into his wallet and handed me a five-dollar bill.

I said, "But Grandpa, they said we're supposed to have ten dollars."

He screamed, "You'd spend every Goddamn penny I have if you had your way!" Regardless of the church, Grandpa's Bible-thumping, and judgment, he was not opposed to cussing.

I felt a sudden and tremendous shame. The unspoken message was that I was a burden on him, and by wanting something, I would be depriving him. I still went on the trip, but half of those five dollars (equivalent to about $40.00 today, adjusting for inflation) was required to get in the gate, and the rest wasn't enough to allow me to do the things other kids were doing such as going to concerts and other activities. I didn't have the money to buy concert tickets. So, I spent the day alone looking at exhibits and losing money on ten cent carnival games. On the way home, I had enough left to buy a corndog with a cup of water for dinner. Other kids were offering me a bite of their burgers, fries, or a sip of their milkshakes, but I refused. Because I was accused of spending all of Grandpa's money, I thought I had to make do with what I had and because the other unspoken message was that I should never ask for or accept help or impose on anyone. That shame about money followed me for a huge portion of my life, and it is still hard to shake. It also instilled a tendency to feel sorry for myself. No matter how much money I made or how well I lived, I couldn't shake the feeling that I was poor. Somebody else always had more: a higher-paying job, a nicer house, the ability to take trips I couldn't take, etc.

As an adult, I discovered that Grandpa had been granted what would be equivalent to about $100,000.00 in today's money from the life insurance policy that my mother had taken out on me. He was also receiving the equivalent of about $2000.00 a month from my mom's Social Security death benefits. It was never *his* money in the first place. It was mine, and there had been plenty for him to give me the minimal amount recommended for the trip and more. He proclaimed himself poor when he was not poor at all. He made us live poorer than any of us had to because he had income from the farm, which was completely paid off, as well as my benefits.

Because I grew up feeling poorer than I actually was. I accounted for every penny and dreaded every bill. I tried to change my shame about money by saying affirmations and keeping a gratitude journal, but it was not until I realized how wealthy I have always been that I realized the difference. I may have grown up in a four-room house with no running water, but that was more due to Grandpa's stinginess and penny-pinching than a necessity due to lack. His penny-pinching was so extreme that when I was in college, the termites had gotten so bad that on Christmas break in 1974, I went to a built-in bookshelf to get something to read, and when I pulled on the binding of the book, it fell apart because the termites had eaten up to the binding. Grandpa had refused to pay for termite treatment, knowing that there had been a problem for years. It took a catastrophe for him to do something about the problem. The termites swarmed the house when I was on the college choir tour during Easter of 1975. Granny described that it happened during Easter dinner with other family members present. She said that wallpaper began to fall, and thousands of termites swarmed the house, flying into the food and flying into them. It took this event for Grandpa to finally decide to do something about the termites. What did he do? He paid cash upfront to build a new three-bedroom house and abandoned the old one. Still, he cut every corner he could cut. He had enough cash to build a new house, and plenty was left over in his bank account after that. We never had been poor.

I had been trained for my entire childhood to think that I was poor, but we weren't poor. I grew up feeling sorry for myself that I was so deprived while others had so much. I think I picked that up from Grandpa and his constant fear of lack. I developed the same fear. However, we lived poorer than we needed to because Grandpa had more than enough money to support us comfortably. Yet when I look back, I never went hungry. There was always food from the farm, and we received commodities in addition to that, probably because Grandpa had lied about his actual assets. I had a comfortable bed to sleep in, a roof over my head, a clean home, and clean clothes to wear, but my fear of poverty lingered well into my adult years. It took way too long before I began to consider how lucky and wealthy I have always been and for the fear of poverty to go away. Rather than saying, "I am grateful for (fill in the blank)." I began saying, "I know I am wealthy because (fill in the blank)." It finally changed my perspective. Regardless of my abuse and struggles in my upbringing, I am well aware that I am luckier than a great many who suffer far worse than I have ever suffered.

I have many things I didn't have in my childhood, and I no longer look at the whole issue of having or not having the same way. Between 1995 and 1997, I faced a financial challenge in which I lost my home, my savings, and all my retirement. I had creditors calling me several times a day demanding more payment than I had already sent them, and I paid as much as I could afford every month. I worked several odd jobs just trying to keep my head above water. One day, I was lying on my sofa looking up at the ceiling fan and thought, "What if I go bankrupt?" A voice in my head came back saying, "You grew up poor. You know how to do poor. You'll be fine." In other words, trust that it will all be okay. So, At the age of forty-two, I started over from scratch. When my house sold, $60,000.00 of equity (around $120,000.00 adjusting for inflation) went to pay off creditors. I got a job in September of 1997 that paid more than anything I was offered in Nashville, moved back to the Ozarks, and worked that job from the middle of September through December. Yet, my taxable income for 1997 was only slightly over $900.00. Nonetheless, after losing so much, I landed on my feet and, within a little over a year (thanks to my tax return), could buy another house. It wasn't much and cheap, but it was still a lovely, comfortable little house. It was about a third the size of my house in Nashville, but it served me well.

The truth is that I have never really been poor. Many people (like myself) whine and complain about various things when they are much better off than most people in the world, and too many don't take into account the suffering of others. Having visited Mexico a couple of times and gone outside the parameters of the tourist locations, I saw what poverty really looks like. I saw people living in dirt floor huts, looking like they had not had a proper meal in a long time. Yet, Mexico is better off than a third-world country, where people often support themselves on as little as five or six dollars a day, and those are the lucky ones. If I want to see real American poverty, all I have to do is take a take a look at the homeless. Yet, even our homeless are better off than many in third-world countries. Personally, I think that every American should be required to live for at least a month as a homeless person or someone from a third-world country so they can understand how incredibly lucky most Americans are by comparison. The truth is that Americans, in general (self-included), are spoiled absolutely rotten. There is so much that we take for granted. There is, among many, the idea of *"I've got mine. So, screw them."* We often feel sorry for ourselves when there is no actual need. We often have little compassion for others or do nothing about our compassion. At times, our arrogance causes us to judge without realizing or thinking through what it is like to walk in the shoes of another. We often take not just white privilege but American privilege and the privilege of wealth for granted. One thing I have always been able to do is mentally walk in someone else's shoes. I can't know how they feel given their situation, but I can imagine how I would feel if I were in that situation. I think more of us need to take the time to imagine what life might be like for those who don't have it as good as we do, whether that is related to financial status or any other type of privilege.

This is a poem about what is too often the American attitude.

THE LUCKY ONE

My heart aches for humanity,
But I am the lucky one.
I hate that grocery prices are getting so high.
What a luxury that I have never experienced
Famine or homelessness.
What a luxury to complain that I don't like beets
When others would scrounge for them
Out of my garbage.
What a luxury to fill up before finishing my plate
And dump the rest in the disposal.
What a luxury to have
A disposal, a kitchen,
A grocery store,

Money to buy food,
A roof over my head,
And a comfortable place to sleep.

My heart aches for humanity,
But I am the lucky one.
Sure, I know teachers don't get paid enough
But I don't want my taxes to go up.
What a luxury that I have never had to work a second job
To support my family and pay for supplies
That the school does not provide.
What a luxury that
I have never had to rush children to safety
And concern myself
More for their lives than their education.
What a luxury that I have never been shot at
Or had to hide beneath my desk
With terrified children
Shivering in fear
Because some angry lunatic
Came parading through our school
With an assault rifle
Killing everyone in sight.

My heart aches for humanity,
But I am the lucky one.
The biggest conflict I've ever seen was a fistfight in a bar.
What a luxury that I have never had tanks
Plowing down my street, blowing up houses;
That I have never had to hide in a basement,
Clutching my children to my chest
While mortars,

Rockets,
Or bombs
Pummel the city above us.
What a luxury that
I have never fallen to my knees weeping
Because mortar fire mutilated my five-year-old child
In a war that neither I
Nor my children
Ever wanted.

My heart aches for humanity,
But I am the lucky one.
I'm safe almost everywhere I go,
But there are certain neighborhoods
I don't drive through at night.
What a luxury that I can walk about as a privileged person
Never concerned about being profiled
Or having to live in one of those
Neighborhoods that I won't drive through.
What a luxury that
I have never had to sit down with my teenagers
And give them a talk about how to behave safely
If the cops pull them over,
Or worry that my kid might get beaten or shot
After getting pulled over for speeding.
What a luxury that I never have to worry
About having my door kicked in
Having a knee to my neck, being piled on or shot
More because of my skin color than for any crime
I never committed.
What a luxury
That I don't have to live in a gerrymandered district

That takes away the power of my vote and gives it
To those who seek to restrict my rights further.

My heart aches for humanity,
But I am the lucky one.
My husband and I love our children
And we look forward to the birth of our next baby.
What a luxury that I have never had to
Figure out how I could get an abortion
After I was molested at twelve years old by my father
Or raped by a brutal and gruesome man
Who was the consummate example
Of malignant misogyny.
What a luxury that I have never had to consider
That pregnancy could kill me,
Or that my doctor, my husband,
And I will not be given a choice by our state
To abort a pregnancy
that, while endangering my life,
Would produce a baby
That has already died inside me.

My heart aches for humanity,
But I am the lucky one.
You know, guys will be guys, and boys will be boys.
What a luxury to never have been raped
By a bunch of college boys,
Called whore, cum bucket, and slut,
And then told nothing can be done about it
Because I got drunk with them.
What a luxury to never have been a child enduring
Sexual abuse with no one taking it seriously

Because they think Uncle Joe would never do that.
What a luxury to never have
Been a boy manipulated into a sexual encounter
At ten years old
Only to have it swept under the rug
Like so much other garbage,
And then told as an adult that I was lucky
Because it happened
Or asked, "Was she hot?"

My heart aches for humanity.
But I am the lucky one.
I'm so proud of my loving family.
Sure, we get in a spat now and then,
But it never amounts to much.
What a luxury that I don't have to
Cower in fear, knowing that
My husband will come home drunk,
Beat me again, and threaten to
Kill me and my kids if I try to leave.
What a luxury that I don't have to be
A child watching my mother get pummeled
And feeling completely helpless
Because there is nothing I can do about it.
What a luxury that I never have to fear
That once he is done with my mother,
He'll come after me.
So, I try to be as quiet as possible
Because I don't want to make him mad.

My heart aches for humanity,
But I am the lucky one.

I think that being gay is a sin
And they should straighten up.
What a luxury that I have never had
My family and friends or church shun and deny me
Or vote against my rights while they don't even try to understand.
What a luxury that I have never been
Put out of my home onto the streets, homeless at sixteen
Because my parents say the feelings that I can't help
Are a choice and an "abomination."
What a luxury that I've never lived in a country
Where I could be put on trial,
Then, imprisoned or executed simply for being who I am.
What a luxury that,
Even in my own country,
I have never been beaten in the streets or murdered
Because some assholes thought I was too feminine,
My gender didn't match my assignment at birth,
Or because I dared
To hold hands with or kiss my spouse in public.

My heart aches for humanity,
But I am the lucky one.
I think our veterans need to be honored,
So, I wave flags and say, "Thank you for your service."
What a luxury that I have never had to fight in a war,
Or awakened screaming with horrific nightmares
About my buddies being killed
And mothers weeping because their children
Were brutally annihilated, even if by accident,
In the name of freedom and democracy.
What a luxury that I have never gotten up
Three, four, or more times a night

With my gun by my side
To check every door and window,
To check and recheck every lock
Just to be sure that my family is safe
When we live in one of the safest
Neighborhoods of the city.

My heart aches for humanity,
But I am the lucky one.
My buddies and I have a drink once in a while.
Hell, I've even tried marijuana.
What a luxury that I have never had
Narcan sprayed up my nose because of
A fentanyl overdose
Or convulsed in withdrawal
Because my addiction
Has gained an ever-increasing stronghold over my body,
And I have no way to pay for treatment.
What a luxury that I have never had to
Battle cravings so strong that I thought
I would die if I couldn't
Get another fix or a drink.

My heart aches for humanity,
But I am the lucky one.
Okay, so I poke a little fun at some people.
They should be able to take a joke.
What a luxury that I have never had to lie on the floor
With my screaming, nonverbal autistic child
Soothing and gently talking to him
For half an hour before he finally calms down.
What a luxury that I have never had to

Roll around in a wheelchair and
Struggle to use a gas station restroom
That has no handicapped facilities.
What a luxury that psychosis has never caused me
To be unable to tell what is real and what is not,
Unable to stop hallucinating or stop thinking that
People are saying horrible, degrading things
When they aren't even talking.
What a luxury that, Even when I'm feeling down,
I never get so down that I don't want to get out of bed
For days at a time, take a bath or talk to anyone,
And then I start thinking that my family
Would be better off if I was dead.

My heart aches for humanity,
But I am the lucky one.
I love that I can hop on a plane and
Vacation practically anywhere I want.
What a luxury that I have never had to
Relinquish my home and everything I own
To flee government corruption,
Drug cartels,
Or senseless murders.
What a luxury that I have never had to flee
On foot for thousands of miles with my children
Hoping that the promise of America might
Give my family another chance,
And then be arrested as an illegal
And separated from my children
That I tried so desperately to protect.
What a luxury that I was not brought to America
Illegally, at three years old

And now, at twenty-three, I have to worry
About being deported from
The only country I've ever known.
What a luxury that my kids
Have never been abducted and
Sold at the age of thirteen or younger,
Into human trafficking and hauled to random hotels
Where men pay to come in
One by one, or as a gang,
And rape them.
What a luxury that my kids will never have to live a life
That when they're too old, and the pedophiles
are through with them,
With no identity,
Their only option is
The streets,
Drugs,
And prostitution.

I could go on and on
About how lucky I am.
Yes …
I am …
The lucky one.
Yet …
How petty that
I concern myself
With the benign things
That others do.
How petty that I
Assume the arrogance
To tell others how

To live their lives
When I have no clue
What they are going through,
What they have been through,
Or what it feels like to live in their skin.
How petty is my hatred and merciless indifference
To the suffering of others
When I proclaim that I follow
The principles,
Morals,
Ethics,
And laws
Of God.
How petty that I
Strain at gnat and swallow a camel,
Focusing my attention
On judgment and ridicule
Instead of compassion.

I am …
Indeed …
The lucky one …
For I have never had to walk
In the shoes of the oppressed.

Poem Introduction – THEY ALWAYS BREAK YOUR HEART

I have always had pets, which have always been a comfort to me. When I was little and experiencing abuse, I made up my own language that I would use to talk to the cats. In my mind, the cats understood what I was saying, but the adults didn't know the language. That way, I could tell my troubles to my cats, at least the ones who would listen. Some of them had other things to do, and they didn't want to take the time to listen to me complain about what the adults were doing. However, it was wonderful when they listened because I could stroke them behind their ears and neck as I got things off my chest. I had dogs, too, but they didn't understand cat language, and I never seemed to find it as comforting to talk to them. Besides, I had no dog language.

During the time that I was in college, I didn't have pets except for visiting the ones I had before going to school. There was one cat that I had raised from a kitten over the summer break from school, and I had spent a lot of time with him all summer. After I left to go back to college and couldn't take him, Granny said he would wander all around crying. She thought he was crying for me, and within about a month after I left for school, he died for no apparent reason, even though he was only a few months old. Perhaps it is possible for pets to die of a broken heart. I loved him dearly and hoped to have him when I came home for my visits, but he didn't understand and never lived to see his first year through or my first visit home.

I haven't even bothered to count the number of pets I have lost over the years, but we always lose them because we almost always outlive them. If we don't outlive them, we are challenged at our dying to let go of everything unless we die suddenly. I have had some pets that were truly amazing companions. Some have just been enjoyable to have around, but some have left indelible marks on my heart. I have grieved for the loss of my pets as heavily as I have grieved for family, friends, or lost relationships. They always break your heart. If you are willing to let them in, even a little, they are going to win your heart, and then, without wanting to or trying to, they are going to break your heart simply by passing away, always too soon. However, in the end, the love is always worth it.

This is a poem about my experience with pets. I wrote it after my last beloved cat died, and I grieved for her horribly.

THEY ALWAYS BREAK YOUR HEART

They always break your heart, you know,
Always.
Yet, you can't help yourself.
They always win your heart, you know,
One after another,
And then another.
They always make sure your heart is full
Before shattering it into fragments.
Yet, what joy they bring
Between the shatters.

Everything passes away.
Everything is temporary.
Love is the only thing that endures,
Endures long past the shattered heart.
For even though the heart is broken, love remains.

Long after they are gone,
You still love them,
Still miss them.
You fall in love with them as deeply as with anyone,
And letting go,
When we have loved,
Is one of the most difficult things
That anybody ever does.

They always break your heart, you know.

You can't help but be aware
That the time will come
When you have to let them go.
Yet, you dismiss that knowledge,
And pretend it isn't there.
Go on, engross yourself with them,
But you have to be prepared.
Still, you can't really be prepared.
No one is ever prepared.
The time will come when you feel their love
Only in your memories.
And that is the time when love
Tastes slightly bitter.
That is the time when
Even the fondest memories
Are also aching and tender.

You learn to cherish every precious moment
Of every precious one,
The cuddles, the licks, the purrs, the pats,
The adoring looks, the bounces of excitement
Over the tiniest thing.
You learn to cherish them
Because they fill you with
Overflowing joy,
And they always win your heart,
Before breaking it.

Try to be prepared for that broken heart.
It's coming.
You always know it's coming.
You know that they love you
Because they prove it, always.

When they love,
They love fully
And wholeheartedly,
And forgive your every mistake.
When they love,
You can feel it
In every moment of every day.

You know they are going to break your heart,
But what a tiny price to pay
For every exquisite moment
Of every exquisite day
In which they graced you
With their blessings
Before they went away.

Poem Introduction – TO BE HONEST

Much of my life was a lie. I pretended to be straight. I pretended to like things that I didn't like, such as hunting or sports. I pretended to like girls and to be genuinely interested in the prospect of marriage. I pretended not to be interested in men when attracted to them. I pretended that the condemnation of the church didn't hurt me when it tore me to my core. I pretended to have the courage that I did not have. I pretended that I was tough when I felt like a marshmallow inside. I pretended that certain derogatory things that people said about gay people, when they didn't know I was gay, didn't bother me. I kept silent while I listened to their judgment, criticism, and ignorance without the courage to speak up and correct them. I tried to fit into the mold society had created for me instead of being honest and courageous enough to be myself. I know everyone lies somewhere, sometimes, for some reason, but perhaps the biggest lie is when we pretend to be something we are not instead of claiming our true, authentic selves. Despite those who would deny us the right to live as our authentic selves, we must still claim who we are and learn to cherish who we are regardless of the opinions of others.

TO BE HONEST

People lie.
Why do they lie?
Some lie big,
Some lie small,
But let's face it,
Everybody lies, sometimes.

For some, it's like an addiction.
You wonder what it does for them.
Is there some thrill to
Maybe getting away with something?

Is there some thrill
In seeking ways to hurt and deceive others?

Maybe they lie because they're angry.
Maybe they're lashing out,
Lashing out like a hurt animal,
Snapping at anything that comes close.
Maybe it's calculated and conniving.
Maybe they lie for some perceived selfish gain
And think if they lie repeatedly
You might eventually believe them.

Maybe it's just for fun –
Tell a lie about someone,
Then, watch to see the story unfold.
What happens?
Often nothing,
But sometimes, a plot unfolds,
And the liars get to watch it
With entertainment,
As though they wrote the script
Of a pathetic soap opera.

Often, those who are chronic liars
Are known for their antics,
And their lies are dodged.
Like balls thrown bouncing down the court.
It's more of an amusement
Than an actual danger.
But,
Sometimes, they cause harm
To the unsuspecting and the innocent.

What then?
Does the liar get some thrill out of creating suffering
For those who never harmed him?
Perhaps so.
Perhaps he doesn't care.
There are so many motivations for lying,
Everything from keeping a secret about a surprise party
To avoiding embarrassment,
To covering an error,
To manipulating,
To seeking some kind of gain,
To unadulterated malicious and vicious intent.
Some people lie when it would be easier
To tell the truth.

Human beings lie.
We all do,
And it is telling the truth to admit that we lie.

Some may do it subconsciously
Without even realizing they are doing it.
Some lie to themselves first
Before they ever lie to anyone else.

What if we made truth our goal?
No more lies,
Especially lies to ourselves.

My goal is honesty,
Clear, direct, and kind
But up-front, direct, honesty.

My goal is to have no fear
Of truth or exposure.
You can't blackmail the one who has no secrets.

My goal is to be done
With omission or commission,
And simply live my life
With full frontal
Spiritual and emotional nudity.

As terrified as I am to try it,
My goal is to show
Who I am.
Love me or leave me.
Hate me or respect me.
I'm not in charge of what you think.

Even if you think my honesty is a lie,
When the veil falls,
And I am exposed
To your judgment or criticism,
I will not seek to hide again.

I will not seek the safe cover of pretense.
This is who I am,
My faults, my mistakes, my talents,
My thoughts, my misgivings,
My dreams, my hopes,
My fears and frustrations.

This is who I am,
And I am willing

To be honest.
Even if you leave me or judge me.
Even if you lie about me,
Even if you think you can't handle my honesty,
For once in my life,
I am willing to be honest.

Yet, even as I say this,
Fear tugs at my heart
And whispers,
"Be quiet."

Poem Introduction – HEROES

The hero is an archetypal symbol in humanity, a part of many myths, fairy tales, novels, films, and stories, as noted in the books of Joseph Campbell. Yet, could it be that we all have a hero within us, and all it takes is the courage to release that part of ourselves? There may be heroes on a grand scale, but most are probably ones no one has ever heard of. They are teachers, doctors, nurses, neighbors, grandparents, mothers, fathers, police officers, firemen, childcare workers, social workers, housekeepers, maintenance workers, and friends. They are the average people whose gifts to humanity may never even be recognized, much less praised. They may never cure cancer or rescue a child from a burning building, but they are heroes, nonetheless. Their contributions may seem small by what we consider hero standards, but they are still heroes. My granny was a hero. Marcy was a hero. My dad was a hero, and many other heroes lifted me up and taught me to stand up for myself.

Take a look around. You may find that you are now and always have been surrounded by heroes, even in your darkest hours. They may not have been able to save you from trauma, but perhaps they might have been able to teach you how to save yourself from the effects or teach you at least to cope with it. Take a look around. There may be times when you have been someone's hero, even on a small scale. Did you hand down that product on the grocery shelf that the little old lady couldn't reach? Did you say something affirmative and uplifting to someone, especially a child? Did you console someone who was grieving? We are all, potentially, someone's angel.

HEROES

Where do heroes come from?
Flesh and bone mean nothing
If not directed by a mind of
Character and commitment.

How are heroes made?
Without a refiner's fire,

The clay will not harden.
So, the strength of a hero
Is often forged by overcoming challenges
That others may never see.

The character of a hero
Is one of love and respect for humanity.
The goal of a hero is to save
And never to destroy.
The Life of a hero
Is not in some grand comic book tale of
Adventure and excitement.
There may be no accolades or praises.
There may never be recognition.
Often,
Heroes are anonymous,
Quietly contributing,
Little by little,
To the fabric of humanity,
And the sanctity of life
Without ever claiming recognition.

The true hero does not seek praise.
Instead,
The hero is often the one giving praise.
Building up, encouraging, and cheering on.

The one who seeks praise,
Rather than being a hero,
Is more likely addicted
To his own arrogance,
Addicted to the need for affirmation
And ego feeding

When he cannot feed
His own ego
enough.

"Look what I did."
These words never fall
From a true hero's lips.

"Look what he did,
Look what she did.
Look at what wonderful things
They did."
These words fall
From the lips of those
Who recognize
That a hero has been
In their midst
And are often spoken
By the silent hero
Who dares to affirm
Rather than condemn.

The hero does not judge,
Does not seek,
Does not demand,
But quietly respects
And honors the rights
Of everyone.
The hero respectfully
Defends and upholds those rights.

Sometimes, a hero's actions take courage.
More often than not,

Those actions are quietly applied as needed
And left to take effect
Without expectation
Of anything in return
Because
The hero understands that true giving
Expects nothing.

What are heroes made of?
Strength and humility
Love and respect,
Honor and dignity,
Ethics and commitment.

Where do heroes come from?
Your own backyard,
Your own street,
Your own home,
Your own school,
Your own workplace.
Perhaps,
The hero you are looking for
Is looking back at you
From your mirror,
Thinking with your thoughts …

Dare to smile at that hero.
Dare to affirm.
Dare to claim the hero in you.

What makes someone a hero?
It's very simple.
The choice to be one.

Poem Introduction – I LINGER

Have you ever considered what it actually means to be alive, what it took to come into this existence in the first place? Have you ever stopped to cherish your existence and recognize that even if there are over seven billion people on this planet, your existence is absolutely unique? No one has ever or will ever experience life the way you experience it. This is one of the reasons why it is important not to judge; we can never understand what it is like to live in another person's skin or witness the world from their perspective. Even if there has been trauma, despite the trauma, the majority of your life is better than your traumatic experiences. Your life may be as good as you are willing to make it, but that may require you to reevaluate your concept of *good*.

First, it is a miracle that anyone exists. Existence itself is a miracle. Our mere awareness of existence is a miracle. Yet, even to be born at all is statistically infinitesimally small. At birth, a woman has approximately one million eggs. By puberty, she has about three hundred thousand left. Out of those, only three or four hundred will ever be ovulated. If the eggs are fertilized, 30-50% fail to implant or will not become viable and are often passed before the woman realizes she is pregnant. Out of the remaining, a woman will bear an average of 2.4 children. In his lifetime, the average man will produce five hundred and twenty-five billion sperm, and there are anywhere between two and seven million in each ejaculation. Out of that gigantic number, he will still only have 2.4 children, on average, and many men and women go through life without bearing children at all. What this means is that you are a miracle. I am a miracle. Everyone is a miracle, and the fact that we can even experience existence, in and of itself, is an incredible miracle!

Every life has value, and every life is worth a novel. Every life has a collection of unique stories that no one else ever experiences. Every life has meaning and matters. Therefore, linger here and rejoice in this miracle that is your existence. Milk life, exude life, and revel in life for as long as you can because the time will come, soon enough, when this miracle will pass.

You don't need greatness or wealth, accolades, or awards. All you need is the willingness to perceive with gratitude the daily miracles that unfold in your life.

I LINGER

How long will I be here?
Who knows how long?
I have been here for a long time,
By some estimations,
And not very long at all,
By others.

Some die before they are born,
Or barely spend a moment outside the womb.
Yet, here I am all these years upon years
After that first traumatic event—birth.
I am still here.
I linger.

I was the one who waited almost a year
To press my head against my mother's cervix
And silently announce,
"Let me out!"
I was the one who came into the world
With a squall and a scream
After the doctor slapped my ass!
I was the one who endured,
Endured more than you know!
I am the one who endures, still.
I am the one who lingers still.

I linger, yet another moment,
Moment by moment,
For as long as I can.
I am the one who lingers in this moment,
Seeing, smelling, tasting, feeling, and hearing.
I am the one who lingers for yet another moment,
For as long as I can.

I am the one who lingers,
Living this moment,
Milking this moment,
Being who I am,
Existing for as long as I can
Before I retreat
Once again,
Into the silence of nonexistence.

Poem Introduction - STORM

There are things that we notice when we practice mindfulness that are otherwise passed up. When we are walking through life tied into our thoughts, there is a lot that we miss. There are things that others may notice or take into account that we don't notice, and some people are generally more mindful than others. In many ways, mindfulness is a simple matter of slowing down. Think of it like this: Are you most likely to notice a quarter on the sidewalk if you are riding a bike, running by, strolling by, or just casually walking by? We notice more of the world when we slow down than when we are rushing through life. One of the most common complaints with anxiety is a racing mind, and one of the best remedies for that is to learn to practice meditation, specifically mindful meditation or meditative walking. Simply slow down or sit without extraneous noise or distractions. Pay attention to life. Even cleaning a litter box can become a mindful meditation. A Buddhist saying is: *"Before I became enlightened, I chopped wood and carried water. After I became enlightened, I chopped wood and carried water."* The world and our place in it do not change through enlightenment—only our perception and perspective of the world change. Also, when I speak of enlightenment here, I'm not talking about becoming someone like a guru or the Dali Lama. I am talking about developing awareness and the ability to encounter the world through a more peaceful and loving perception.

This and several other poems to follow are about mindfulness and its practice. They are poems about being aware of the moment, experiencing life as it unfolds, witnessing life, learning to let life speak to us, and honing our awareness of being alive.

STORM

The storm is coming.
Smokey drifting mist hangs in the air
Like clouds moving upon the ground.

Limbs of trees whip in gusts of wind,
And wind chimes clang more than tinkle.

The storm is coming.
Quiet stillness interludes the flipping gusts of wind.
The air is moist and cool,
With microscopic pellets of water.

The storm is coming.
Will it blow and bellow,
Shout with clasps of thunder
And streaks of light across the summer sky?
Will it clatter with a false bravado,
Posturing on the horizon
Like the schoolyard kid
Who thinks he can take on the coach,
but then drops his head and retreats?

The storm is coming.
Will it blow through with torrents of rain
Dumped from God's bucket,
Or will it simply pretend to come,
Then, go the other way?

Regardless, I sit and observe
For as long as possible,
Drinking in the breeze,
And the cool solitude.
I sit with the wind on my cheeks
And watch leaves dancing to storm music.
I sit and wait for the very last moment
To dash inside before getting soaked.

Poem Introduction - MUSIC

Mindfulness is awareness. Mindfulness is recognizing that this moment is the only moment we are living, right here, right now, whatever it contains. Mindfulness seeks those quiet moments of tranquility, especially when the past or future has nagged at our awareness. Mindfulness is milking as much essence from the experience of life as we possibly can. I have said that art is where you find it, and I often take photos of simple things, such as light streaming through the fluid in a glass or autumn leaves that have fallen onto the deck, but music is also where you find it. An instrument is not required, nor are specific rhythms to have music. Music is all around us every day. Music is in the ticking of a clock, the sounds of birds, the sound of a breeze through the trees, the sound of traffic, and even the sound of a distant siren. It is all music. The world is never completely still nor completely silent, and mindfulness calls us to be aware of the music, the art, and the dance of life that surrounds us in every moment of every day.

MUSIC

Let this be your music,
The whisper of wind through the billowing trees,
The soft tinkle and resonate harmonics of windchimes,
The chatter of hummingbirds,
The call of a mockingbird in the tree over the fence
Which calls the call of all birds in one variant song.
Absorb the transient noises of the city in the distance.
Let this be your art, your peace,
The crimson and golden glimmer
Of blooms against a backdrop of varying shades of green,
The pillows of clouds drifting across the bluest sky.
Let this be your moment,
Still and peaceful,
Yet filled with nature's activity.

Let this be your contentment
As leaves sway in gentle breezes of softly fragrant air.
Let this be your passion,
To melt into this moment,
One with all there is.
With gentle breezes on your skin,
Let nature make love to you.
Let this be your surrender,
Your moment in the dance of awareness,
Your bliss beyond all bliss,
The kiss of this moment
Lingering sensually upon your soul.

Poem Introduction – JUST LIVE

Many people, and perhaps most trauma survivors, walk through life completing daily activities while their minds are somewhere else. Sometimes, the body goes on autopilot, and the day after you lose it, you find the TV remote in the kitchen cabinet by the snacks. We all do it, to some extent, especially when stressed or distracted. Still, trauma survivors have more of a tendency to check out, dissociate, and become unaware even when their bodies are walking around doing 'normal' things. Certain things may trigger them to check out and not be present.

Getting caught up in fear, worry, anger, resentment, guilt, regret, trepidation, and foreboding is easy. However, the one truth about all those things is that they are not real at this moment. They are not happening now. *A Course in Miracles* says, *"The one truth about the past is that it is not here."* To fear or worry, we must fantasize that something terrible will happen. Often, that is based on having experienced terrible things in the past. If it were happening now, we would be dealing with it, not winding up anxiety over some thought about an event that will probably never occur. When we are angry or resentful, we are thinking about the past and how we have been wronged or treated unjustly. When we have guilt or regret, we are thinking about something that we wish had not happened or a mistake we wish had not been made. With trepidation and foreboding, we feel as though some horrible happening may fall on us at any moment, even though we have no idea what it may be. None of this is really being in life. Life is what is happening right now. Life *is* this moment, this experience, even if it is unpleasant.

When I was a kid, being raised by grandparents who both had dentures before their forties, I was, of course, never taught to brush my teeth. Before I was a teen, we had a zinc bucket in the kitchen for water drawn from a stone well at the base of the hill. So, tooth brushing would have been a little more complicated with that. Still, I was never taught to care for my teeth. As a result, by the time I was a teenager, I had terrible dental health and even a couple of abscessed teeth. The only dentist within fifty miles was a quack who let one of my abscessed teeth go for almost two years while telling my grandparents that I was making up the pain so I could get out of school. Meanwhile, I went through repeated eruptions of infection. Even though it was a gross experience, I was always grateful when the abscess burst because I got some relief for a while. When that dentist finally admitted that I had an abscess, he decided to do a root canal. I don't recall any gas or anesthesia, so it felt like he was pulling my brains out through the roof of my mouth. That same dentist put a filling on top of another abscess that caused a grapefruit-sized swelling that ran down my neck. That occurred just before I went to college, and when I got there before I ever started classes, a different dentist had to do an emergency extraction of that tooth. As a result, I had shooting pains down my neck for over ten years and had to have a bridge between my teeth to replace the one that had been extracted. Given all that, one might think I would be terrified of dentists. However, I have been fastidious about my dental care since I was eighteen, having regular checkups, and I learned to practice mindfulness.

When I visit the dentist, I close my eyes, breathe deeply, and relax. I trust that the dentist knows what he or she is doing until proven otherwise. If they were to prove that they are not kind or competent, I now have recourse that I didn't have as a child. So, I lean back and feel my body against the chair. I notice things like the hygienist's lab jacket touching my wrist or the dentist's stomach growling as he leans over to do his work. I focus on the sensation of their fingers in my mouth, even the sensations of the instruments, and I allow. I allow even that to be my moment and repeatedly place myself back into the moment. The one truth about what happened to me with that dentist from my childhood is that it is not happening now. Since my childhood, only one other dentist has mistreated me, and I fired him quickly. The flip side is that I once had a dentist who was so gentle that I could fall asleep during procedures, and his fillings were as smooth as silk. When I am at the dentist, it is a different dentist at a different time than my childhood. I define how now differs from then, and if any trepidation should arise, I may ask myself, "How is now different from then?" Next, I answer that question mentally and notice anything I can that is different from that time when a quack dentist mistreated me. Another thing I do when I catch myself ruminating is say to myself, "This is my moment. This is the only moment I am living. This is the only moment that exists. I bring my awareness to this moment." Neither the past or the future exist in this moment. This is always the only moment that exists.

Being alive is being present and being aware, not jerking around with anxiety and hypervigilance, but relaxing into this moment, right here, right now. If someone were unethical or had toxic behavior, I would eliminate my contact with them. However, I have learned to give almost everyone a chance before I assume they will hurt me. Unless there are overt and clear danger signals (which many trauma survivors can misread through anxiety), I give people a chance. I don't trust all at once because that would not be wise, either. However, I gradually extend trust to deeper and deeper levels as long as the other person continues to show that they are worthy of that trust. Yet, even if they have made it into my most intimate inner circle, I will still stop associating with them if they betray me. As I previously mentioned, the first rule for maintaining healthy, stable relationships is, *"If you don't treat me right, you will not treat me at all."* I will not disrespect or harm you, but if you don't give me the respect, honor, and dignity that I deserve as a human being, I will stop having anything to do with you. I can forgive a snake for biting me, but I will not go near the snake again. When I eliminate time spent with people who are toxic to me, I open a space for those who can be trusted and those who will treat me with respect, honor, and dignity. When we learn to love ourselves, we accept nothing less than treating ourselves with respect, honor, and dignity and accept nothing less from others.

It is especially effective when we can practice mindfulness during peaceful times. However, when stressed, that is the most important time to practice and often the time that people are least likely to practice. Peaceful times can be achieved in almost any peaceful setting. I have done it in my living room by shutting off all extraneous noise and just listening to the clock ticking, children playing across the street, or the simple essence of silence, which is never completely silent. My favorite place to do it is on my back deck, where I have flowers and hummingbird feeders. Weather permitting, I do that for about an hour every day.

We are not truly alive when we check out to either past hurts or future fears. We are truly alive when we check in and are aware; when we live in and focus our full attention on the current moment.

JUST LIVE

Have you ever considered
What an incredible blessing it is
To feel a breeze on your skin,
A soft, caressing touch of nature,
Comforting and crisp?

Have you ever considered
What an incredible blessing it is
To feel the sun on your face,
A warm brilliance
That twinkles through the tree-top canopy
And shines upon the grass?

It is a blessing
To be able to see the lucent blue sky,
Or the sparkling dew on morning rose petals
Before the day has left the dew to dry.

It is a blessing
To breathe,
To feel air inflating you,

To be aware of your body,
Your breath of life,
The evidence that you are here.

It is a blessing
to hear birds singing,
With variant calls
From breeze-blown branches,
Or even to hear,
On distant roadways,
Rolling waves of traffic.

Life is a blessing to be savored
And when we learn how to live it, we savor it.
When we learn how to encapsulate ourselves
Into the moment,
Letting all else go,
We learn to be in life
Rather than simply
Watching it pass us by,
When we learn how to live life
Instead of regretting, fearing, or resenting,
We may finally realize
How good it is to be alive.

Poem Introduction – THE HUMMINGBIRD

Think of this. No moment that has ever existed in anyone's life, or in the life of anyone who has ever lived, has ever repeated itself, and there are billions of moments in billions of lives going on at this very moment. When they say the past repeats itself, they mean that human behavior patterns tend to repeat, but the past never repeats. The moment comes and becomes the past immediately. The instant it is created, it passes into the past, and the process is unending. As soon as we experience the moment, it is gone, and no two human beings or creatures ever experience the same moment. Even if they stand side by side at the same moment on the same day, their experience is different. No day we have ever lived can be identical to any day we lived before, and every day we live becomes an adventure into the unknown. We may make plans and determine what we intend to do on a given day at a given time, but we have absolutely no control over how that unfolds. Even if things are going as planned, we still have no control over the outcome, and anything could happen at any moment that might redirect what we had planned. For instance, I may plan to vacuum the rug before I leave for an appointment, but the power goes out and does not come back on until hours after my appointment. The rug will have to wait, and my plans will have to change. Regardless, I cannot vacuum the rug when I originally planned.

Hummingbirds, to me, are magical. They are an example of how quickly one moment can pass into another, yet a kind of eternity is felt when watching them. They are the only birds capable of flying backward. They are gentle (except when fighting each other over a feeder) and zip through time, always in a hurry. Once in a while, one will perch to drink nectar or guard a feeder, but even that does not last long. I love to stand when the hummingbirds are plentiful, with my nose up to a feeder, and watch as they buzz around my head, but one of the most amazing things I ever experienced was when I was meditating on my deck one morning with my palms up, and eyes closed. I felt the gentlest sensation on the fingertips of my left hand and opened my eyes to see a hummingbird licking at my fingertips. I don't think I'm that sweet, but there it was. It flew away a few seconds after I opened my eyes. Having been deep in meditation, I had no clue what was happening until I opened my eyes to see the hummingbird. Sometimes, hundreds of hummingbirds come to my feeders, so I paid no attention to the buzzing sound when the hummingbird found my fingers. However, the memory of that moment is one of my most treasured, a miracle moment. Talk about a soul encounter!

The Tao says that any spiritual lesson can be found in nature if we observe. Training ourselves to observe is one of the first steps toward awareness. Training ourselves to observe is learning mindfulness, but it is also learning to let the moment be the moment, suspended of expectations. When we learn to observe, we find that epiphany is frequently repeated.

THE HUMMINGBIRD

The hummingbird comes
And flies away,
Comes again and flies away,
The hummingbird comes,
But just a moment,
Just a moment,
Then, it flies away again.
The hummingbird comes,
For only a moment
That disappears
Almost as quickly as it arrived.
The hummingbird perches,
For less than a moment,
Lingers in time
Like a whisp of wind.
The hummingbird comes
And flies away,

Flies away,
Again and again.
Pay attention,
Or you might miss it.
Pay attention
Or the moment is gone.
Pay attention.
You could miss it,
Gone forever,
Never to repeat again.
The hummingbird comes
And flies away,
Flies away again.
The hummingbird comes
And flies away,
Yet, it lingers on my awareness,
The awareness of now
Becoming a winking memory
Of magical experience.
The hummingbird comes
And flies away.
Eternity passes in only a moment.
Awareness of eternity
Lasts for only a moment,
Then flies away,
Again.

Poem Introduction – SHADOWS

This is another mindfulness poem inspired by sitting on my deck on a late autumn afternoon, watching long Maxfield Parish-style shadows drift across the lawn as darkness crept in. I cannot emphasize enough that there is a beautiful peace to be found in mindfulness.

SHADOWS

Here come the shadows
Sneaking up on daytime,
Turning it into night
Making love to the light.
Here come the shadows
Laying long and slender
Drifting off into the yonder
Creeping slowly by.
Soon, the light surrenders,
Allows the night coitus.
Soon, the light is ravaged
By this sensual consummation.
The night engulfs the tree lines
And brings a restful sleep.
Deep into the slumber
Existence seems to cease.
Yet, soon, the light comes creeping
Sneaking up on night
Spreading glorious morning
Across the clouds and sky.
Here, the light awakens,
And shoos the night away
Giving birth to morning
And a beautiful new day.

You've had your time asunder
Now come and claim the day.
Soon, the light comes shining,
Like a smile across the sky
Another day is dawning
As it will forever,
And ever,
By, and by, and by.

Poem Introduction - SEAGULL

Before moving to The Coastal Bend of Texas, I had little experience with seagulls. There might have been a few encounters on the occasional vacation near the ocean, but I had never lived where others came to vacation, and I hadn't paid that much attention when I was on vacation. I had never had ongoing observation of gulls before.

When I first moved into that horrible apartment, I would take my camera across the street to the bay side. I discovered that getting a good shot of a seagull is about as difficult as capturing a hummingbird photo. They are generally very active, but occasionally, they are found scurrying along the shore or perching on a light pole.

It seemed to me that they were having a good time, and since I wasn't having a very good time with my transition to Texas and didn't know a soul there, I decided to go hang out with the gulls and join their party.

SEAGULL

If I were a seagull,
I would play on currents of air
That rise above the ocean waves.
I would float above,
And sail below.
I would revel in each day.
If I were a seagull,
I would wing about the sky
Simply for the joy of being able to fly.
I would sit atop a light post
And cheerfully watch all passers-by.
If I were a seagull,
I would feel the warm sun
Reflect across my beak
And watch for any morsel

That life provides
For me to eat.
I would not seek,
But only find,
And always trust that life provides.
I would have no worries,
Should I eat this,
But not that.
I would scarf up the bounty
Like a feathered aristocrat.
If I were a seagull,
I would fan my wings
For no other reason
Than the sensation of such things.
I would have no worry
Of what anyone might think.
For how could that
Have anything to do
With the life that was given to me?
If I were a seagull,
I would teach the world,
Don't worry.
Don't think about
What tomorrow might bring.
Instead,
Play all day
Above the waves
Shouting
be—be—
just be—be
Just be.

Poem Introduction WHITE FEATHER

The most difficult move I ever made was to The Coastal Bend of Texas; I have described that torment previously. I was frustrated, pissed off, stressed, and overwhelmed. I had to use every tool in my spiritual and mental health maintenance toolbox to get through all of that. One of those tools was going for a walk any day when the weather cooperated. Even then, I would ruminate with anger and frustration rather than enjoying the beauty around me, the rolling teal, white-tipped waves, golden sand, and magenta sunsets. One of those happiness tools, being one that I had to remember to engage, was gratitude. An attitude of gratitude elevates mood altitude. Gratitude is particularly important when many things are going wrong. Then, we need to try to identify what is going right. Many people don't realize there is a healing aspect to appreciation and awe. The simple experience of awe positively changes our brain chemistry. One of my favorite quotes is from *The Color Purple* (on my top-ten list of all-time favorite films, also a brilliantly written novel by Alice Walker): *"I think it pisses God off if you walk by the color purple in a field somewhere and don't notice it."* We need to notice life and all the beauty contained within it. Especially when stressed, we need to focus on anything we can appreciate. I tried to practice mindfulness on my walks, but I also had to remind myself that gratitude is one of the most effective tools in the spiritual and mental health toolbox. On one of those walks, I found a large white feather when I was ruminating about how I had been deceived and mistreated. It was my reminder to return to the moment.

WHITE FEATHER

Crisp wind
Fills the short hairs on my head
With just a touch
Of cool breeze.
Sea birds play on the wind

Like kites over the current
At the ocean's edge.
My feet sink into the warm sand,
As I wobble on uneven gait.
The evening tide caresses my feet,
With gentle ocean's kiss.
Clouds of white, lavender and gold
Contrast the blue sunset sky,
And I almost miss it all.

Instead, I ruminate
About my grief and anguish,
My thoughts of attack
And fear of attack.
I almost miss it all
While,
In my selfishness,
I fail to consider that
I have a roof over my head,
Food in my belly
And a comfortable bed for sleep.
As well,
I have a beautiful location
Where I can walk along the beach.

I am not a refugee
Fleeing brutal conflict of unrelenting war.
I am not a family
Watching everything thing they own
Rise into the smoke of callous flames.
I am not a victim
Of flood,

Landslide or famine.
My loved ones are not being
Gunned down on the street.
I am only pissed off
That I did not get my way.

I feel victimized,
Yet I come and go as I please.
I get to watch hummingbirds and gulls
Or take a walk safely on the beach.
In the center of nature's splendor,
I can stop,
Take a deep breath of salty air,
And relax,
If I choose.

As I ruminate about the wrongs
Done to me
Instead of laughing
That the joke of life
Is when we take
Anything too seriously,
I come upon a white feather
Lying peacefully in the sand.
It brings me back,
This symbol of air
And free spirit,
This symbol of rising above it all.

The message?
Come back!
Live this moment.

Relish this moment.
Cherish this moment.
Languish in this moment.
For as soon as we perceive it
This moment is gone.

Feeling stunned,
Yet comforted and reassured,
I bend down to pick up
The white feather.
I hold it in my hand
Close to my heart
And face the rolling blue ocean.

A breeze flicks the short hairs on my head.
Warm, wet sand gathers between my toes.
Then,
I turn,
Carry the feather home,
Place it in a vase,
And proceed,
Once again,
To forget
That I am not
A victim.

Poem Introduction - BLESSED

My best friend is a Baptist Christian, heterosexual man, married with several children, and he has been the most loving and faithful man I have ever met. However, my husband matches his standards of loving and caring. I have had other heterosexual male friends, but only a couple who were very close. In fact, in 1982, I prayed to have a heterosexual male friend to help me overcome my fear, specifically of straight men, but men in general. My abuse had taught me to fear men, even if I was attracted to them. After I prayed, the next Sunday at Unity Church in Little Rock, a man turned to me at the end of the service and began a conversation. We immediately recognized many things in common, including our appreciation for Jimmie Spheeris's music when others didn't seem to know who he was. My prayer was answered. He was a wonderful friend, and we maintained that friendship for several years beyond my move to Nashville in 1984, but we lost contact over time and distance. Even though he was supportive and affectionate and helped me through my fear of men, he was not as loving and affectionate as my best friend, whom I met in 1998.

After I moved back to the Ozarks in 1997, I had a lonely period for about a year. My partner initially did not move there with me, and I was alone again for a short time, although I did have family in the area, I was familiar with everything, and I made friends quickly. I had inherited a couple of dogs (a long, separate story), and I was walking my dogs one day when I saw a new friend I had recently met standing in the alley behind the old movie theatre, which had been converted into a community playhouse. I detoured and walked down the alley to say 'hello' and find out what play they were working on. That friend introduced me to a man who was also in the play. It was a simple 'hello, nice to meet you' and a brief conversation. I took little notice and continued my walk. Then, I started getting emails from the man my friend had introduced me to. He had lifted my email from a group email that other friends had sent around. At first, I thought, from the content of his emails, that he was gay and that he was coming on to me. However, I was to be pleasantly surprised that he was not gay. The whole relationship might have been more confusing and difficult if he had been. Instead, he had been advised by his therapist that he should consider establishing friendships with people of a better character than he had previously been involved with. His therapy had followed an ugly divorce, and initially, without knowing I was gay, he had concluded that I was of the character his therapist had recommended and pursued a friendship with me.

We met and, over time, established a genuine, affectionate friendship with frequent social visits. Yet, we are very different. First, he is a fundamentalist Christian and has had almost the opposite political views from myself. Still, he has never pushed either his religious or political views on me, even though we have had some heated discussions over politics. His politics were never anti-gay, and he was never demeaning of my sexual orientation. In fact, I learned that the Supreme Court had legalized gay marriage when he called to inform me and offer congratulations that my rights were honored. Over the years, we have seen each other through break-ups, moves, and marriages. To this day, I still cannot understand what he sees in me, but I have been and continue to be the grateful recipient of deep and abiding love from him.

In 2003, he moved to another city, a 2-hour drive from where I lived. He had remarried and bought a house there. That was the Christmas after my break up with my first long-term partner. Granny had passed the year before, and I had used my inheritance money to renovate a Victorian farmhouse. The renovations were still ongoing when I moved into it on the sixth of December. I got the flu during the move and had to go to bed while friends completed moving my stuff in, and it would be weeks before I got everything unpacked. Having lost Marcy the previous June, barely over a year after I lost Granny, that was a particularly difficult year. So, I didn't do Christmas that year. I was too overwhelmed. On Christmas day, my aunt brought me a black walnut pie (It's an Ozarks thing) and went on to other celebrations. So, I was home alone. My friend called and asked what I was doing.

I said, "sitting here by myself watching television."

He said, "That's what I thought. I'll be there in a couple of hours." He then hung up the phone and drove two hours to my house.

His wife had taken his step-children to Illinois to visit their grandparents, but he chose to stay home because of his work schedule. So, he was home alone for Christmas, as well. He drove to my house to pick me up. Then, we drove the 2 hours back to the town where he lived to see his new house. Then he drove from there an hour to Springfield, Missouri, a triangle point from each of our homes. There, I had my first *Jewish Christmas*. We saw a bad movie and had bad Chinese food. I understand that a *Jewish Christmas* in New York is going out for Chinese food and watching a movie on Christmas Day. That's what we did. Even if the movie and the food were not the best, that Christmas goes down in the books as one of my most wonderful Christmases simply because I was the recipient of his loving rescue. After that, he drove me two hours from Springfield to drop me off back home and then returned to his own home. He had driven nine hours that day to have Christmas with me. When my second partner broke up with me, he called and said, "Get your ass up here!" I then drove to his house, where he and his family made sure that I was not alone in my initial grief. Those are only a couple of the thoughtful and wonderful things he has done for me over the years, including taking time off work and coming to help me move to The Coastal Bend. Since 2003, I have spent several Christmases at his home with his family. He also presided over my marriage, which was held at Bethesda Fountain in Central Park, New York. He flew to New York with his wife and sister-in-law to conduct the service for us, and my sister was also present. To say that I am blessed to have him as my friend would be an understatement.

BLESSED

Intimacy is a bond of trust
Built and nourished within relationships.
We have that, have had that
For almost thirty years,
But you were not what I thought.

Love is a bond of acceptance,
Wanting the greatest and highest good,
Not idolizing but cherishing each other.
We have that, have had that
For almost thirty years,
But how did it happen?

Of all the people I have ever known,
You are among the most loving, considerate, and giving.
Your affection, sincere and strong,
Comforts me like a warm blanket over my soul.

That you love me unconditionally is not in question.
But we are not now and never have been lovers,
Nor will we ever be.
Still, our love for each other is boundless and strong.

Of all the men I have ever known,
You are among the angels,
And there are very few.
You are an anomaly
exuding unbridled, unconditional love.
You are not like other men.
You require nothing of me,

Desire only good for me,
And love me despite my faults.

You never let me down.
Even when I have assumed
That I could handle things
All by myself,
You were still at my side to help me.

You took me in,
Made me part of your family.
You nurtured and nourished my spirit.

When I went through heartache and disappointment,
You lifted me after others had cast me down.
You are yet another angel, another anchor
Who has helped me through life's storms,
And I know that you were sent to me
By a loving God with a miracle performed.

Our political differences notwithstanding,
We became close and loving friends
Each one able to see beyond ideology
To the glimmering soul within.
Our religious views notwithstanding,
We share a spiritual bond of loving trust
Each one able to respect and honor
That spirituality transcends religiousness.
Our sexual orientations notwithstanding,
We became affectionate and considerate friends,
Each one able to respect boundaries,
And love without fear, without end.

How could I have made it without my way showers,
And you among them?
Of those glistening souls,
Those angels on the earth,
Those nurturing spirits
Who teach us what love really is,
Your light shines brilliantly.
How could I have made it without you?

You are a diamond in a world of stones,
A pot of gold at the end of my rainbow.
You are the illuminating essence of genuine friendship.
You are a rose in a field of thorns,
And you are among the few
That I have allowed to touch my soul.
You enrich my life and shower me with blessings,
And I am wealthy to have you as my friend,
For in this, I am blessed beyond measure
Beyond this life, forever and ever again.

Poem Introduction – THE GULLS ARE ALWAYS LAUGHING

When I began to spend more time around the gulls, I realized that their call sounded like laughter. Since one of my favorite quotes is by Oscar Wilde, *"Life is too important to be taken seriously,"* I began to allow the gulls to remind me not to take things too seriously when undergoing significant stress. Taking life too seriously has been one of my biggest obstacles. I think that it may often be an obstacle for those who have experienced abuse or trauma and sometimes for those who haven't. Those of us who have been victimized and have perceived ourselves as victims rather than survivors take most things too seriously. When abuse teaches us that we are a victim, cursed, worthless, useless, unworthy, unsafe, and unloved, it is very easy to take even little things too seriously and to forget to laugh when we need to lighten up and have some joy. It becomes even more important for those who have had very little joy in their lives. Sometimes, we have to create joy. Whenever we find joy, learning how to wallow in it is important instead of wallowing in our heartache. I have also said that we need to wrap our lips around the tit of life and suck it for all its worth. There is a quote from the old Broadway show *Auntie Mame*, *"Life is a banquet, and most poor suckers are starving to death!"* We have to permit ourselves to step up to life's banquet, and we can find it on any given day if we look for it.

No life is without sorrow. No life is total joy and laughter; some lives have more sorrow or joy than others. Yet, when they say laughter is the best medicine, they are not kidding. Laughter is one way that people cope with excessive stress and trauma. During times of extreme stress, people may laugh at things that are gruesome, grotesque, and awful such as military service people laughing when horrible things have happened, not because those things are funny but because the experience is overwhelming. Laughter gives some relief to the one who is overwhelmed. People also laugh when mildly stressed. I recall being in the dorms on the night before finals and rolling in laughter on the dorm central room floor with my friends. It was a way of blowing off steam and mitigating the stress and worry about passing finals.

Laughter, like all human emotions, serves a purpose. It does something for us. It literally can improve mood and reduce depression and anxiety. It can benefit us physically, as well. When we laugh, it forces us to process more oxygen, stimulating our circulation. There is often a relaxed feeling after laughter because the brain releases endorphins, which can diminish our perception of pain and act as a mild sedative. So, endorphins reduce our experience of stress. Laughter improves our immune system because it causes the release of neuropeptides. Emotionally, it helps us connect with others who may enjoy humor. People are more likely to laugh in the presence of others, and the shared experience of laughter can increase a feeling of bonding and belonging. This is entirely different from being laughed at by bullies, which is demeaning and ridiculing of the one who is bullied. That is not a shared experience because the one who is bullied does not perceive the experience as humorous or funny, and in truth, neither do the bullies. True humor contains no malice, and so-called humor expressed with malice is not humor at all. This includes cutting little passive-aggressive digs at one another while telling the other, "Lighten up. It's a joke!" If the other person is not taking it as a joke, regardless of the intent, it is not a joke. Suppose the one who says it was a joke didn't mean to offend. In that case, it is their responsibility to communicate compassionately that they had no intent to offend rather than demanding that the one to whom it was directed has no sense of humor.

In gay culture, there is a thing called *"reading,"* as in *"To read for filth!"* If you don't know what it is, watch RuPaul's *Drag Race* a few times, and you will learn that *"reading is fundamental."* When you watch these queens read each other, you can tell when some of them aren't joking, and the remarks are cutting and demeaning, while remarks from others may be unflattering but funny and are not taken with offense. The same is true when you witness a roast of a comedian by fellow comedians. This is not bullying but poking fun, and some comedians are masters at it. Joan Rivers and Betty White come to mind as masters. You can tell the difference between derogatory humor and bullying, and even if it was intended as humor, if the other person takes offense, it is time to back up and genuinely affirm your respect for that person instead of continuing to disrespect them by telling them things like, "You can't take a joke."

Regarding laughter affecting the immune system, I swear that the film *"Dumb and Dumber"* with Jim Carrey and Jeff Daniels cured me of a chest cold. When it first came out in the theaters (1994), a friend invited me to see it, and I initially refused because I had bronchitis or some respiratory bug. However, she convinced me to go, which became a healing experience. I may have spread whatever germs that had caused my chest congestion to others in that theatre, but I laughed so hard during the film that my chest had cleared by the time it was over. Every time I laughed, it caused me to cough deeply, clearing my chest congestion. Laughter was my expectorant. Of course, this was in the days before face masks to reduce the spread of things like COVID-19. My apologies to anyone who may have caught my chest cold at that Nashville theatre in 1994.

Humor is more than just a belly-bust of laughter. Humor may produce only a giggle or a smile. It is still beneficial. Looking at things on the lighter side is not just about humor. Positive thinking will never hurt us, but negative thinking will. When we think negatively, it is not just our emotions that get dragged down but our physical well-being. For instance, people who have habits of anger and getting pissed off at every little thing are more likely to have heart attacks than people who don't. Believe me when I tell you that I have done my fair share of that—thankfully, without a heart attack and thankfully with a continuing reduction of outbursts as I have matured.

Pessimism, in general, can create a chronic condition in which our hormone balances and immune responses are disrupted. The brain chemicals necessary for a good mood are depleted by a pessimistic outlook on life. It is like this. Every thought we think, even those we don't notice, has an emotional effect—that emotional effect results from a biochemical reaction in the brain caused by the thought. The thoughts will either bring us up or bring us down. Try a simple experiment of imagining the most horrible thing that could ever happen to you and notice your feelings when you imagine that. You might even film yourself doing this with your phone, and your eyes closed while recording, and then review your facial expressions after you imagine something terrible. Then, try the same thing while imagining some wonderful situation, perhaps the most fantastic thing you think could ever happen to you. Then, watch that playback. There are over seven thousand micro-expressions on the human face. So, our faces react to what we think, as do our moods and bodies, even if we don't realize our expressions are changing.

One of the most important things we can ever learn is to manage our thinking. Granted, it is easier said than done because the mind habituates. This means that turning around old, ingrained habits, especially habits we learned in childhood, is a very difficult thing to do, and it may only partially be accomplished. Still, it can become something that improves our lives and emotions when we diligently practice. The important thing is that we practice in an uplifting, reassuring way. Studies have shown that the neural pathways in our brains can be rewired by what we practice and habituate. If we, therefore, practice things like love, thoughtfulness, and compassion, our brains will rewire to those influences. When we get our happiness blockers out of the way and practice the skills of happiness, we change our brains to habituate to new thinking. We need to learn how to become, for ourselves, the loving, comforting, nurturing, protecting, and disciplining parents that we may not have had as a child.

All of us essentially parent ourselves every day. We tend to pick up where our parents left off. They got us up for school. Now, we get ourselves up for work. We must engage in discipline and learn to make ourselves do the things our parents might have made us do when we were kids. That means setting the alarm, getting up, going to work/school, devoting ourselves to accomplishing our tasks, and fulfilling our obligations. If our parents were not disciplined themselves and didn't discipline us, we are likely to be undisciplined as adults. Suppose our parents were critical and condemning of us. In that case, we probably tend to be critical and condemning of ourselves within our inner dialogue, as well as having a tendency to be critical and condemning of others. Recovery can mean learning to self-parent and provide ourselves with what we may not have received as children or did not receive in balance. A child's four basic emotional needs are nurturance, comfort, protection, and discipline. When we do not get those things in balance during our childhood, we tend to be out of balance as adults. For instance, I had some protection as a child, but Granny could not fully protect me. I received nurturance from Granny but not from Grandpa and my uncle. Granny sometimes comforted me, but I never received comfort from either of the men in the family. Granny disciplined me appropriately but what was labeled as discipline from the men was harsh and punitive. That, in addition to the condemnation I felt from the church, left me unbalanced as an adult. I was lucky to have loving mentors who taught me how to self-parent and love the little boy who still resided beneath all the resentment accumulated throughout my childhood.

Nurturance is affirmation and encouragement. If we didn't get that as children, we must learn to nurture, affirm, and encourage ourselves as adults. That might mean recognizing and affirming ourselves when we know we have done a good job or appreciating our satisfaction at completing some chore, like doing the laundry. It might be that we account for our good qualities and affirm ourselves for our efforts at positive change. In many respects, it means learning to be our own cheerleader. It may also mean surrounding ourselves with friends and family who nurture us and limiting time with those who are not nurturing, especially those who have toxic behavior.

Comfort might be a hug, reassurance, edifying talk, or distraction. For instance, when my nephew was about three or four years old, he fell on the sidewalk and skinned his knee. His grandpa picked him up and said, "Look at that hole in the sidewalk! Did you make that hole with your knee? You must have a really powerful knee!" His grandpa was trying to comfort him by distracting him from his pain, so comforting ourselves appropriately as adults might be a healthy distraction, such as taking a walk, a hot bath, or putting our feet up at the end of a stressful day. It might also be calling on friends and asking for some time, maybe for a hug or validation. However, it is very easy for trauma survivors to engage in some very unhealthy ways of distraction as self-comfort. That is likely to include things like excessive drinking or drug abuse, gambling, gaming, spending, sexual addictions, compulsive eating, or other ways of shutting down. Unfortunately, those who engage in these distractions can get into a chronic habit of creating an additional problem from which they need to escape. The primary error is confusing pleasure with happiness and comfort. Pleasure is addicting, but true happiness is not. The pleasure or euphoria is a distraction, and it becomes easy to assume that we are 'happy' when engaging in self-destructive avoidance because, for a moment, we are not feeling the pain that we need to face. Since pleasure is temporary, once the euphoria wears off, we are back to the unhappiness we were trying to avoid in the first place, and that is often made worse by the ongoing and increasing consequences of addiction. True comfort does not cause additional problems.

Protection is probably the most important task for trauma survivors because when we are not safe with the very ones who were supposed to be protecting us, we may not feel safe with anyone, including ourselves. There is a song, for instance, by Pink, "*Don't Let Me Get Me*," which addresses being self-destructive. When we are not protected as children, we can begin to incorporate the hatred directed at us into ourselves. Often, abuse and trauma survivors become self-destructive and self-sabotaging because they buy into the idea that they are worthless, that they are discards of society. Why bother taking care of ourselves if we don't believe we have any actual worth in the first place? When we are not protected as children or not taught how to protect ourselves, we may go way overboard into rage and violence or make inappropriate demands and think that we are protecting ourselves by that behavior. On the flip side, we may put up with way too much because we are afraid of communicating our feelings or setting boundaries with people who continue to take advantage of us. Maybe by not being protected as children, we didn't learn about boundaries, how to set them, or that we even deserve them. We may get into too much conflict or try to avoid conflict, thereby allowing ourselves to have others take advantage of us. Appropriate protection of ourselves as adults (not extremes) begins to reverse the effects of not being protected as children.

A loving parent protects their children and teaches them how to protect themselves appropriately. That might include teaching children that they have a right to say 'no' and that they have a right to certain boundaries and feelings. I've heard it said that if you want to set a child up for exploitation, teach them that it is not okay to say "no." Of course, there are times when parents have to take authority, but it is important for children to know that they have choices and a right to protect themselves. Protecting your child might mean going to the school to talk to the principal about the problem of your kid being bullied and defining, with the school and/or parents of the bullies, what needs to happen to intervene in the problem. It might also mean that you teach your child that another person's behavior is never about them, whether the bully is another child or an adult. It might mean teaching your child to protect their spirit by teaching them to keep from taking on the negativity directed at them. It might mean teaching them effective communication skills and how to assert themselves. As a last resort, it might mean teaching them to protect themselves physically if needed. Many survivors of trauma don't know how to appropriately protect themselves, especially emotionally, or they don't protect themselves at all and place themselves in dangerous situations. It is also not unusual for kids who are being abused at home to be bullied at school. Abuse subdues children and makes them vulnerable to mistreatment from others.

Self-discipline is another thing we must learn if we were not taught that as a child or didn't have appropriate discipline. Some people may have been overindulged as children and given very little discipline. So, they grow up with a sense of entitlement, expecting others to kowtow to their expectations, or they grow up with a sense of dependency, expecting others to take care of them instead of stepping up to care for themselves. Some people may have had parents who vacillated between abusing them and overindulging them after feeling guilty about the abuse. This is often a pattern of behavior found with domestic violence where the perpetrator overindulges after feeling guilty and swears that he or she will never do it again. Some may have grown up with perfectionism, where they were severely punished for the slightest infraction and therefore have felt that they can never do anything good enough. Some grew up with an enabling parent where one parent set appropriate, disciplinary boundaries and the other bailed the child out of responsibility. There are all kinds of ways in which childhood discipline can be screwed up and, as a result, produce an adult who continues to have problems with authority or self-discipline. One of my imbalances was created by Granny. Because she felt sorry that I had lost my mom, she tended to rescue me. On the one hand, I was being abused by my uncle, but if I bitched and moaned about something, Granny would swoop in and fix it so I wouldn't be upset. The result was that I maintained a habit of bitching, complaining, and demanding well into my adult years. I was overindulged, in addition to being abused. I do believe in the fine art of bitching, but there are limits.

Many don't understand what discipline is. It absolutely *is not* screaming at a child or punishing a child, and it, most assuredly, is not abusing a child. Appropriate discipline gives choices within certain parameters and provides consistent, reasonable consequences if the child does not comply. It is never doing for a child what he or she can do for themselves. Discipline may be affirming or rewarding a child for appropriate behavior while never rewarding inappropriate behavior. Discipline is sticking to a rule if it is reasonable, even if there is a protest. There are many good books on parenting, and it might be a good idea for those adults who did not get appropriate parenting and discipline as children to read those books and think about how healthy parenting principles might be applied to their self discipline. Some books to consider might be *Love and Logic* and *One, Two, Three, Magic*. I am reminded here, also, of my friend who was disabled yet so skilled because his parents required him to learn to take care of himself. When he dropped his fork on the floor, they told him, "Pick it up. You can do it." I'm sure he was also praised for each of his accomplishments. As a result of his parents' *tough love*, he was a very self-disciplined and successful person.

Our living is much more comfortable when it is balanced. There will, of course, be times when things push us off track. The key is to get back on track as soon as possible. Like driving a car, the goal is to stay within our lane and safely transition from one lane to another until we reach our destination. If we see ourselves headed for the ditch or an animal runs out before us, we compensate to get back into the lane. If we end up in the ditch, regardless of our reaction, the important thing is to get ourselves out of the ditch and get back in the lane. We can whine about it, scream about it, pout about it, cry about it, or whatever. Eventually, we have to do something about it. The problem requires the same process to resolve regardless of our reaction. Our happiness requires learning how to stay in the lane. When I moved to The Coastal Bend, I had a problem drifting out of the lane due to the stress, and I had to review and renew ways to get back in my happiness lane.

There is a phenomenon that I call "*The hornet effect.*" That is when you can't swat one problem before you are stung by the next, and the problems keep coming. I had a severe hornet effect in Nashville between 1995 and 1997 when I lost everything and had to start over. I was in a mild hornet effect when I moved to Texas. However, another phenomenon often follows the hornet effect, which I call "*the domino effect.*" That is when the circumstances of life get stacked ahead of us like those domino sculptures where one tip causes everything to fall perfectly into place to create the artistic effect. Just as there are times when life seems to be falling apart, there are times when everything seems to be coming together for our best benefit. Regardless of whether life is going well or not, one of the ways that we can live it more effectively is by learning the skill of detachment. With detachment, we let go of expectations, worry, or regret and let life be life. We learn to remove our happiness blockers, such as guilt, shame, anger, resentment, regret, entitlement, judgment, perfectionism, criticism, and contempt. When we get the obstacles out of the way, happiness is a natural experience that can occur regardless of our external circumstances.

When I moved to Texas, I had to work on my detachment. I had to work on getting my happiness blockers out of the way again because I quickly fell into allowing external circumstances to interfere with my comfort and peace of mind. I was mentally and emotionally in the ditch and had to figure out how to get back in my lane. Previously, I thought I had it together. I thought I was happy, except that I was not comfortable living in the cold of Missouri. I looked forward to a warm climate and practiced my faith and affirmation that everything would work well. However, life had other plans. It often does. I had to be challenged, once again, to test my spiritual and mental health skills. I had to learn how to let go, and I had to learn how to laugh again, even though my circumstances, at the time, gave me multiple reasons to be unhappy.

Since I am a writer, I wrote about the experience. I wrote it in poetry at first because that was a quick way of expressing what was going on in my mind without getting bogged down with too much detail, and I enjoy writing poetry. When I realized that the lesson the gulls were trying to teach me was the same lesson proposed by Oscar Wilde, *"Life is too important to be taken seriously,"* I worked on not being so serious. It was a lesson that Marcy had tried to teach me years earlier, a lesson I needed to relearn. Granny had taught me to take a break when I was a child. So, the gulls reminded me of the lesson to lighten up. Then, I began to let go, practice mindfulness, and laugh in the face of difficulties, and in time, things fell together again.

Of course, this one last poem inspired the title of the book. It is a poem about reminders that life/spirit presents to us when we are open to receiving them.

THE GULLS ARE ALWAYS LAUGHING

No matter what the day may bring,
The gulls are always laughing.
Tragedy or treasure matters not to them.
The gulls are always laughing.
They sail above the rooftops and parking lots.
They glide over the beaches and the stones.
They laugh whether the sky has clouds or sun.
No matter how the day unfolds,
The gulls are always laughing.

Carefree in all they seem.
The gulls are always laughing.
Laugh it off and go on, they call.
Laugh it off and go on.

Whether my heart breaks or mends,
The gulls are always laughing.
Whether my world goes on or ends,
The gulls are always laughing.
They laugh above my head and play on joyful wings.
They laugh at all those silly, trivial human things.
The gulls are always laughing.
When my heart a moment bears
The weight of hurt or regret
The lesson of the gulls, I claim
As one that I will conquer, yet.
The gulls are always laughing.
The gulls are always laughing.
The gulls are always laughing.

*Even today, A voice within
me pleads, don't tell.*

Epilogue

While struggling through healing from my own traumas, I realized that trauma is a liar. As I said in the introduction of the poem *Diamond*, it takes an insane experience or a series of insane experiences and then perpetrates a set of lies about ourselves and the world. When we believe those lies and live according to those lies, trauma keeps us trapped. To heal, we have to stand up to the lies of trauma. We have to refuse to believe the evil of trauma in order to escape from it. We have to stand up to it just as we would stand up to a schoolyard bully. Some of us never stood up to our bullies, but we don't have to let those bullies live in our minds. We can kick them out repeatedly if necessary. One way to defeat a bully is to stand up to the bully, even if that bully is within our own thinking. Every time we do what trauma tells us to do, we strengthen its hold over us. If trauma says, "Don't go out to eat. It's dangerous," and we don't go, then we are telling trauma, "Yep, you're right. It's dangerous." If we listen to the anxiety of trauma instead of challenging it, we don't give ourselves a chance to learn that it's safe to go out. We forget or deny that literally millions of people go out to eat every day without consequence. Is it possible for something bad to happen? Of course, it is, but the chances are infinitely small. We must learn to challenge the trauma to defeat it. It may take a great deal of courage and strength to stand up to it, but we have to stand up to it if we can ever escape it. One of the ways we defeat it is through truth and logic. Then, once we get even a tiny glimpse of the truth, we can no longer deny it, and we will no longer be satisfied by sitting in the dark prison that trauma creates for us. Initially, our feelings and reactions may get worse. It takes a lot of energy to hide from the imaginary tiger, but it takes even more energy to fight, and when we begin to fight the trauma, it initially comes back at us. Ego defends the existing belief, not the truth. When the Bible says, "*Seek, and you will find, knock and it will be opened unto you*," *Matthew 7: 7-8*, it means (to me) that we find what we look for. Ego will seek and find "*evidence*" that trauma was right, but we have to counter it with truth because when we seek evidence of the truth, we find that, as well. Once we have found it, there is no turning back. Once we understand it, we will never again believe the lies of trauma, even if we momentarily slip. Let me note here that the generalized social shaming of LGBTQIA+ people, even if they were not physically or mentally abused or bullied, is trauma in and of itself, and what we have to do as queer people is stand up to shaming, especially as we have internalized it into our own thinking.

There are three primary lies of trauma. The first lie is: *You can never be safe again*. When we have been traumatized, everywhere feels unsafe. We find ourselves hypervigilant, checking every corner, the nearest exit, and the quickest way to get to it if we allow ourselves to go out at all. Instead, we may opt for isolation by staying away from people as much as possible or by disconnecting whenever we are in a group of people, even family. The truth is that the majority of people are safe the majority of the time in the majority of places around the world. Of course, there are places that are not safe, and of course, there is no perfectly safe place, but we are all still safe most of the time in most places. When we put it into perspective, trauma is just one small speck in the totality of our lives, but those who have been traumatized focus on that speck like a dot in the middle of a piece of paper instead of realizing that the rest of the sheet of paper is blank. We can decide what to write on the rest of it instead of assuming that the one speck is all there is.

The second lie of trauma is: *No one can be trusted.* It feels like everyone is our enemy or a potential enemy, and we may subconsciously set ourselves up for one rejection or betrayal after another so our ego can *"prove"* that it was right. We may put up an emotional wall to keep other people at a distance; there can be several ways to accomplish this. Because human beings need connection, some may drop their wall, open themselves at the wrong time to the wrong people because that's all they know, and then put the wall back up and refuse to let anyone in again after being hurt. This may go back and forth for a lifetime. The problem with a wall is that it keeps out those who can be trusted as well as those who can't, and because ego tries to prove the belief, we may sabotage our chances of developing relationships with people who can be trusted. The truth is that there are a lot of good, ethical people in the world. The truth is that healthy people don't have walls; they have filters and boundaries. They check things out gradually and allow people into their circle little by little. Remember, the first rule for establishing and maintaining healthy relationships is, *"Treat me right (with the respect, honor, and dignity I deserve as a human being), or you won't be allowed to treat me at all."* Healthy people don't make spaces in their lives for those whose behavior is toxic, and the more we allow toxic people to take up space and time in our lives, the less space and time we have for those who would treat us right. If someone comes into the outer edges of a healthy person's filter and betrays their trust, they are not allowed to get any closer. They will likely be completely disconnected from the healthy person's social circle. If someone gets all the way in and betrays trust, they are marked off the list just as anyone else who betrays trust would be. That is not to say that people are not allowed to make mistakes or be given a chance to prove their trust again after making a mistake. Still, repeated infractions should not be tolerated, especially after giving those chances. A healthy person does not expect others to be perfect but will not tolerate overtly toxic behavior. An unhealthy person goes back and forth between putting up their wall, lowering it to experience toxic behavior, and then putting the wall back up again. Until they recognize what they are doing, that can go on unimpeded. One key to recovery is to remove the wall and install a filter by learning healthy boundaries, setting and maintaining those boundaries, and knowing that you have a right to boundaries.

It is also important to understand that when you begin to eliminate contact with toxic people, there will be a wilderness period. I think the Bible story of Exodus is a perfect metaphor for escaping the slavery of trauma or addiction. Like Pharoh in the story of Exodus, addiction, trauma, and unhealthy coping keep us enslaved rather than free. First, the children of Isreal were enslaved, and it took seven plagues for Pharoh to let them go. In other words, it isn't easy to get out of trauma and/or addiction. There may be multiple slips in early recovery, and it takes a tenacity to break free. When the Children of Isreal were finally released after the plagues, Pharoh sent his troops after them. This means toxic people will usually continue to come back, and healthy boundaries have to be set over and over. Then, the Children of Isreal crossed over the Red Sea and made a big break but wandered in the wilderness. There is always a wilderness period when we escape trauma reactions, an addiction, or a situation of being around toxic people. There is a time of loneliness when we no longer have toxic social contacts but haven't yet developed healthy relationships. The Children of Isreal feared the wilderness and how long it took to reach the promised land. So, they thought they should return to Pharoh and that they were better off as slaves. Recovery is not an easy process; when we commit to new playgrounds and playmates, it can take time to find them, and there may be multiple temptations to give up—those in the Bible story who endured the wilderness eventually crossed into the promised land. So, the longer we hang in there, the more skilled we become at maintaining our happiness, and the less difficult it becomes to resist the temptation to return to whatever had enslaved us.

The third primary lie of trauma is that because the trauma treated you as worthless and meaningless, or you could not control what was happening, you must, therefore, be worthless and meaningless. Any form of shaming sends this same message. Those who abuse, shame, and traumatize use others as objects rather than treating them as human beings. Those who traumatize treat human beings as though they own them for their purpose, whether that is sexual exploitation, control, or violence. Those who traumatize will degrade, demean, and devalue other human beings. So, those who have been traumatized tend to blame themselves and tend to feel as though they are somehow unworthy because of the trauma. They think it was their fault that they were violated. Adult survivors, having been abused as small children, often blame themselves even though there was nothing that they could have done to prevent what happened. Little children can neither defend themselves against an adult physically nor understand how to deal with adult manipulation. The self-loathing that comes out of trauma is far more than just low self-esteem. It is literally hating oneself and believing that nothing we do matters, that we don't matter, or that we deserved to be abused. We may continue to believe that we deserve mistreatment and, therefore, make ourselves vulnerable to it as adults. However, the truth is that there is no such thing as a worthless or meaningless human being. This was addressed in the poem *A Single Step* and the poem *Diamond*. You can throw a diamond in the trash, and it is still a diamond. Its value is not affected by what was done to it. Just because an abuser or some trauma threw you in the trash does not mean that you have lost your value. The opinions and actions of others cannot change your intrinsic human value, and no degree of shaming can change your value. Not even your mistakes can change your value, and regardless of how others treat you, what you have done to yourself, or how you have treated others, your value remains unchanged. Reclaiming and recognizing your rightful inheritance of equal value to all is important. It means that you have greater honor and respect for yourself and others and that because you recognize their value and your own, you choose not to mistreat them or yourself. Even those who perpetrate trauma are behaving that way because they continue to believe the lies of trauma. They don't get it. They don't realize that it is not possible for one human being to have greater or lesser value than another. Yet, those who do not believe they are loveable don't have relationships; they take emotional hostages. Sometimes, they take physical hostages or stalk. Only those who know their worth and learn to love and honor themselves can have healthy, stable, loving relationships. Only those who stand up to the lies of trauma and refuse to believe the so-called "*proof*" of the ego come to heal from trauma.

As much as therapy, my spiritual study brought me healing and comfort with myself and my life. The Presbyterian pre-ministerial student at Lyon had gotten me to question, and my guide and mentor, Marcy, had taught me about the importance and value of all religions. I was introduced to *Love is Letting Go of Fear* by Jerald Jampaulski in the 1980's. I had also read Marianne Williamson's *A Return to Love* and purchased a series of her lectures that I repeatedly listened to while driving to and from work. From there, I was introduced to the writings of Thich Nhat Hanh, a Buddhist monk who founded *Engaged Buddhism* in Vietnam in response to the Vietnam War. He traveled to the United States in 1966 and met Martin Luther King Jr. Later, Dr. King nominated him for the Nobel Peace Prize in 1967. I read his book *Peace is Every Step* in my early to mid-thirties, also noted in the poem, *A Single Step*. I have read multiple other enlightening books. Also, I received a lot of guidance from Unity churches and *A Course in Miracles*.

Oddly enough, some of my greatest spiritual breakthroughs came when I was visiting back at the family farm in northern Arkansas, where I had been raised in such a rigid authoritarian church and where I had been traumatized. However, let me post a disclaimer here. Just because the religion I grew up with was rigid and authoritarian does not mean that everyone who subscribed to it was. Many were good-hearted and loving people, including my grandmother and Aunt Estelle. The church, however, condemned me for being who I am. Nonetheless, it was back there, visiting that farm, where breakthroughs in spiritual understanding often came to me. I even remember a time when visiting home that I attended church with Granny and, during Bible study, I espoused principles of *A Course in Miracles* to receive affirmation of agreement among congregants attending. Truth is truth wherever you find it. How do we know it is truth? Truth is irrefutable. It cannot be argued. It is what it is. Beliefs can be argued; the one truth about beliefs is that no belief can ever be truth. This is why so many religions conflict with one another. The practitioners allow their egos to get them caught up in the beliefs they defend, depriving them of witnessing the truth. Whatever we defend, we keep, and our ego will defend belief and indoctrination rather than questioning indoctrination. Freedom does not come with defense. It begins with questioning.

Because the works of Jerald Jampaulski and Marianne Williamson were based on *A Course in Miracles*, I also began to study the course. Initially, it tore me up. Much like being gently confronted by the Presbyterian pre-ministerial student back in college, it reminded me that many of the beliefs I had been taught and had subscribed to for much of my life did not match the truth or make sense. My torment was that I could recognize the truth; I knew it was the truth, and yet, my ego still defended the lies and old beliefs. Those beliefs, however, began to fall apart in the light of truth. For instance, *A Course in Miracles* admonishes the relinquishment of guilt as a useless and harmful emotion. Yet, I continued to find myself experiencing guilt and personal shame on many levels. I thought it a bit humorous, washing dishes in Nashville one evening, shortly after I started studying *ACIM*, when I realized I was feeling guilty about something. Then, because *ACIM* admonishes that guilt is not helpful, I felt guilty for feeling guilty. I had to smile when I realized what I was doing. Guilt is an internal emotional punishment for a perceived wrong. It doesn't even have to be a legitimate wrong, simply a perceived infraction, and when we start to break patterns that we have been taught for life, even if we consciously know the ideas are ridiculous, we still feel guilty when we defy them. Guilt does nothing to correct any mistake and does nothing to uplift us. It is one of those emotions that drags us down rather than something that lifts our spirits and brings us to an enlightened awareness. Guilt, shame, and fear mongering are authoritarian tools used as ways of maintaining control rather than teaching love.

Think of it like this. If you were taught from early childhood that sitting on a stool is grievously wrong and you should never do it, what would happen if you attended a function and the only place to sit was on a stool? You might consciously know that there is nothing wrong with sitting on a stool because you have seen people do it without consequence for years, but you would still hesitate simply because you were taught that it is wrong. Being taught that it is wrong doesn't make it wrong. However, the ego defends the belief even if it is erroneous. So, you would feel very hesitant to sit on a stool; you might choose to remain standing. Let's say you convince yourself that it is okay to sit on a stool. After all, good people do it all the time. How would you get comfortable sitting on a stool? The answer is that you would have to make yourself do it, and guess what? Then, you will feel guilty and anxious for quite some time whenever you sit on a stool. Even though you consciously know that sitting on a stool is okay, the ego will nag at you that you are breaking the rule instilled in you since childhood. Therefore, the ego will tell you it's a sin and that you should be ashamed. If you give in and stop trying to sit on a stool, your ego wins, and you keep the erroneous belief that sitting on a stool is wrong. You must repeatedly sit on stools to get comfortable until the guilt finally disappears. The ego's defense of beliefs, regardless of their relevance or validity, is why so many people are trapped in authoritarian religions with so much guilt. They usually don't question or challenge their beliefs, even though those beliefs are often contrary to the laws of love. Those who tell you that you are not allowed to question are the very ones who need to be questioned most. The basic definition of wrong is any intent or action to cause harm. Therefore, if there is no intent to do harm, and no one is harmed by your actions, it is not wrong. Yet, when we entertain thoughts and intent to do harm, even if we don't act on it, we harm ourselves.

After I had learned to relinquish guilt, I moved back to the Ozarks and had power of attorney over Granny as she deteriorated into dementia. It became obvious that she could no longer live alone when I walked into her house one winter day to the smell of gas. The burners on the gas kitchen stove were on but were not lit. Yet, the gas heater in the living room was lit. She hadn't even noticed. I turned off the burners and opened the windows for a while. I'm not sure how close the house came to exploding, but that, plus aunts finding maggots in food that Granny had saved, brought us to the decision to place her in a nursing home. One of my aunts tried to keep her at her house and care for her, but it soon became obvious, due to her dementia, that this would not work. We had to pick a nursing home for her. Two of my aunts wanted her in nursing home 'A,' while another aunt, who wanted to tell everyone else what to do, wanted her in nursing home 'B.' I had worked as an aide in a nursing home 'A' during college summers and was familiar with it. It was a fine nursing home and the most convenient location for all three aunts and me. So, I placed Granny in nursing home 'A.' Yet, this one aunt couldn't stand the fact that she had been outvoted. She called me one evening and proceeded to chew me out and tell me what a horrible person I was for placing Granny in the nursing home that was not her preference. I told her, "You might as well stop with the guilt trip. I don't go on guilt trips."

She said, "Well if you don't feel guilty, how are you going to correct what you do that's wrong?" (Note: This is the same aunt who tattled to Granny that I was gay.)

I calmly replied, "First, I'm not doing anything wrong. I am making the best decision I know for Granny and everyone else involved, and everyone agrees with this except you. Just because you don't like it doesn't mean it's wrong. Second, if I make a mistake, I will correct it because I care, not because I feel guilty." By then, I had learned I didn't have to get on the plane because someone handed me a ticket for a guilt trip.

She had little else to say, and it didn't matter. The decision had been made. Like her, too many people think that guilt is supposed to be there and that it serves a purpose, but more often than not, it serves the purpose of selfish people who use it to manipulate others, including their children, into doing what they want them to do. For instance, people who accuse you of being "selfish" are usually selfish people. That is exactly how my aunt was trying to use it when I confronted her. There had been a time when I would have felt guilty and would have been fairly easily manipulated. However, that time no longer existed.

The authoritarian church I had grown up in utilized guilt and fear. I mentioned earlier about Grandpa telling me that I would go to hell for studying A Course in Miracles. I had learned before that time not to go on guilt trips and that I don't have to be perfect to be spiritually aware. When I told Grandpa that no one has the right or authority to condemn anyone to hell, that was the last time he ever jumped my shit about religion.

The interesting part is that he never set foot in church himself. However, he would sit with his Bible on his lap and talk about what other people were doing wrong. When asked why he didn't go to church, he said it was because he was a sinner and was undeserving of participating. I reflected that if it weren't for sinners, there would be no reason for church and that maybe religion is about trying to improve yourself instead of waiting till you are perfect before going. Nonetheless, he never went.

Not long after having the experience with the stone beneath my foot, as described in the poem *A Single Step*, I realized that hate begets hate. For the longest time, I had hated my uncle for what he did to me. I resented not just him but others like him. Yet, after attending Al-Anon meetings, I began to have other revelations. One of those revelations was that if I hated just as my uncle hated and resented just as he resented, I had accepted his legacy, and therefore, even if I didn't drink heavily or become violent, I had become like him. I began deliberately attempting to be the opposite of him. I set about learning what genuine love is about. I'm still learning, but I realized that hate for hate creates only more hate but love for hate brings healing. It is easier said than done, even within myself, where the biggest battle is fought. Marianne Williamson said (and I can't find the exact quote), "*Is the devil going to do more harm stalking Africa or between your ears? Where is the damage done? Where does the work need to be done?*" She was talking about dealing with our egos, issues, fears, resentments, etc. She talked about how we focus on fixing others when we need to focus on fixing ourselves. She was talking about that part of us that is selfish, self-serving, demeaning, demanding, and fearful. The work we need to do with the devil (ego) is within our minds, including no longer listening or responding to the deceptions. Our egos are tricksters. They deceive and trick us. They demean us and cause us to be arrogant. They judge others and focus on what they are doing so that we don't have to examine ourselves, and all this is done internally. The work we need to do spiritually is between our ears. While doing that, we let others do their work in their own time. Our lives belong solely to us, and their lives belong solely to them. What they do with their lives is none of our business, and only the ego's arrogance would assume any right or authority to correct others. Any focus we place on them is a distraction from the work we need to do within ourselves.

One day, another thought occurred to me: "*What would the world be like if everyone were to adopt one simple goal? Relinquish all malicious intent.*" What a simple goal that is. Yet, simple is not necessarily easy. Often, we don't realize how many tidbits of malice corrupt our thinking. It may not seem malicious when we wish that someone who has upset us would "*get theirs,*" but if we are honest with ourselves, those are thoughts of malice just as surely as desiring to kill someone or take something from them. Carl Jung noted the importance of facing our "*shadow,*" that part of us that we don't like and carries resentful and malicious thoughts, our inner Gollum. We don't like admitting that we have that shadow self within us, but we all do. That shadow is our ego. When we get honest with ourselves and begin facing those parts of us that we would rather pretend are not there, we begin to make real progress. If we are to truly learn self-love, we have to learn to love all parts of ourselves, including the parts we would rather not have.

If I am honest with myself, regarding my childhood and growing up in that rigid authoritarian church, it was back there, on that old farm, where my spiritual development began, and it wasn't just about what I learned in church that I later could reinterpret. It was learning from Granny to take a break. It was learning to sit in nature. What I didn't realize was that, even as a child, I was learning to practice mindfulness and meditation, which is one of the things that got me through a difficult childhood. Sitting on that huge boulder at the edge of our farm, up in the tree line, I could see the squirrels and birds. There, I first learned to be silent and listen to nature. I was practicing mindfulness meditation without even realizing it. I was still angry and confused, but I had a solace that comforted me. I allowed Mother Nature to rock me in her comforting arms.

Now, I have shared some of those lessons with you. I have given you a piece of my heart, a glimpse into my experience. I hope it helps to know that it is possible to overcome, but it is not possible without realizing that there is a better way and becoming determined to find it. That's what I did. There is a saying in the Twelve Steps, "*If you keep doing what you always did, you will keep getting what you always got.*" To feel differently, we have to think differently. To manifest a better life for ourselves, we have to believe differently, and all the while, we have to practice, practice, practice the skills of recovery and happiness. I have said that recovery is like learning to play a musical instrument. First, you must take lessons; the early lessons are the most difficult part. It usually means learning to read music, and learning the instrument, and how to interact with it. Then, you have to practice diligently every day to get good at it. Then, you have to practice diligently every day to stay good at it. If you ever put the instrument down and stop playing, you will begin forgetting how to play. As they say to the studio musicians in Nashville, "*You've got to keep your licks up.*" In other words, If you stop practicing, you lose your skill. For instance, I stopped playing guitar in 1989 after playing for sixteen years, and now, I can barely recall two or three chords. So, if we want to obtain and maintain recovery, if we want to overcome trauma, we have to keep our licks up. We have to practice the skills of happiness every day, and when we learn the skills of happiness and then practice them every day, we find that despite our trauma, we can overcome it and still live happy and fulfilled lives.

If you ever find a feather in your path, hear a gull laughing, or if you aren't around gulls, and hear the call of a blue jay, a mockingbird, a crow, or any other bird, look up at the sky and smile because the universe is reminding you that you are meant to be here, your worth is as valuable as anyone, and you deserve to be happy.

THANK YOU, AND BLESSINGS!
Karlyle Tomms

There is no such thing as the end.

"When I despair, I remember that all through history, the way
of truth and love has always won. There have been tyrants
and murderers, and for a time, they seem invincible, but in
the end, they always fall - think of it, always."
MAHATMA GANDHI

"An eye for an eye
makes the whole world blind."
MAHATMA GANDHI

Crisis Lines:
National Suicide Hotline is to call or text **988**
Suicide Prevention Lifeline: 800-273-7386
National Sexual Assault Hotline, operated by RAINN, for free, confidential counseling, 24 hours a day: 1-800-656-HOPE(4673)
Trevor Project (LGBTQIA+ Crisis): 866-488-7386
It Gets Better Project for LGBTQ+ youth: https://itgetsbetter.org/
National Domestic Violence Hotline: 800-799-SAFE (7233)

Resources:
Anyone can contact their state department of mental health. Often, Addiction Recovery Services are within the same department. Also, looking up your state department of mental health can help you with guidance to licensed professionals in your area and other resources in your home state. Mental health providers with specific specialties may also be located through the online search option *Psychology Today* provides. Many other resources and organizations are available for contact by searching any related topics.

Recommended Self-Help Books:
These are only a few of the possible options for self-help books available. However, these are my favorites.
Codependent No More – Melody Beatty
Healing The Child Within – Charles L Whitfield
Love is Letting Go of Fear - Jerald Jampaulski
Say Goodbye to Guilt - Jerald Jampaulski
Teach Only Love - Jerald Jampaulski
A Woman's Worth - Marianne Williamson
A Return to Love - Marianne Williamson
Your Sacred Self - Wayne Dyer
Adult Children of Alcoholics - Janet Woititz
On the Family - John Bradshaw

Healing the Shame that Binds You - John Bradshaw
Getting the Love You Want - Harville Hendrix

Other Books of Interest:
Stranger At the Gate – Mel White
Caste – Isabel Wilkerson
The Velvet Rage – Alan Downs PhD
A New Earth – Ekart Tolle

About Karlyle Tomms

*K*arlyle Tomms grew up in rural Ozarks poverty. He completed his master's degree in 1981. He has written for regional magazines and newspapers, and is often invited to speak at both professional and non-professional events, as well as radio talk shows. However, he had never published fiction until completing his first novel in 2014. His general method for fiction has been to define a character and allow that character to tell his or her own story from first person perspective as though the character is presenting an autobiography. Through his characters he explores the psychology of the human condition as well as the various elements and entanglements of personalities. Incorporating the social and historical influences surrounding his characters, Karlyle's stories explore overcoming social, emotional, and spiritual challenges.

Fresh Ink Group

Independent Multi-media Publisher

Fresh Ink Group / Push Pull Press
Voice of Indie / GeezWriter

✸

Hardcovers
Softcovers
All Ebook Platforms
Audiobooks
Worldwide Distribution

✸

Indie Author Services
Book Development, Editing, Proofing
Graphic/Cover Design
Video/Trailer Production
Website Creation
Social Media Management
Writing Contests
Writers' Blogs
Podcasts

✸

Authors
Editors
Artists
Experts
Professionals

✸

FreshInkGroup.com
info@FreshInkGroup.com
X: @FreshInkGroup
Facebook.com/FreshInkGroup
LinkedIn: Fresh Ink Group
Instagram: @FreshInkGroup and @FIGPublishing

Fresh Ink Group
FreshInkGroup.com

EDGE OF SMOKE

Karlyle Tomms

In the Pruitt Igoe slums of St. Louis in the 1960s, a heroin-addict mother breaks her son's dolls and screams, "You are not a girl!" However, no one can convince Stephanie to live as Stephen. Her mother pimps her out to a man who rapes her and takes pictures of her as others rape her. After finding her mother brutally murdered, she is placed in Christian foster care, where they also try to convince her to accept being male. Her mother's lover is sentenced to life in prison for the murder. Famed Televangelist Pastor Ronald Dennison sets up a trust that allows a compassionate old neighbor to adopt her out of foster care. Still, she is violently bullied at school for identifying as female. The trust pays for transition surgery at eighteen, and she begins to live fully as a woman. Frightened by men, she remains a virgin until she falls in love with Jordan, but she runs into the man who abused her and remembers her childhood pledge to kill him. Will her lust for murdering the man who brutalized her as a child cause her to lose the man she loves, or will she come to her senses before it's too late?

Jacketed Hardcover
Softcover
All Ebooks Editions

Fresh Ink Group
FreshInkGroup.com